The Bumper Book of

RUDE AND POLITICALLY INCORRECT JOKES

Stories to embarrass your mother

ALLAN PEASE

PEASE INTERNATIONAL

Published by Pease International Pty Ltd
P.O. Box 1260,
Buderim, Qld 4556, Australia
www.peaseinternational.com

National Library of Australia
Cataloguing-in-Publication data
Pease, Allan
Rude and Politically Incorrect Jokes
ISBN 1 920816 08 9

1. Australian wit and humour - 20th century.
2. Ethnic wit and humour. I. Title

A828.302

Edited by The Peases and Diana Ritchie
Organised by The Peases
Illustrations by John Hepworth

Cover Design by Tiffany Cruickshank
Printed by McPherson's Printing Group
Distributed by Harper-Collins Pty Ltd
in Australia and New Zealand
Text designed and typeset by Murray Child & Bookhouse
Send complaints or abusive e-mail letters to
allan@dontcare.com

ACKNOWLEDGEMENTS

I can't recall when most of the jokes in this book were told or by whom, but here's a list of those who personally told me some of the most memorable or made me laugh the hardest.

Anita Kite, Barbara Pease, Barry Markoff, Terry Butler, Mike Goldring, Ben Gaze, Ray & Ruth Pease, Graham Dufty, Bert Newton, Kerri-Anne Kennerley, Max Walker, Rosanna & Simon Townsend, Frank Boggs, Rob Edmunds, Dave & Jan Goodwin, Alex & Denise McTaggart, Lenny Henry, Esther Rantzen, Bernard Croft, Sally Jesse-Raphael, Diana Ritchie, Bill Suter, Martin Grunstein, John Tickel, Bob Johnson, Sheri MacRae, Daryl Somers, Peter Draper, Peter Kay, Ron Tacchi, Amanda Gore, Ronnie Corbett, Paula Thompson, Jo Fenwick, John Fenton, Dick Byrne, Roger Dawson, Jim Cathcart, Doc Blakely, Robert Henry, Jack Levi, Max Hitchins, Melissa Pease, Jasmine Pease, Adam Sellars, Gary Skinner, Allan & Anne Parker, Andy Clarke, Raelene Hall, Errol Hibberd, John Macintosh, Bob Geldof, Kamahl, Gay Byrne, Pat Kenny, Don Lane, Ernie Sigley, Denise Drysdale, Nick Owen, Rob Miller, Dennis Waitley, Richard Otton, Iven Frangi, Christine Maher, Leanne Harrison, Chris Ganderton, Michael Pease, Peter & Pat Walsh, Roger Varney, Fat Wilson, John Allinson, Mike Creagan, Bob McLennan, Trevor Otton, Doug & Peter Bailey, Uli Huber, Graeme Shiels, Ron Barassi, Graham White, Derek Morris, Chris Fenton, Cliff Ritchie, Frank Todisco, Nellie Carter, Alan Francis, Tom Manwarring, Steve Harris, Steve Foy, David Hunt, Ian McKay, Gordon Cramer, Kevin Austin, Lee Grice, Mark Stewart,

Deb Mehrtens, Dorie Simmonds, Pandora White, Jeremy Bradbeer, Brian Boggs, Barry Shaw, Graham Rote, Malcolm Edwards, Trevor Dolby, Tono Taylor, Kevin Fraser, Glen Fraser, Mark Bray, Charlie Cusheri, David Smith.

DEDICATION

To The Peases who, in helping organise and compile this volume, have learned the art of being Rude and Politically Incorrect.

Why not use Allan Pease as guest speaker for your next conference or seminar?

Pease International (Australia) Pty Ltd
Pease International (UK) Ltd

P.O. Box 1260
Buderim 4556
Queensland
AUSTRALIA
Tel: ++61 (0) 5445 5600
Fax: ++61 (0) 5445 5688

Liberty House
16 Newbold Terrace
Leamington Spa CV32 4EG
UNITED KINGDOM
Tel: ++44 (0)1926 889900
Fax: ++44 (0)1926 421100

email: (Aust) info@peaseinternational.com
          (UK) ukoffice@peaseinternational.com
website: www.peaseinternational.com

INTRODUCTION

Picture this scene:

Julius Caesar walks to the podium to address the senate on the state of the Empire. As he begins his address, a senator sitting near the back leans across to two other senators and says "You know, Caesar's parents nearly lost him as a child. Unfortunately they didn't take him far enough into the desert."

The three burst into laughter..."and you can tell when he's lying - his lips are moving!" chides another. Now, 6 of them are sniggering, trying not to be obvious. But Julius is unimpressed. That night, they are thrown to the lions for being Politically Incorrect.

So who told the first jokes? I've heard those same lines used against politicians in most countries as I travel the world giving seminars. And most of the joke-tellers think they've got new or original jokes, yet jokesters were being put to death thousands of years ago for cracking the *same* lines.

I give around 150 seminars and speeches a year and travel to over 30 countries and I reckon I've heard just about *every* joke there is. It's even hard for me to find a new one on the Internet. Whilst I'll take credit for a few original jokes, this book is a collection of the best ones I heard from friends, relatives, neighbours, business associates, clients and conference delegates - but there are few *new* jokes. It usually takes a terrible disaster like a military coup, mass murder, earth-quake or plane crash to give birth to new humour. When the NASA space shuttle exploded there was an abundance of new material being told the **next** morning. "What does NASA stand for? Need another seven astronauts." "NASA's new advertisement - Become an Astronaut - Go Up as a School Teacher, Come Back as a Marine Biologist." "What colour were the Astronaut's Eyes? Blue - one blew to the left, the other blew to the right." I heard these jokes the morning after the disaster as I boarded a plane in Sydney heading for London. When I arrived at Heathrow, my host told me *exactly the same jokes*. This was at a time when the only way of spreading jokes quickly was by phone or telex!

The jokes in this book are politically incorrect, rude or both—but *very* funny. I've omitted crude jokes or anything that I considered gross, slan-derous or obscene because you don't need it to be funny. (Obscene is anything that gives the judge an erection). Most of the humour here deals with attitudes or choices - gays, lesbians, public ser-vants, lawyers, sexists, feminists, discrimination, ethnics, attitudes, farters, bankers and wankers.

"What's the difference between a banker and a wanker? A wanker knows what he's doing." The jokes here are also the ones I'd *never* tell into a microphone.

Lawyers and religious nuts get an extra large serve here. Lawyers because everyone loves lawyer jokes and religion because, as a kid, I had the Catholic Church forced down my throat for years. As a 6 year old, I wanted to be an altar boy - but I'd be buggered if I'd be one now. Thanks to bishops, vicars and priests everywhere dropping their drawers the Church has become the butt of ridicule everywhere. The religious jokes in this book are not intended to denigrate religion but to lighten up its darker sides. Modern Christians appreciate this approach and some supplied many of the jokes. Those who choose to be offended are usually the ones who cause most of the problems in religion.

Sometimes I'm called sexist. It's usually by a feminist. For these women, sexism is anything a man says or does. My wife Barbara will tell you I'm the least sexist man around. When we first met we had a fast and furious affair - I was fast, she was furious. But today, I'm king at our house - she was there the night I was crowned. And one night she came to me on bended knees - and dared me to come out from under the bed.

I don't have any attitude problems with men *or* women. But I have little time for idiots of any sex, race or religion. Some of my best friends are Chinese, English, Africans, Fins and Kiwis. Some of the rudest jokes I've ever heard came from Aborigines, American Blacks and Feminists. And none of them will be spared here!

So how do you remember jokes? Simple - when you hear a good one, write it down. For twenty years I wrote them on napkins, business cards, tablecloths and on my hand. Then I practiced, practiced, practiced.

We're all public speakers. Whether it's on stage behind a microphone, in the pub with friends or over a dinner table. Others are impressed by your ability to recall jokes and tell them well.

A famous comedian once said to me "My ad-lib jokes aren't worth the paper they're written on."

Write them down. Categorise by punch line and practice on everyone. That's what I do. The highest paid people in the world are not those who know the most, it's those who are calculatingly funny. A good humorous T.V. host will be paid 10-20 times more than the head of the local university. We pay more for laughs than facts. We know that a speech which has humorous jokes, lines and cracks every 6-7 minutes is 200-400% more remembered than if the same speech is delivered without the humour. So its a great way to teach facts. I've become so good at it that I've often been described as a cunning linguist.

HUMOUR HEALS
Norman Cousins was diagnosed with a terminal illness. The doctors told him that they could no longer help him and that he would soon die. So he checked into a hotel room and hired all the funny movies he could get and watched and re-watched them over and over, laughing as hard and loud as he could. After 6 months of this self-inflicted laughter therapy, the doctors were amazed to find that his illness had been completely cured - the cancer **gone**! This amazing result led to the publishing of the book "Anatomy of an Illness" by Norman Cousins and the start of massive research into the function of endorphins. Endorphin is a chemical substance that is released from the brain when you laugh. It has a similar chemical composition to morphine and heroin and has a tranquillising effect on the body while building the immune system. This explains why happy people rarely get sick and miserable and complaining people always seem to be ill.

Laughter and crying are closely linked from a psychological and physiological standpoint.

Think of the last time someone told you a joke that made you buckle up with laughter. Where you couldn't control your laughing. How did you feel after? You felt a tingling sensation all over, right? Your brain released endorphins into your blood system that gave you what was once described as a "natural high!!" In effect, you were "stoned". Those who have trouble with laughing at life often turn to drugs and alchohol to achieve that same feeling. Alcohol loosens inhibitions and lets people laugh and release endorphins which is why most well-adjusted people laugh more when they drink alcohol and unhappy people become even more miserable or even violent.

At the end of a big laughing session, you will often cry. "I just laughed until I cried!" Tears have encaphlins which is another of the body's natural tranquillisers to relieve pain.

We cry when we experience a painful event and endorphins and encaphlins aid in self-anethesis.

The basis of many jokes is that something disastrous or painful happens to a person. But because we know that it is not a *real* event happening, we laugh and release endorphins for self-anethesis. If it *was* a real event, it is likely that we'd go immediately into crying mode and the body would also release encaphlins. This is why crying is often the extension of a laughing bout and why in a serious emotional crisis, such as a death, where many people cry, a person who cannot mentally accept the death may begin laughing. When the reality hits, the laughter turns to crying.

The bottom line? - laughter anesthetises the body, builds the immune system, defends against illness and disease, teaches better and extends life. Humour heals.

THE LAUGHTER ROOM

In the 1980's several American hospitals introduced the concept of the "Laughter Room". Based on Norman Cousins' experiences, the room was filled with joke books, comedy films and humorous cassette tapes and had regular visits from comedians and clowns. The results? An improvement in patient health and shorter average hospitalisation time per patient.

The first Laughter Room was set up in Australia in 1995 at Moruya Hospital, New South Wales. Christine May from the South Coast Health Service said the Laughter Room was set up to improve the psychological and physiological well-being of the patients. "Research has now shown the positive effects of laughing such as the release of the body's own painkillers and improvement of the immune system. After laughter, the pulse rate steadies, breathing deepens and the muscles relax. This all helps a patient get through an illness", she said. Executive In Charge of the Project, Margaret Thornton said "We have recorded shorter durations of stay for many patients, a decrease in the number of painkillers required by those in pain and patients are easier to deal with."

So I guess you could say they take their laughter seriously.

Humour Heals. He who laughs, lasts.

FREEDOM OF SPEECH

Suppression of speech. Caesar did it to the Romans, the Sheriff of Nottingham did it to Robin Hood and his Merry Men, Hitler did it to the Germans and Jews. In the '90's, they gave us Political Correctness and the Thought Police were marshalled once again to suppress freedom of speech. Speech is the audio version of thought so how can you suppress people's thoughts? You can't. Just because you can't *say it*, doesn't mean you won't *think it*. When I was a kid at school I got a continual hard time from a teacher called Mr Spencer. I think I must have looked like someone he hated. He was 50 and a mean one. He looked like he'd been weaned on a pickle. In fact, if Moses had seen *his* face, there would have been another commandment.

One day I'd had enough of his cracks about me and in response to a snide remark to the class, I stood up and said "Sir, if bullshit was put to music, you'd be a symphony orchestra!" The class laughed, some ducked for cover. Mr Spencer was not impressed. I was put into detention for a week. I liked school now - it gave me an opportunity to practice the jokes I read in books and Dad's Playboy magazines. Dad read Playboy for the same reasons he read National Geographic - he could see pretty pictures of places he'd never get to visit. And now Mr Spencer had volunteered for target practice. He wouldn't stop so neither did I. I was much better at it than him, because I'd practised.

Mr Spencer loved to brag about his upbringing in the country. "One day I was walking in the wheat field," he told the class. I jumped in with,

14
—

"... and you scared the crows so badly that they brought back the wheat they stole last year." Detention again.

"Before I was born, my mother wanted a daughter and my father wanted a son," he confided to the class on another occasion..."and they were both happy!" I announced. More detention.

"My grandfather worked in a timber mill," he said one day, thinking we were interested in his boring life. "I'll bet he gave the whole town circular saws!" I exclaimed.

There was hardly a week that I didn't bring home a note from school demanding a good excuse for my presence. "He started it ..." I protested to the headmaster. The headmaster, Mr Richards was 65 and mean too. "Do you comb your hair with a sponge?" I asked. That was a poorly timed joke it seemed. He produced a 10 inch leathery-looking weapon, walked towards me with it and said "Bend over". Luckily, this wasn't a catholic school or I might have been given the breathalyser. It was a leather strap and he gave me six of the best. "And to think that I stood up for you this week!" I said indignantly. "Really?" he asked disbelieving. "Yes!" I said. "Some of the kids said you were a fat, ugly slob with a face like a sheep's arse. I told them you were **not** fat!"

And so began my career as a public speaker.

Recently, two of those teachers came to one of my evening seminars and when I spotted them in the audience, I used the same sort of lines on them that I'd used at school. They laughed all night, but I never got detention. And they paid $90 to get a seat.

God moves in strange ways.

Well, the headmaster made me apologise to Mr Spencer. As he walked me back to the class he said "You are never to say those dreadful things about me in this school again!" And I obeyed. I never said them again. Not at that school. I definitely cracked those jokes about him everywhere else. And I thought them and whispered them to my friends.

So - the point? The Thought Police may stop you from saying something publicly but they'll never stop you thinking it or saying it in private. If Mr Spencer had addressed his attitude towards me, the problem would have gone away.

BEING OFFENDED

Political Correctness is a repressive system developed by university boffins, frustrated feminists and other unhappy people who have nothing better to do. As long as there are Irishman, there will be Irish Jokes. Or Asian jokes or feminist jokes.

The English always tell Australian jokes about me "You can tell an Australian - but you can't tell him much!" "What's the difference between Australia and yoghurt? At least yoghurt has some culture!" "Why are Aussies so well-balanced? They have a chip on both shoulders." " ... and they're level-headed. They dribble out of both sides of their mouth."

But I don't choose to be offended. If it's a good joke (or true!) I'll laugh just as hard as the English. And later, I'll tell it against the Kiwis or the Yanks. Or write it in this book. Being offended is a choice. Others can't offend you - you **choose** to be offended. And choosing offence tells the world that you are unable to come to terms with the problems in your world.

So it doesn't make sense to choose offence. Or shame, embarrassment or feeling hurt. These choices show everyone that you have low self-esteem and aren't in control of your emotions. You can feel **offended** that it rains on your birthday party but the rain doesn't care - it just keeps raining.

You can choose to feel **embarrassed** because someone tells a joke that says your country persons are stupid. That doesn't mean that they *are* stupid and even if you agree that they are, abusing the joke-teller won't make them any smarter.

If you're a lawyer, you can choose to **feel hurt** because someone jokes that lawyers are liars. That doesn't mean that all lawyers are liars or that you are a liar. And reporting the joke-teller to the Thought Police won't stop him from thinking it. It only confirms that lawyers are worse than he thought!

You can choose **anger** because the traffic is backed-up. But it won't clear the traffic. If you take a calm analytical approach about why the traffic is backed up you may come up with a solution that can help solve the problem. There's no point in choosing anger. Or telling the Thought Police about it.

Well, when I finished school Mr Spencer said it was a highlight for him to see the back of my head. And he told me so. He said I was a smartarse. I told him that a smartarse was anyone who could sit on an ice-cream and tell you what flavour it was. I guess he was right.

DON'T TAKE YOURSELF SERIOUSLY

Barbara Pease is my significant other - (before

Political Correctness she was my W.I.F.E. which means washing, ironing, fun and entertainment). She runs our company and travels the world. She doesn't, won't and isn't interested in cooking. Where other husbands will get pot roast, I'll get roast pot. If she cooks, we all pray before we eat, even though we're not religious. She gave my penis a name - Willy. She says all men should name their penises because you don't want a complete stranger to make all your major life decisions. Whenever she sees me she smiles - which proves she can recognise a joke. She told me that I was ready for marriage when I met her because I wore an earring. I'd experienced pain and bought jewellery.

The best humour you can tell is on *yourself*.

Take what you do seriously. But never take yourself seriously.

A WORD ON DISCRIMINATION

There's a paradox here - if you insult or offend **one** person or **one** group you can be accused of being discriminatory. If you offend **everyone** you won't be accused.

This book is definitely non-discriminatory. **Everyone** gets a serve.

Allan Pease

P.S. *You're welcome to copy any of the cartoons you like and fax them to your friends.*

CONTENTS

When you're down and out...everyone wants to screw you!!

— from *Rude and Politically Incorrect Jokes* by Allan Pease

LAWYERS AND JUDGES

The lawyer went into the doctor's surgery with a frog on his head.

"That's a nasty looking growth", said the doctor.

"I'll say it is", said the frog. "It started out as a pimple on my arse."

***

What's the difference between a prostitute and a lawyer?

Not much, except a prostitute will stop screwing you once you're dead.

***

What's black and brown and looks great on a lawyer?

A Doberman.

***

"I'm in deep financial trouble and need some advice", said the client to his lawyer. "I'm down to my last hundred dollars and want to know if you can answer just two questions for that amount."

"Certainly sir", said the lawyer, "what's the second question?"

A new law says that solicitors and barristers must be buried in holes forty feet deep.

Deep down, they are good people.

***

"You seem like an intelligent, honest man who wouldn't lie to the court," the lawyer said sarcastically to the witness.

"If I wasn't under oath I'd return the compliment," said the witness.

***

The clerk addressed the prisoner in the dock. "Prisoner, do you wish to challenge the jury?"

The prisoner looked at the jury. "Not all of them at once," he said, "but I reckon I could go a few rounds with the little fat guy in the middle."

***

What's the difference between a lawyer and a football?

You only get six points for kicking a football between the posts.

***

What is it that a lawyer can do that a duck can't?

Stick his bill up his arse.

What's the difference between a catfish and a lawyer.

One's a bottom-crawling scum sucker, and the other's a fish.

***

Did you hear about the lawyer who was so big that when he died they couldn't find a coffin big enough to hold the body.

They gave him an enema and buried him in a hat box.

***

Obscenity is anything that gives the Judge a fat.

***

What do you call a barrister with an I.Q. of 25?

Your Honour.

***

"Do you know how to save a lawyer from drowning?"

"No,I don't."

"Good!"

***

He introduced himself as a criminal lawyer. "Well, at least you're honest about describing yourself", said the client.

***

The University has stopped using rats for experiments. They've decided to use lawyers for three reasons.

1. Lawyers are more plentiful than rats.
2. Some rats are nice and you can get attached to them.
3. There are some things that rats just won't do.

But they had to stop using lawyers and they're back to using rats, because they found that lawyers aren't that close to human beings.

***

What's the difference between a lawyer and a rooster?
   A rooster clucks defiant.

***

What's 12 inches long, transparent and lies in the gutter?
   A lawyer with the shit kicked out of him.

***

The young lawyer had just opened for business. He had been sitting behind his desk for a week when at last he saw a man come into his outer office. Quickly he picked up the phone and pretended to be negotiating a big deal. He spoke loudly about large sums of money and possible Court proceedings. When he hung up, he looked at the visitor and asked, "Can I help you?"

"Yes", said the man, "I've come to connect your phone."

***

Why don't you ever see lawyers at the beach?
The cats keep covering them up with sand.

***

Two lawyers were walking along, negotiating a case.

"Look", said one to the other, "let's be honest with each other."

"Okay, you first," replied the other.

That was the end of the discussion.

***

What do lawyers use for birth control?
Their personalities.

***

A lawyer was visiting Bangkok. He went to the most exclusive Escort Agency and asked if he could take Sue-Lin to dinner.

"Yes", said the Madam. "It will cost you $300 for Sue-Lin's company. No sex. And she must be back here at 11 p.m."

Sue-Lin was the most beautiful Eurasian creature the lawyer had ever seen. He wined her and dined her, but before returning her home, he gave her $1,000. "This is a gift", he said.

Sue-Lin told him that he was a wonderful and generous man.

"Will you have dinner with me again tomorrow night?" he asked.

"Oh yes", she replied. "I will cancel all my previous engagements."

So the next night, the lawyer wined and dined Sue-Lin again. He could not get over her beauty, and at the end of the evening, gave her another $1,000 and said, "Sue-Lin, this is for you."

Sue-Lin was overcome with gratitute and had a tear in her eye. "You are the most generous person I have ever met", she said.

"Would you come to dinner with me again tomorrow night?", asked the lawyer.

"Of course I will!", said Sue-Lin. "I will do anything for such a kind, generous man."

So he wined and dined Sue-Lin again, and took her back to her apartment, where he gave her another $1,000. This overwhelmed Sue-Lin. She fell into the lawyer's arms and then onto the bed, where they made passionate love until three in the morning. The lawyer told Sue-Lin that he had to leave as he was catching a plane for Sydney at six o'clock that morning.

"Sydney!", said Sue-Lin. "You didn't tell me you came from Sydney! I have a sister who lives in Sydney!"

"Yes, I know", said the lawyer. "She sent you the $3,000."

***

When Pope John Paul died, he arrived at the Pearly Gates at the same time as a lawyer. Both were ushered in to see St. Peter. He gave the lawyer a mansion with a swimming pool and the Pope had to share a double room and an old T.V. set. The Pope was disappointed and queried this decision. St. Peter explained.

"We've got a hundred Popes up here, but that's the first lawyer."

***

What do you call a bigot with a wig?

Your Honour.

***

"On what grounds do you want a divorce?", asked the lawyer.

"Cruelty", she replied. "Every night he wants

sex and his donk is as big as a horse. It hurts unbearably."

"If that's the case, I will file your petition", said the lawyer.

"File my petition? Not likely! Let the bastard sandpaper his."

***

It was a sexual harassment case, and it had been a long day. The young lady accusing her boss said that she was too embarrassed to repeat the words that he said to her. The Judge suggested she write them down and that the words be shown to himself and the jury.

She passed the note, which read "Get your pants off and have a drink with me tonight", to the Judge, who then passed it on to Fred, the foreperson of the jury. Fred passed it on to the next juror, a middle aged spinster who had nodded off in the stuffy courtroom. He had to nudge her. She woke, read the note, winked at Fred and put the note in her handbag.

***

"Have you anything to say for yourself?", asked the Judge after hearing the case.

"Fuck all", muttered the Defendant.

"What did he say?" asked the Judge, who was a bit hard of hearing.

The Clerk whispered in the Judge's ear. "He said 'Fuck all', your Worship."

"That's funny", said the Judge, "I'm sure I saw his lips move."

RELIGION

Sister Mary and Sister Barbara were driving along a country road when the Devil appeared on the bonnet of their car and made menacing gestures.

"Quick," said Sister Mary, "Show him your cross!"

Sister Barbara leaned out the window and yelled, "Piss off you bastard! I'll kick you in the fucking balls if you try that again! Don't mess with me you prick!"

***

The Pope's doctor had told him that his celibacy was causing serious health problems. The doctor recommended that the Pope have regular sex with a woman or else he could die. The Pope resisted this suggestion for some time, but finally came to realise that it was the only answer.

"OK, I'll do it," he said, "but on three conditions. First she must be catholic, second she must live in the local parish, and third it must completely confidential."

As the doctor was leaving the room the Pope yelled, "...and by the way Doc, can you get me one with big tits?"

***

A group of nuns arrived at the Pearly Gates and ask St. Peter for admission to Heaven.

"If any of you have seen a man's private parts you will have to wash yourself in holy water before entering Heaven," he said. The first nun came forward and said, "I have seen a man's private parts."

"Wash your eyes in holy water and pass through sister ," said St Peter.

The second nun said, "I have touched a man's private parts."

"Wash your hands sister and pass through" he said.

The fourth nun tapped the third nun on the shoulder and said, "Sister would you mind changing places with me. I'd like to gargle some of that holy water before you go sitting your arse in it."

***

The Evangelist settled into his motel room after a busy day of rousing, table thumping delivery of his message to the public. Before heading downstairs for a nightcap, he flipped idly through the

Gideon Bible which sat on his bedside table, as indeed it does in every motel room throughout the world.

Downstairs in the bar he soon formed a chatty association with the barmaid, and, with his usual gift of the gab, invited her to his room for a blessing. A few more drinks and hands-on healing and it wasn't long before they were getting into a very ticklish situation.

"Are you sure this is alright", giggled the barmaid. "You are a man of the cloth."

He reassured her, "It is permissible, my child. It is written in the Bible", after which he proceeded to have his way with her.

Whilst enjoying a post-coital cigarette, the barmaid turned to him and said, "Show me - where is it written in the Bible that it was alright to do what we did?"

Whereupon he picked up the Bible, turned to the inside cover and showed her the passage written there: "The downstairs barmaid is a certainty."

***

Why was Jesus crucified and not electrocuted?

Because if they had electrocuted him, today, 100 million Catholics wouldn't bless themselves with a cross. They would scream "Aaaarrrrgggghhh!" and shake.

***

As the shop steward passed his local Church, the large sign proclaimed, **"Jesus Lives!"** Hurrying to the Union office, he worriedly queried, "Does this mean no more Easter holidays?"

***

Princess Sophie gave birth and a twenty one gun salute was fired. Sister Mary at the local convent gave birth and they fired a dirty old Canon.

***

The crowd had gathered around Mary Magdalene, preparing to stone her. Jesus held up his hand and said, "Whoever is without sin, let them cast the first stone."

Out of the crowd came a rock. It hit Mary Magdalene on the head and killed her. Jesus looked exasperated and yelled, "Mother, sometimes you just piss me off."

***

Sitting in the plane was a Bishop and a young Priest. The Bishop was doing 'The Times' crossword.

"Four letter word, exclusively female, ends in UNT", he mumbled.

"Aunt", suggested the young Priest.

"Oh", said the Bishop, "have you got an eraser?"

The white missionary was in big trouble. The tribal chief was very angry.

"My sister had a white baby last night and you're the only white man in this area. You must die for this breach of tribal law."

"But Chief!", said the missionary nervously, "I know it looks that way but these things happen. For instance, see your flock of sheep over there? Can you see the black sheep? There is only one."

"Alright, alright", replied the Chief, "I'll keep quiet if you'll keep quiet."

***

O'Brien was dying.

"Sister", he said, "call the Vicar."

"Don't you want a Priest?"

"No, I want to become a Protestant", said O'Brien. "Better one of those bastards die instead of a good Catholic."

***

Pat and Mick were working on the road outside the local whorehouse when they saw the vicar approach, look cautiously around and enter the building.

"Look at that!", said Pat. "That dirty Protestant minister! What a hypocrite!"

Not long after, they noticed a rabbi approach, look cautiously around and enter the building.

"Did you see that?", said Mick. "The bloody Jews are no better."

Half an hour went by, when they noticed Father O'Flanagan looking furtively about before dashing in to the whorehouse.

"Mick", said Pat, "take off your hat. One of those poor girls must be dying in there."

***

Computers go back to the Garden of Eden. Eve had an Apple and Adam had a Wang.

***

The young man entered the confessional box.

"Father, I had sex with a pair of beautiful eighteen year old nymphomaniac twins every night last week."

"Disgusting! What kind of Catholic are you?", reproached the priest.

"I'm not a Catholic", he replied.

"Then why are you telling me this?"

"I'm telling everyone!"

***

Pat and Mick went into Dublin every Saturday night together. Pat always went to confession at the local church on the way while Mick waited outside.

"It's been a week since my last confession, Father", said Pat, "and I must confess that I have sinned of the flesh again."

"Was it Mary Fitzgerald, that hussy from the

dairy?"

"No, Father."

"Was it Maureen O'Connor from the fruit shop then?"

"No, Father."

"Then it must have been Kathleen Dwyer."

"No, Father."

"Well, do your usual fifty Hail Marys and thirty five Our Fathers and be off with you."

Pat joined Mick outside the church and Mick asked, "What did you get?"

"I got three certainties for tonight!", replied Pat.

***

Mary was entering the church. She had no head covering and was wearing a see-through blouse.

"You can't come into church like that!", exclaimed the priest.

"But I have a divine right!", replied Mary.

"You have a divine left too, but you still can't come in without a hat."

***

"What's this?" (hold your palm up to your mouth and make biting gestures.)

Jesus biting his nails.

***

The Hindu rushed into St Patrick's Cathedral and cried, "My Karma has just run over your Dogma."

The drunk boarded the bus, took a seat next to a priest and began reading his newspaper. After a while, in a slurred voice, the drunk asked the priest, "Do you know what causes arthritis?"

The priest looked at the drunk disdainfully. "Yes, my man. I can tell you. It's too much alcohol! Too much immoral living! Too much smoking. How long have you had it?"

"S'not me", said the drunk. "It sez here the Pope's got it."

***

Adam was the world's first butcher.

He was always chasing Eve with his meat waggin.

***

Eve was the first carpenter.

She made Adam's banana stand.

***

The evangelist decided to knock on the new neighbour's door. A boy opened the door and just stood there, speechless, staring at him. When he asked the boy where his mother was, the boy pointed to the bedroom. The evangelist opened the bedroom door and found the boy's mother in bed with a goat!

Stunned, the evangelist charged down the stairs, grabbed the little boy by the shoulders and yelled, "Do you know what's in bed with your mother? Do you know what they're doing? Doesn't it bother you?" The boy looked at him, shook his head and answered, "Na a a a a-a."

The Sunday School teacher asked the class, "Who went to Mount Olive?"

"Popeye!", came the quick reply.

**

The proud father handed the baby to the Priest for the christening.

"And what name have you given this little boy?", asked the Priest.

"It's a girl", said the father out of the side of his mouth, "You've got hold of my thumb."

**

What's the difference between a woman in Church and a woman in the bath?

One has a soul full of hope.

**

They were a very religious couple. They had attended Church and prayed together for many years, and this was their wedding night. He changed into his pyjamas in the bathroom and when he came back into the bedroom, his bride was naked between the sheets.

"I thought I would find you on your knees", he said.

"Oh, we can do it that way too, but I thought tonight I'd like to see your face", she replied.

41

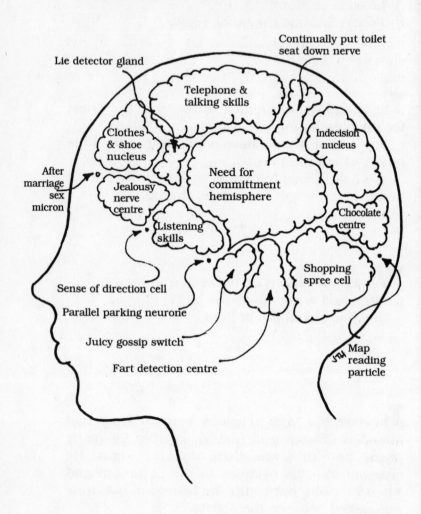

The female brain

Because We Are Men

If we put a woman on a pedestal and try to protect her from the Rat Race, we're a male chauvinist pig. If we stay at home and do the housework, we're a pansy. If we work too hard, there is never any time for her and the kids. If we don't work hard enough, we're a good for nothing layabout. If she has a boring repetitive job with low pay, that is exploitation. If we have a boring repetitive job with low pay, we should get off our butts and find something better.

If a man gets a promotion ahead of her, that is favouritism. If she gets a promotion ahead of a man, that is equal opportunity.

If we mention how nice she looks, that is sexual harassment. If we keep quiet, that is typical male indifference. If we cry, we're a sheila. If we don't, we're an insensitive bastard.

If a man thumps her, that is wife bashing. If she thumps him, that's self defence.

If he makes a decision without consulting her, he's a chauvinist. If she makes a decision without regard for his feelings, then she's a liberated woman. If he asks her to do something she doesn't enjoy, that is domination. If she asks him it's a favour.

If we appreciate the female form and frilly underwear we're sexual perverts. If we don't notice, we're poofters. If we like a woman to keep in shape and shave her legs, that is sexist. If we don't care, that is unromantic. If we try to keep ourselves in shape, that is vanity. If we don't, we're slobs.

If we buy her flowers, we're after something. If we don't, we're forgetful. If we are proud of our achievements, we're up ourselves. If we aren't, we're not ambitious. If we ask for a cuddle, we never think of anything else but sex. If we're totally wrecked after a bad day at the office, we never give a stuff about other people's needs.

If she has a headache, it's because she's tired. If he has a headache, it's because he doesn't love her anymore. If we want sex too often, we're over sexed. If we can't perform on cue, there must be someone else.

***

Why are pubic hairs curly?
So they don't poke you in the eye.

***

I can't get over a girl like you... so answer the phone yourself.

***

What's the difference between a woman with her period and a terrorist?

   You can negotiate with a terrorist.

***

What's the definition of 'making love'?
It's what a woman does while a man's screwing her.

***

A woman's best friends are her legs, but even best friends must part.

***

Man cannot live on bread alone. He must have a bit of crumpet.

***

Why does it take a woman with P.M.S. three hours to cook a small chicken?
   BECAUSE IT JUST FUCKIN' DOES !!!!!!!

***

What's the difference between a woman and a washing machine?

   A washing machine doesn't ring you up constantly after you've left a load in it.

Jenny Jones woke up one night to find her husband pushing aspirin into her mouth.

What do you think your doing?", she screamed at him.

"It's for your headache", he replied.

"I haven't got a headache", she gasped.

"Great! Let's fuck!"

***

Have you heard about the latest bra for middle aged women?

It's called Sheep Dog. It rounds them up and points them in the right direction.

***

Why was alcohol invented?

So ugly women could get laid too.

DOGS ARE BETTER THAN WOMEN BECAUSE......

- Dogs don't cry
- Dogs love it when your friends come over
- Dogs don't care if you use their shampoo
- Dogs think you're a great singer

- Dogs don't expect you to call when you run late
- The later you are, the more excited dogs are to see you
- Dogs will forgive you for playing around with other dogs
- Dogs don't notice if you call them by another dog's name
- Dogs are excited by rough play
- Dogs don't mind if you give their offspring away
- Dogs understand that farts are funny
- Dogs can appreciate excessive body hair
- Dogs like it when you leave things on the floor
- A dog's disposition stays the same all month long
- Dogs never need to examine the relationship
- Dogs parents never visit
- Dogs love long car trips
- Dogs understand that instincts are better than asking for directions
- Dogs never criticise
- Dogs agree that you have to raise your voice to get your point across
- Dogs never expect gifts
- Dogs don't worry about germs
- Dogs don't want to know about every other dog you've ever had
- Dogs don't let magazine articles guide their lives
- Dogs would rather you buy them a hamburger dinner than a lobster one
- Dogs don't keep you waiting
- Dogs enjoy heavy petting in public
- Dogs find you amusing when you're drunk

A man and a woman were in an elevator in the Empire State Building when the cable broke. As the elevator plummetted down, the woman looked at the man and said, "Is there one more chance of being a woman?"

"There sure is", said the man as he quickly pulled his trousers off. He threw them at her, saying, "Here, iron these!"

THE LAST 10 THINGS A WOMAN WOULD EVER SAY

1 Could our relationship be more physical? I'm tired of just being friends.

2 Go ahead and leave the seat up. I love the feel of cold,wet porcelain.

3 I think hairy bums are really sexy.

4 Wow, get a whiff of that one! Do it again.

5 Please don't throw that old t-shirt away. The holes in the armpits are just too cute.

6 This diamond is much too big!

7 I won't even put my lips on that thing unless I get to swallow!

8 Wow, it really is ten inches!

9 Does this make my bum look too small?

10 I'm wrong. You must be right again.

***

What do women and cow-pats have in common?

The older they get, the easier they are to pick up.

***

The woman of the 21st century is well educated, well dressed, highly motivated, professionally oriented, drives a B.M.W. and thinks that cooking and fucking are cities in China.

***

Women have only got themselves to blame for all the lying that men do.

They ask too many questions.

***

They've just released a new Barbie Doll called Divorced Barbie.

It comes with all Ken's stuff.

***

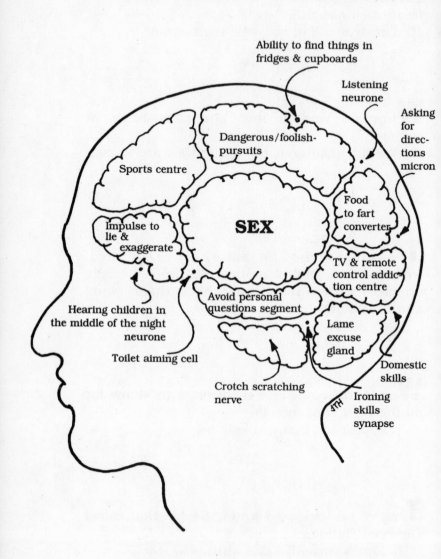

Ability to find things in fridges & cupboards

Listening neurone

Asking for directions micron

Dangerous/foolish-pursuits

Sports centre

Food to fart converter

SEX

Impulse to lie & exaggerate

TV & remote control addiction centre

Hearing children in the middle of the night neurone

Avoid personal questions segment

Lame excuse gland

Toilet aiming cell

Domestic skills

Crotch scratching nerve

Ironing skills synapse

The male brain

JOKES ABOUT MEN
The Rules According to a Woman

1. The woman always makes the Rules.

2. The Rules are subject to change at any time without prior notification.

3. No man can possibly know all the Rules.

4. If the woman suspects the man knows the Rules, she must immediately change some or all of the Rules.

5. The woman is never wrong.

6. If the woman is wrong, it is due to misunderstanding, which was a direct result of something the man did or said.

7. The man must apologise immediately for causing said misunderstanding.

8. The woman may change her mind at any time.

9. The man must never change his mind without the express written consent of the woman.

10. The woman has every right to be angry and/or upset at any time.

11   The man must remain calm at all times unless the woman wants him to be angry and/or upset.

12   The woman must, under no circumstances, let the man know whether or not she wants him to be angry and/or upset.

13   The man is expected to mind-read at all times.

14   The man who doesn't abide by the Rules can't take the heat, lacks backbone and is a wimp.

15   Any attempt to document the Rules could result in bodily harm.

16   If the woman has PMT, all the Rules are null and void.

17   The woman is ready when she is ready.

18   The man must be ready at all times.

Adam came first. But men always do.

***

What's the difference between a 21st century woman and a computer?

A 21st century woman won't accept a three and a half inch floppy.

***

"Of course there's nobody else!", she said to her doubting boyfriend. "Do you think I'd be going out with a dickhead like you if there was?"

***

What's the difference between a new husband and a new dog?

After twelve months the dog is still excited to see you.

***

What is a major conflict of interest for men?

When pizza arrives during sex.

***

How do men practice safe sex?

They meet their mistress at least 30 kilometres from where they live.

What can you say to a man whose just had sex?

Anything you like - he's asleep.

***

Why do men find it difficult to make eye contact?

Breasts don't have eyes.

***

"God, why did you make woman so beautiful?" he asked.

"So you would love her." God replied.

"But God, why did you make her so dumb?" he asked.

"So she would love you."

***

The feminists were all hailing the Miracle Birth - the baby had both a dick and a brain.

***

Bob was going over the household budget and was complaining to his wife about her expenditure.

"You can clean the house yourself", he said. "That will save on the cleaning lady."

"You can also learn to cook. That will save on restaurants."

"And while you're at it, you should learn to iron, so we won't have to pay the ironing lady."

"And you should learn to fuck", said his wife, "then we could get rid of the gardener."

***

When a woman marries she expects three S's: sensitivity sincerity and sharing. What does she get? The three B's: burps, body odour and beer breath.

***

What's a man's idea of helping to make the bed?

He gets out of it.

***

Marriage is the price men pay for sex and sex is the price women pay marriage.

***

Why are men like public toilets?
They're either vacant, engaged or full of shit.

***

24 Reasons Why Women Prefer Chocolate to Sex:

1   You can get plenty of chocolate.
2   Chocolate satisfies you even when it goes soft.
3   You can safely have chocolate while you're driving.
4   You can make chocolate last as long as you want it to.
5   You can have chocolate anywhere (even in front of your mother).
6   If you bite the nuts too hard, chocolate won't mind.
7   You can have chocolate on your desk without upsetting your workmates.
8   Two women can have chocolate together and not be called dykes.
9.   You can ask a stranger for chocolate and not get a bad reputation.
10   You won't get hair in your mouth when you suck on chocolate.
11   "If you love me, you'll swallow it" has real meaning with chocolate.
12   With chocolate there's no need to fake enjoyment.
13   Chocolate doesn't make you pregnant.
14   You can have chocolate at any time of the month.
15   It's easy to find good chocolate.
16   You can have as many different chocolates as you like.
17   You're never too old for chocolate.
18   When you're having chocolate, it doesn't keep anyone awake in the next room.

19 Even small chocolates are good.
20 You don't have to beg to get chocolate.
21 You can have chocolate with kids and not go to jail.
22 Chocolate doesn't keep you awake snoring after you've had it.
23 You can have chocolate all weekend and still walk OK on Monday.
24 It's easy to find eight inches of chocolate.

***

He was very suave and as he slid up to a blonde at the singles bar, he thought he'd try out his new pick-up line.

"Hi beautiful. I'd love to get into your pants."

"Why?", she replied, "there's already one arsehole in there."

***

The elderly spinster was asked why she never married.

"I have a dog that growls, a parrot that swears, a fireplace that smokes and a cat that stays out all night. Why would I want a husband?"

***

I believe in circumcision - it's no skin off my nose.

***

THE LAST TEN THINGS MEN WOULD EVER SAY

10   I think Barry Manilow is really cool.

9   While I'm up, can I get you a cup of coffee?

8   I think hairy legs are really sexy.

7   Her tits are just too big.

6   Sometimes I just want to be held.

5   That chick on "Murder, She Wrote" gives me a hard-on.

4   Sure, I'd love to wear condom.

3   We haven't been dress shopping for ages. Let's go now. Can I carry your purse for you?

2   Fuck Monday Night Footy. Let's watch Pride and Prejudice!

1   I think we're lost. I'll pull over and ask for directions.

***

What's the definition of the perfect male lover?

He makes love until 2 a.m. then turns into chocolate.

***

Why do most men prefer women with big tits and tight twats?

Because most men have big mouths and small dicks.

***

Why do men cum quickly?

So they can rush down to the pub and tell their mates.

***

The marriage counsellor asked her why she felt the relationship was over.

"Because he's a lousy lover", she replied.

The counsellor asked the husband how he felt about it. He replied, "How can she tell that in three minutes?"

***

"Darling", he said, "am I the first man to make love to you?"

"Well you could be... were you behind the stage of the Rolling Stones concert in 1993?"

"Darling, am I the first man to make love to you?"

"You could be... you look kinda familiar."

***

"I went to the doctor about my piles and he told me I had beautiful firm breasts, just like an eighteen year old."

"Oh yes?", smirked her husband, "but what did he say about your forty five year old arse?"

"Your name wasn't mentioned", she replied.

FEMINISTS ON MEN

Why does a woman need an arsehole? Someone's got to put out the garbage.

***

How many men does it take to change a light globe?

Ten. One to change the bulb and nine to pin the medal on his chest.

***

"Your boobs are too small."

Why do men have holes in the end of their penises?

To get air to their brains.

**

When a woman makes a fool of a man, it's usually an improvement.

**

Men prefer looks to brains because most men see better than they think.

**

A woman only wants to have a child, not marry one.

**

Some women get excited about nothing, then marry him.

**

Why is a pig better than a man?

Pigs don't turn into men when they have too much to drink.

Women can take a joke - they get married to prove it!

***

What do you call a man who has lost 99% of his brains?
A widower.

***

When you look at the worms we pick up, it's no wonder men call us Birds.

***

What is the useless bit of skin at the end of a penis called?
A man.

***

"Doctor, I have a small embarrassing wart."
"Then divorce him."

***

Modern women think of having children at age 35.
At age 35, modern men think of dating children.

Why did Dorothy get lost in the Land of Oz?

Because she had three men giving her directions.

***

What's the difference between a man with a mid life crisis and a circus clown?

A circus clown knows he's wearing funny clothes.

***

What's the best way of making sure your man doesn't make a fool of himself at a party?

Leave him at home.

***

What can you immediately tell about the guys down the gym who parade around showing off their perfect bodies?

They're unemployed.

***

Why is it a waste of time telling a man to go to hell?

He'd get lost on the way.

***

What do men and pantyhose have in common?
They cling to women but one rough spot and watch them run!

***

How can you be sure a man is planning for the future?
He buys two cases of beer instead of one.

***

How are men like bread?
They're easier to take when you butter them up.

***

Why are men like babies?
They make a fuss when you try to change them.

***

Why are men like vending machines?
They'll take your money and half the time they won't work.

***

What's a man's idea of helping out around the house?

He drops his clothes where it's easy for you to pick them up.

***

What recycling do most men do?

They use their beer cans as ashtrays before throwing them on the side of the road.

***

Why did Moses spend 40 years wandering in the desert?

He refused to ask for directions.

***

Why are bachelors like used cars?

They're easy to find, cheap and unreliable.

***

What's the difference between a clitoris and a hotel bar?

Most men can find a bar in under four minutes.

***

Any woman who thinks that the way to a man's heart is through his stomach is aiming too high.

***

What do men and floor tiles have in common?
   If you lay them properly, you can walk over them forever.

***

She was looking for a husband so she put an ad in the Lonely Hearts column. She got fifty replies, all saying "You can have mine."

***

Why do men always have a stupid look on their face?
   Because they are stupid.

***

"My boyfriend's a SNAG", said Jody. "A Sensitive New Age Guy."
   "That's nice", replied Carol. "Mine's a Caring Understanding Nineties Type."

***

Why do men like masturbation?
Because it's sex with someone they love.

***

What do you call a man with 99% of his brain missing?
Castrated.

***

Why are all men like blenders?
You need one, but you're not quite sure why.

***

How can you tell if a man is sexually excited?
He's breathing.

***

What's a man's idea of foreplay?
Half an hour of begging.

***

Why is food better than men?
You don't have to wait an hour for seconds.

Why are men and parking spots similar?

The good ones are already taken and the ones that are left are handicapped.

***

What do men and beer bottles have in common?

They're both empty from the neck up.

***

How many men does it take to screw in a light bulb?

One. Men will screw anything.

***

Why do women rub their eyes when they wake up?

Because they don't have balls to scratch.

***

Why don't men have to use toilet paper?

Because God made them perfect arseholes.

***

How do you save a man from drowning?
Take your foot off his head.

***

What do you call a man with an I.Q. of 50?
Gifted.

***

How many men does it take to change a roll of toilet paper?
It's unknown 'cos it's never happened.

***

What do toilet seats, anniversaries and a clitoris have in common?
Men miss them all.

***

How do you keep a man interested after marriage?
Wear perfume that smells like beer.

***

Why do men marry women who remind them of their mothers?
Who else would put up with them.

Colleen had just accepted Paddy's proposal of marriage and had asked him home for the week-end to meet her parents. Innocently she burst into the bathroom and saw Paddy standing naked. She ran to her mother and asked "Mother, what's that thing hanging between Paddy's legs?"

"Don't worry, that's his penis, it's nothing to be concerned about."

"But what's that big purple knob on the end?" asked Colleen.

"That's just the head", her mother replied.

"And what are those two round things about 18 inches back from the head?" asked Colleen.

"Well", said mother, "for your sake, I hope they're the cheeks of his arse."

***

The annoyed wife phoned her husband at the club, told him how late it was and politely suggested he should come home. Now.

"But darling", the man pleaded, "I'm playing the pokies. I can't quit now. I'm on a winning streak. I've got a stack of 20 cent pieces as long as my dick."

"Huh!", snorted his wife. "You mean to tell me all you've got left is a lousy two bucks?"

***

What is the difference between medium and rare?
Six inches is medium, eight inches is rare.

CATHOLICS

"I'd like a bottle of Johnny Walker please."
Sister Mary asked the surprised bartender. "It's
OK...It's for Mother Superior's constipation."
Later that day the licensee was shocked to see
the nun sitting in the park, pissed.
"Didn't you say that whiskey was for Mother
Superior's constipation?" he asked.
"It is," slurred Sister Mary, "...and when she sees
me she'll shit."

***

The old nun was lecturing the drinker on the
evils of drink as he tried to enter the pub.
"Listen Sister," he said, "Don't knock it if you've
never tried it! If you'd tried even one drink
you'd know what you are talking about," he
said.
    She agreed that he had a point.
    "OK, I'll try just a small drink then," she said.
"I don't want to be seen drinking from a hotel
glass so can you get me some in this water flask?"
she asked.
    He went up to the bar and asked for a gin in the
flask.
    The barman laughed, "Don't tell me that damn
nun's still out there!"

" ... and as I caressed her soft, white, pulsating mound, she gasped as she stroked my throbbing loins, and then I ..."

— from *Rude and Politically Incorrect Jokes* by Allan Pease

The Priest found a quiet corner for his usual morning fondle and got so carried away he didn't see the tourist looking through the window and the flash of a camera told him he'd been sprung. He chased the tourist and begged, "I'll buy the film."

"No, you'll buy the camera!" said the tourist smugly.

"How much?"

"$3,000."

"That's robbery!" said the indignant Priest. But he had little choice so he paid it. Later, Sister Beatrice noticed the Priest's new camera.

"How much did you pay for that?" she asked.

"$3,000!"

"My God," she said. "Somebody must have seen you coming!"

***

Two nuns are walking down an alley at night when two guys jump out and start raping them. The first nun looks to Heaven and says, "Forgive them, Father, for they know not what they do." The second nun looks up and says, "This one does!"

***

Two nuns are cycling down a cobblestone street. The first one says to the other, "I haven't come this way before." The second replies, "Me either. Must be the cobbles."

How do you get a nun pregnant?
Dress her up as an altar boy.

***

Mother Superior walked into the fruit market and asked for 120 bananas.

"If you want a large quantity, it's more economical to buy a case of 144", said the fruiterer.

"Well...O.K... I suppose we could eat the other 24."

***

Father Ryan was giving the nuns their last bit of advice before they set forth into the wide world from their Convent.

"There will be many a wicked man trying to take sexual liberties with you", he said, "but always remember that one hour of pleasure could ruin the whole of your careers. Has anyone got any questions?"

"Yes, Father. How do you make it last an hour?"

***

Zoos are a place for the most unusual accidents. One day, Sister Mary leant too close to the gorillas cage. The big silverback reached out and grabbed her, pulled her through the bars, tore off her habit and screwed her.

When she was finally rescued, she was admitted to the hospital in a state of shock. It was a week before Mother Superior could speak to her. Sister Mary was crying uncontrollably.

"What's wrong?", asked the Mother Superior. "Why are you still so upset?"

"How would you feel?", sobbed Sister Mary. "It's been a week and he hasn't written, hasn't phoned."

***

Christian Brothers are dedicated to the education of children. One Brother and a lay-teacher were taking a class of children on a holiday. They were travelling by plane. The pilot rushed into the cabin and shouted, "We're out of fuel. The plane is going to crash. There are only two parachutes on board. I've got one. You must decide who is going to have the other one."

The Christian Brother said, "We can strap two children together in the one parachute."

The lay-teacher said, "Fuck the children."

The Christian Brother replied, "Do you think we've got time?"

***

Six year old Susie comes home and announces "Mum, God's got a name."

"Really!", said the mother. "How do you know that?"

"In school today, they taught us that God's name is Harold."

"Harold?", replied the mother. " Why Harold?"

"Well", said the six year old, "they taught me this poem -

Our Father, who art in Heaven
Harold be thy name...................."

***

There was an earthquake and the Christian Brothers Monastery was levelled. All fifty Brothers were transported to Heaven at the one time.

At the Pearly Gates, St. Peter said, "Let's go through the entry test as a group. Now, first question. How many of you have played around with little boys?"

Forty nine hands went up.

"Right!", said St. Peter. "You forty nine can go down to Purgatory and take that deaf bastard with you!"

MAGIC LAMPS

A drunk walked into the bar carrying a small case. He put the case on the bar and said to the barman, "I bet you a double scotch I can show you the most amazing thing you've ever seen."

"I've seen some pretty amazing things", said the barman, "but I accept the bet."

The drunk opened his case and there was a pianist 12 inches tall, sitting down playing a piano.

"I've never seen anything like it!", said the barman, "where did you get that?"

"Well", said the drunk, "I dug up this old lamp and when I rubbed it a genie appeared and said I could have one wish."

"What did you ask for?"

"A 12 inch penis!" said the drunk.

***

"**C**ould I rub the lantern?", said the barman.

"Certainly", said the drunk.

The barman rubbed the lamp and a genie appeared.

"What is your one wish?" said the genie.

"I wish I had a million bucks", said the barman, and instantly the bar was full of ducks - a million of them.

"I forgot to tell you", said the drunk, "the genie's got very poor hearing."

***

A man is walking along a deserted beach and finds a bottle and rubs it. A genie appears and grants him any wish.

"I wish I was always hard, and could get more arse than anybody."

So the genie turned him into a seat in a public toilet.

Ray was on holidays in Bangkok when he visited an antique shop and spotted a little ivory idol in the corner of the shop. As he studied it closely he was surprised when it spoke to him.

"Please help me kind Sir. I'm not really an ivory idol, I'm a beautiful young princess, trapped in here by a wicked witch's spell. I need someone to have sex with me to break the spell."

"I'll talk to my brother-in-law about it" said Ray, "He's an idle fucking bastard."

***

John sat still as the fortune-teller gazed into her crystal ball. Suddenly, she started to laugh uncontrollably so John leaned across and punched her in the nose.

It was the first time he had struck a happy medium.

***

Three men are walking down the beach when they find an old lantern in the sand. One gives it a rub and a genie appears. The genie says, "You can have one wish each."

The first guy thinks for a few minutes and says, "I would like to be a hundred times smarter than I am now."

"Your wish is granted", says the genie.

The second guy blurts out, "I'd like to be a thousand times smarter than I am now."

"Your wish is granted", says the genie.

The third guy thinks hard and long and decides, "I would like to be ten thousand times smarter than I am now."

The genie grants his wish, and he turns into a woman.

***

A man is walking on a beach when a bottle washes up on the shore. He opens it and a genie appears and grants him any one wish.

But he's a little embarrassed about his wish, so he whispers it in the genie's ear.

"Tonight at midnight," says the Genie, "your front doorbell will ring and your wish will be granted." He rushes home and waits excitedly. As the clock chimes twelve, the doorbell rings. He opens the door and sees 3 jockeys standing there wearing white hoods and holding a noose.

"Are you the guy who wants to be hung like a donkey?" they ask.

***

The tourist was visiting a Greek fishing village and noticed that a local fisherman had a head no bigger than a tennis ball.

"Why is your head so small?", asked the tourist.

"Well", said the fisherman, "many years ago, I caught a mermaid in my nets. I was going to sell her to a marine park when she said, "Let me free and I will grant you three wishes."

"I would like a beautiful new fishing boat", he said, and lo and behold, a lovely big trawler appeared.

"I wish to be wealthy", he added, and instantly the deck of his new boat was covered with gold ingots.

The fisherman thought how beautiful the mermaid was and said, "For my third and last wish, I wish to make love to you."

"But you can't", replied the mermaid. "I am only half woman."

"Well", said the fisherman, "how about giving me a little head?"

***

Harry was shipwrecked on a tropical island for twelve months. One day out of the surf came a stunning blonde dressed in scuba gear. Slowly, languidly, voluptuously, she walked down the beach and laid down beside Harry.

"Would you like a cigarette?", she purred in his ear.

"Are you kidding!", said Harry.

"She unzipped a pocket of her wetsuit, pulled out a packet of cigarettes, lit one for Harry and put it in his mouth.

Then she asked, "How about a nice cold beer?"

"Yes! Yes! Yes!", cried Harry.

She unzipped another pocket, produced two glasses and a bottle and poured them both a drink.

She moved closer to him, whispering seductively in his ear, "How would you like to play around?"

"Oh God!", said Harry disbelievingly, "don't tell me you've got golf clubs in there too!"

ACCOUNTANTS

What do you call ten accountants buried up to their necks in sand?

Soccer practice.

ACUMEN

Doctor Watson was told by Sherlock Holmes' gardener that a schoolgirl was in Holmes' bedroom. Watson heard muffled sounds coming from the bedroom and, fearing that Holmes was in danger, broke down the door to find Holmes and the girl having a 69.

"Holmes!" said Watson, "What kind of a schoolgirl is this?"

"Elementary, my dear Watson, Elementary."

***

Two young men were in Court on charges of heroin trafficking. Before sentencing, the Judge said, "We have just designed a rehabilitation program, and if you two are prepared to become involved, I will consider not ordering a jail sentence. What I want you to do is spend a hundred hours of your own time trying to reform drug addicts. Do you accept this challenge?"

Both men accepted. "Further", said the Judge, "I want you to report back to me on a monthly basis."

At the end of the first month, the first man claimed that he had influenced thirty five men to enter into a rehabilitation program.

"Remarkable!", said the Judge. "How did you accomplish that?"

"Well", replied the first man. "I draw two circles - a large circle, which I mark 'A' and a small circle inside the large circle which I call 'B'. I explain to the drug addicts that before they start taking dope, their brain is as large as 'A' but after they've been on dope for a couple of years or so, it finishes up the size of 'B', which means you finish up a moron. Then you'll go to jail. This seems to have the required impact and they consent to go onto a rehabilitation program."

"Excellent!", said the Judge excitedly. "Now, how did you go?", he said to the second man.

"Well, I got nine hundred men to enter the rehabilitation program, using the same method but a different story."

"That's amazing! How?", enquired the Judge.

"I draw a large circle 4 inches in diameter, and mark it 'A', and put a small circle in the centre which is about one inch in diameter and mark it 'B', and I tell them that after they've been on dope for a few years, they'll get caught and go to jail. Before they go to jail, their arsehole will be as big as circle 'B', and after they've been in jail for three months, it'll be as big as circle 'A', and this seems to have the desired effect."

He was an uneducated youth. He left school at thirteen and there weren't too many job opportunities available to him. The only thing going was the job of a shit-house cleaner.

"Fill out this form", said the prospective employer.

"But I can't write", said the boy.

"Well", said the prospective employer, "you don't qualify for this job, so be on your way."

On the way home, the lad bought a box of apples for $2. He sold them around the neighbourhood for $6. He developed this idea and years later, finished up with a chain of 20 fruit and vegetable markets.

One day, his bank manager asked him to sign some papers.

"Can't write", he said.

The bank manager was amazed. "You can't write? My God! What would you have been if you had been able to write!"

"A shit-house cleaner", came the reply.

***

A good looking, husky young man walked into the barber shop and asked, "How many before me?"

"Three hair cuts and a shave", replied the barber.

The young man left, but returned the next day and asked, "How many before me today?" "Two hair cuts and three shaves", replied the barber.

This happened five days in a row. Eventually the barber sent his apprentice to follow the young man to see what he did. When the apprentice returned, he said, "I dunno, boss, he just goes 'round to your house."

***

The lonely traveller pulled into a motel and asked the reception clerk for a single room. As the traveller filled out his registration form, he saw a beautiful redhead walking across the lobby. He went over and talked to her. A few minutes later, he came back to the desk with the girl on his arm and said, "Fancy meeting my wife here! Looks like I'll need a double room now."

Next morning he came to the desk to pay his bill but was confronted with an account for $3,000.

"What's this for?" he yelled at the clerk, "I've only been here one night."

"Yes", said the clerk, "but your wife's been here for three weeks."

***

Business was bad. The boss had to dismiss one of his employees. It came down to Jack or Jill. He called Jill into his office and said, "Jill, I have to either lay you or Jack off."

"You're going to have to jack off then, 'cos I've got a bloody headache", Jill responded.

***

Reggie loved dangerous activities, so he went to the pet shop and bought sixty budgerigars, took them home and, using Super Glue, stuck them on the back of his leather jacket. He then went to the top of the tallest building in town and jumped.

Reggie spread his arms. The budgerigars flapped their wings, and down he went.

When the ambulance men arrived to put him on a stretcher, he was still conscious.

"That's the last time I'm going to try budgie jumping", he gasped.

AIRLINES

The 767 was coming in to land and the pilot had forgotten to turn off the P.A. system.

"As soon as I clock off", he said, "I'm going to have a nice cold beer and then screw the arse off that blonde flight attendant."

The horrified flight attendant made a dash toward the cockpit, but tripped over a suitcase in the aisle. A little old lady sitting in an aisle seat whispered, "There's no need to hurry dear, he said he was going to have a beer first."

ALCOHOLICS

10% of all road accidents are caused by drivers under the influence. Does that mean 90% of accidents must be caused by non-drinkers?

***

"Drinking makes you look beautiful, darling."
"But I haven't had a drink."
"No, but I have."

***

What's the difference between a drunk and an alcoholic?

A drunk doesn't have to bother about going to all those boring meetings.

***

Two drunks were having an argument as to who made the best home brewed beer. They eventually decided to send samples for chemical analysis. A week later the reply came. It said "After exhaustive tests of both samples, we are unanimous in our conclusion. Neither of these horses should ever race again."

What happens when you drink milk instead of beer.

— from *Rude and Politically Incorrect Jokes* by Allan Pease

ALL MIXED UP

The fisherman called his guide on his mobile phone to make arrangements for the following day.

"I need two punts and a canoe", he said.

When he arrived, there were two young ladies waiting for him at the fishing lodge.

"What's this?", he asked his guide.

"Well", replied the guide, "when you phoned, there was static on the line. I managed to get a couple of local girls, but what in the hell is a panoe?"

***

The farmer from Louisiana told the lawyer he wanted a divorce.

"Do you have grounds?" asked the lawyer.

"I do", he said, "600 acres."

"Do you have a case?" asked the lawyer.

"No" said the farmer "I have an International Harvester."

"No, no. Do you have a grudge?"

"Yes, we have a double garage, because we have two cars."

"No!" said the lawyer, "Do you have a suit?"

"Only the one I'm wearing." was the reply.

"No, no.", said the lawyer impatiently. "Does your wife beat you up?"

"Never. I'm always up early, and she sleeps in until nine some mornings."

The lawyer was tearing his hair out. "Is she a nagger?"

"No" said the farmer "She's a white gal, but she gave birth to a boy yesterday and he's a nagger, so I want a divorce."

***

Their marriage had been shaky. He was looking shifty and she was sulking. They were washing the dishes. She was washing, he was drying. She handed him a saucer and it broke as he dropped it on the floor.

"Why don't you admit it!", she shouted. "Tell me, where do you go on Tuesday and Thursday nights?"

The husband looked embarrassed and blushed.

"Nowhere much", he said.

"You liar" she said "You're playing football for South Australia! I demand an explanation!" she said.

Still looking embarrassed, the husband said, "I'm going down to the local massage parlour for extra sex and excitement. I'm having sex with prostitutes for money, and that's all. Then I come home."

"You're a liar!", screamed the wife. "You're secretly playing football for South Australia. You're going to practice during the week and playing on Saturday afternoons, aren't you?"

"No! No!", protested the husband. "I just go out for a bit of extra sex! I'm just looking for a stray screw down at the singles bar or a prostitute."

"Do you swear you're not playing football for South Australia?", she demanded.

"I swear I'm not. I'm just spending $400 or $500 a week on professional sex", he continued.

Sobbing with relief, she threw herself into his arms.

"Forgive me", she said, "I'm sorry I didn't trust you."

They continued washing the dishes. She handed him a cup and it slipped from his fingers and smashed on the floor.

"You liar!", she screamed, "You **are** playing for South Australia!"

(Or any other team or club that suits the story)

***

Irene was suspicious that her husband, John, was fooling around with other women. They'd had an invitation to a fancy dress ball so Irene devised a plan to catch John out.

"I've got a headache", she said to John. "Why don't you go to the fancy dress ball on your own?" So John donned his gorilla suit and left for the ball.

Irene put on a monkey suit and headed off to the ball later in the night. Soon after she arrived, there was John, carrying on like a sex maniac and flirting at every opportunity. She made her way over to him and whispered in his ear, "How would you like to take me out in the garden and give me a good screw?"

So he rushed her outside and screwed her on the lawn.

Irene left the ball early to be sure she was home before John.

When they awoke the next morning, she asked him, "How was the ball last night?"

"Pretty boring", he replied. "I finished up playing cards with a couple of other fellas upstairs. Do you remember Alan Jones? Well, I lent him my gorilla suit, and he told me that he had a great time!"

***

Scratching his head and totally confused, the gorilla left the zoo library. He had just finished reading Charles Darwin's 'Origin Of The Species' and 'The Bible' and didn't know whether he was his keeper's brother or his brother's keeper.

***

Custer's last words at the Battle of Little Big Horn: "I'll never understand these damn Indians. Just a few minutes ago they were singing and dancing."

***

Maureen was most surprised to find out that she was pregnant.

"When did you have your last check up?", asked the doctor.

"Never!", insisted Maureen. "An Italian, a Frenchman and a Yank, but never a Czech!"

ALTERNATIVE MEDICINE

Colin was completely bald and clean shaven. He was seeking a remedy from the naturopath for his baldness.

"Every night for three months, rub the secretion from a woman's vagina on your head", advised the naturopath.

In three months, Colin returned.

"You dirty bastard!", exclaimed the naturopath when he saw Colin's luxurious moustache.

***

The doctor dropped into his Club most nights to have his favourite cocktail, an almond daquiri.

One night, Dick the bartender found he was out of almonds, so he added some crushed hickory nuts instead.

The doctor took one sip and beckoned to the barman. "Is this an almond daquiri, Dick?"

"No", said Dick, "it's a hickory daquiri Doc."

ANIMALS

Jim had been Mayor for 20 years and was cheesed off for not receiving appropriate recognition.

"See that suspension bridge?" he complained to a fellow councillor. "I not only designed it, I also put thousands of dollars of my own money into its construction. I've worked on the hospital committee, town planning committee, the school committee. And I get no gratitude or thanks from anyone! Not even 'Well Done'. Do they ever talk about me? No! ... but fuck just one sheep ..."

***

"**A**re you worried about this Mad Cow disease that's going about?" said one cow to another.
"No", replied the other, "cos I'm a goat."

***

Why do black men keep pidgeons?
To teach them how to walk.

***

The local spiritualist church was being addressed by an eminent spiritualist from overseas. After a spine tingling talk about the supernatural, he asked his audience if anyone had had an intimate relationship with a ghost. "Come forward", he said, "and tell us about it."
A hand went up in the middle of the audience. "I have, though I'd prefer not to discuss it."

After great applause and encouragement from the rest of the congregation, the shy, introverted little man came forward and introduced himself as Timothy.

"Well now, Timothy", said the spiritualist, "Tell us about your intimate relationship with a ghost."

"Ghost!", exclaimed Timothy, "I thought you said 'goat'!"

***

Johnny's parrot had just fallen off its perch and died. It was lying on its back on the bottom of the cage, its legs pointing upwards. Johnny asked his father, "Dad, when birds die, why do their feet always point upwards?"

"Well, Johnny, they do that so that God can reach down, take them by the claws and pull them up into Heaven."

Next day when Dad got home from work, Johnny rushed over to him and said, "Gee Dad, we nearly lost Mum today."

"What do you mean?" queried his father.

"Well, I heard these noises upstairs so I rushed up to see what was happening. There was Mum, lying on the bed, with her legs pointing straight up and she was yelling, "God, I'm coming." If it hadn't been for the gardener holding her down, we'd have lost her for sure."

***

There is a car accident, and six people are killed. The only survivor is a chimpanzee that is handcuffed to the steering wheel. The Police arrive. The chimpanzee starts making signs and gestures to the Police.

"I think this chimp is trying to tell us something! Do you understand what we are saying?", the cop asks the chimp.

The chimp nods his head. So they begin to question the chimp.

"Just before the accident, what were the people doing?", asks the cop.

The chimp raises his hand to his mouth and makes drinking gestures.

"Drinking alcohol?", asks the cop.

The chimp nods his head.

"What else were they doing?"

The chimp shows smoking gestures.

"Smoking dope?", asks the cop.

The chimp nods again.

"Anything else?"

The chimp makes hip thrusting gestures.

"Having sex?", said the cop.

The chimp nodded again.

"And what were you doing during all this?", asks the cop.

The chimp grabs the steering wheel and begins to steer the car.

***

A white horse goes into a bar.

"Did you know", said the barman, "that you have a brand of Whisky named after you?"

"Great! I'll have a double Neddy!", said the horse.

***

Two zebras were debating, 'Were they black with white stripes, or white with black stripes?' So they went to see the King of the Jungle, Leo the Lion,

"Are we black with white stripes, or white with black stripes?", they asked.

The lion pondered the question and replied, "You are what you are."

This confused the zebras, who sought clarification from the wise old Owl.

"It means that you are white with black stripes", said the Owl, "otherwise he would have said, 'Yo is what yo is'."

***

Did you hear about the transexual donkey?

It had a hee in the morning and a haw at night.

***

A woman walked into the pet shop and asked the pet shop owner for a pet with a difference.

"How about this bullfrog? He's going out at $500."

"$500 for a bullfrog! You've got to be kidding!"

"This is a special bullfrog", said the shop owner. "It is trained in the art of cunnilingus. Just put him between your legs and he gets straight into it!"

"Wow!", said the woman, paying her $500 and heading for home as fast as possible.

At home, she removed her panties, put the bullfrog between her legs and said "Go for it!"

The bullfrog didn't budge, but croaked "Rrrrbitt, rrrbitt."

The woman nudged the bullfrog a few more times but she could get nothing more than "Rrrbitt."

Disappointed and angry, the woman stormed back to the pet shop, asking for a refund.

"You told me this frog was trained in the art of cunnilingus, but he does nothing but croak."

"No way!", said the shop owner, "He's the best frog I've ever trained."

Incensed, the woman removed her panties, jumped on the counter and placed the frog between her thighs.

"See", she said, "I told you so."

The shop owner put his head between the woman's legs and said to the frog, "Alright you little bastard, I'm going to show you just one more time."

***

If you have a green ball in your right hand and a green ball in your left hand, what do you have?

Kermit the Frog's undivided attention.

***

The crocodile sauntered into the menswear shop.

"Do you have any shirts with faggots on the pocket?", he asked.

***

An elephant and a monkey had become good friends. While wandering through the jungle one day, the elephant fell into a deep pit. The monkey rushed to the nearest road and flagged down a Mercedes Benz. With the help of a rope, the Mercedes pulled the elephant out of the pit.

Some time later, the monkey fell into a pit and it was the elephant's turn to rescue him. The elephant just stood over the pit and dropped his dick down so that the monkey could climb out.

This story proves that if you've got a big dick you don't need a Mercedes Benz.

***

It was bedtime, and as the young boy snuggled under the covers, his Union shop steward father began telling the nightly bedtime story. "Once upon a time and a half..."

In their daily English class, the teacher asked her young pupils for an example of the word 'contagious'. Little Adrian's hand shot up to respond.

"Last weekend, a big truck full of pumpkins nearly ran my Dad's car off the road. When it went round the next bend, all the pumpkins fell off, and Dad said it'd take that contagious to pick them all up again."

***

What's the difference between a University and a Technical College?

At University they teach you to wash your hands thoroughly after going to the toilet. At Technical College they teach you not to piss on your fingers.

***

The teacher was asking her third grade students for a three syllable word and to use it in a sentence. Several students raised their hands.

"Beautiful", said Barbie. "My teacher is really beautiful."

"Wonderful", said Susie. "My teacher is wonderful."

The teacher was quite flattered, and then chose Johnnie.

"Urinate", said Johnnie.

"What?", replied the shocked teacher.

"Urinate, but if your tits were bigger, you'd be a ten."

The young man was trying hard to impress his date. He called the drink waiter over and asked for a bottle of Chateau Neuf du Pap 1985. Upon tasting it, the young man refused the bottle, saying it was a 1987 vintage from the north coast vineyards.

"Please bring me exactly what I ordered."

The second bottle was opened, and the young man took a mouthful and once again, impatiently exclaimed, "This is not what I asked for. This is a 1983 vintage, and it's from the vineyards of Cote d'Azur."

An old man was listening to the conversation from the bar. He went over to the table and said to the young man, "I'm most impressed by your knowledge of liquor. Try this and see if you can tell me what it is."

The young man swelled up with pride, took a mouthful of the contents in the glass and swilled it around.

"That tastes like piss!", he cried as he spat it out.

"You're right!", exclaimed the old man. "Now tell me what age I am and where I was born."

***

The attractive young lady was attending a sales motivation class. There was a ladder in the hall leading to a balcony which had a notice, "Climb the ladder to success."

Intrigued, she climbed to the balcony where she found a man with his penis in his hand.

"What's this?" she cried.

"I'm Cess", he replied. "Start sucking!"

Charlie was in grade one and he went over to check the new kid out.

"How old are you?", he asked.

"I don't know", said the new kid.

"Do women bother you?"

"No", said the new kid.

"Then you are five."

***

"Dad, where do I come from?"

This was a question Dad dreaded hearing. He explained all about the birds and the bees, about sperm and ejaculation, egg and ovulation and childbirth.

"Do you understand now?", asked Dad.

"Not really", said the boy. "Angelo said he comes from Italy and Jimmy Lee comes from Hong Kong. So where do I come from?"

***

Tyrone, a young Aboriginal boy, was asking his father what an I.Q. test meant.

"When your I.Q. is over 120", replied his father, "you are considered to be very intelligent. When it's around 100, you are average. When it's below 50, you're stupid. You wouldn't even be able to tie up your shoelaces."

"Is that why white fellas wear thongs?", asked Tyrone.

***

"**M**ummy, where did I come from?"

"The stork brought you."

"And where did you come from, Mummy?"

"The stork brought me, too."

"And what about Grandma?"

"Yes, the stork brought her too."

"Gee, doesn't it ever worry you to think that there have been no natural births in our family for three generations?"

***

"**W**here do babies come from, Mummy?"

"The stork brings them, of course."

"Well, who fucks the stork?"

***

The primary school teacher had just finished showing a video on sex education and was discussing the subject with her class. Little Johnny had his hand up.

"That video's wrong", he said. "My Dad's got two penises."

"Don't be silly, Johnny. That's impossible."

"It's true, Miss", he persisted. "Dad's got a little one that he pees out of and he's got a really big one to clean Mummy's teeth."

***

The teacher was asking the nature study class what they knew about birds. Johnny put up his hand and claimed that birds had spare parts.

"What do you mean, Johnny?" asked the teacher.

"Well, I heard Dad tell Uncle Bill that he would like to screw the arse off the bird next door."

***

Two twelve year old boys walked into the chemist shop. "A packet of tampons please", they said.

"Are they for your mother?"

"No."

"Are they for your sister?"

"No. They're for us."

"What do you want them for?"

"On TV it says if you use tampons, you can swim and dive, play tennis and ride horses."

ANNIVERSARIES

It was their first wedding anniversary, and he was laying back watching television. As she walked past, she whacked him with a magazine.

"Why did you do that?", he complained.

"For being such a lousy lover", she replied.

He thought about this, stood up and gave her a thump in the ear.

"What was that for?", she cried.

"For knowing the difference", he replied.

***

Family and friends had gathered together to celebrate the couple's silver wedding anniversary when the inebriated husband took the floor and loudly roared, "FORNICATION".

"For an occasion like this, we need more champagne!"

***

Barry was blind. Someone had just given him a silver coated nutmeg grater for his birthday. When asked how he liked it, he said it was the most violent story he'd ever read.

MULTICULTURAL

AFRICAN

"There are three important tribes in Africa", said the anthropologist.

"Firstly, there are the Masai, who grow to 6'6"

or 195cm. They live in the pastural areas. They tend cattle. They are a very proud people. They thump their chest and cry, "We are the Masai!"

"Secondly", he continued, "there are the Pygmy, who live in the dense forest. The Pygmy are 4'6" or 135cm. They are hunters and a very proud tribe. They beat their chest and cry, "We are the Pygmy!"

"And lastly, there are the Fukawi. They are 5'6" tall and live in the lush grasslands where the grass grows 6' high. They are also a very proud people who jump up and down, beat their chest and cry, "Where the Fukawi?"

AUSTRALIAN

The new player from Kickadingo was having his first game, but was not getting his fair share of kicks. The coach sent a runner out.

"The coach said he will pull you off at half time", said the runner.

"Great!", said the country boy. "You only get oranges at Kickadingo."

***

An Australian gentleman is a man who gets out of the bath to piss in the sink.

***

Why wasn't Christ born in Australia?

Where would you find three wise men and a virgin?

***

In the remote parts of Australia, "Tie me Kangaroo Down Sport" is considered a boundary rider's love song.

***

The coach of Aussie footballers was travelling through Dublin when the guide announced, "We are now passing the biggest pub in Ireland."

A voice called from the back of the bus..."Why???"

***

An old swagman was walking down a dusty outback road. A farmer pulled up in a beat up old truck and said, "Would you like a lift, mate?"

"No way!", replied the swaggie. "You can open and close your own bloody gates!"

***

What's the difference between an Australian wedding and an Australian funeral?

One less drunk at the funeral.

How do you tell if a Tasmanian girl is old enough for sex?

Put her in a barrel. If her chin comes to the top, she's old enough. If it doesn't, cut the barrel down a bit.

***

Terrence had just returned to Ireland after a holiday in Australia. His family wanted to hear about his trip. Terry told them that Australians were the most hospitable people he had ever met.

"They will share their home with you, they will share their grog with you, they will share everything." he said. "It's those white bastards you've got to watch."

***

Why do Aussies put XXXX on a can of beer?
Because they can't spell beer.

***

Why do Aussies wear shorts?
To keep their brains cool.

CHINESE

What do Australians keep that Asians throw away?
Snot.

***

"**I**'ve just been sexually molested by a Chinese laundry man!" she screamed to the copper.
"How did you know it was a Chinese laundry man?" asked the sergeant.
"Because he did the whole thing by hand."

***

A man rang the Chinese restaurant to order some food.
   "Can I speak to Ha-Fin?"
   "No. Ha-Fin is out."
   "Is that Ha-Fout?"
   "No. Ha-Fout is not in."
   "Well, who's that?"
   "I'm Ha-Fup, the receptionist."
   "Sorry, I'll call you back when you're not busy."

***

EGYPTIAN

Mohammed el Caribe was in the village market one day when he felt a great rumbling in his stomach. He could not control himself and let go a fart that could only be described as a triple thunderclap. Everyone in the market stopped what they were doing and stared at Mohammed. He was so ashamed that he left the village and wandered the desert for many years, too embarrassed to return to his home.

Now in his seventies, he felt that he would like to return to the place of his birth. He was sure that no-one would recognise him. Back in his home town again, he headed for the marketplace, and was surprised to see a big supermarket standing in its place. He asked one of the shoppers how long the building had been there.

"Ah!", replied the man, "this building was completed twenty years to the day after Mohammed el Caribe farted in the market place."

FRENCH

Two tourists wandered into a cannibal restaurant and perused the menu. It read:
Italian with garlic sauce - 5 shells
Roast sirloin of Englishman - 10 shells
Sweet and sour Chinese - 12 shells
American, hamburger style - 8 shells
Sauteed Frenchman - 30 shells
The tourists called the waiter over. "How come

the Frenchman is so expensive?", they complained.

"Have you ever tried to clean a Frenchman?", replied the waiter.

GREEK

How do Greeks separate the men from the boys?

With a crowbar.

***

How do Greek mothers teach their children to put on their underwear?

Yellow to the front, brown to the back.

IRISH

The curfew in Belfast started at 10 p.m. At 9.30, the British soldiers were leaving their barracks to enforce it. A sergeant in charge of one of the patrols heard a shot ring out at 9.35. He soon discovered that Private Connolly had shot a man.

"It's only 9.35", roared the sergeant. "Why did you shoot him?"

"I know that man", said Private Connolly. "I know where he lives. He would never get home by 10 o'clock."

Two Irishmen were visiting London and were walking down Pall Mall.

"This is not such a bad place", said Sean. "Where else could you walk down the street, meet a complete stranger, have dinner with him and then be invited to spend the night at his house."

"B'golly, did this happen to you?", asked Seamus.

"Agh, no, but it did happen to my sister."

***

Irish John was complaining to his mates in the bar. His wife was pregnant again, and he already had eight kids.

"I'll bloody well hang myself if this happens again", he said.

But sure enough, one year later, John announced that his wife was pregnant again.

"You said you'd hang yourself if this happened", one of his mates reminded him.

"That I did", said John. "I got the rope, tied a noose in it and threw it over a branch of a tree, then I thought to meself, begorah, maybe I'm hanging the wrong man!"

***

The Irish Maiden's Prayer: "Dear Lord, Please have Murphy on me."

***

Michael O'Regan was on his deathbed. He had not long to go. One night, the smell of a lovely Irish stew wafted into his bedroom and the nostalgia brightened him up. He called his son.

"My last request, Sean, is to have a bowl of that Irish stew that I can smell your mother is cooking."

Sean returned in a few minutes. "Mum says you can't have any. It's for the wake."

Why do the Irish call their basic currency the Punt?

Because it rhymes with Bank Manager.

***

Did you hear about the Irishman who went to the toilet?

He wiped the chain and pulled himself.

***

An Irish family was sitting around watching T.V when the father leaned over to the mother and said, "Let's send the kids to a S-H-O-W so we can fuck."

***

Paddy was standing at the bar with a rottweiler at his feet.

"Does your dog bite, Paddy?" asked Mick.

"No", replied Paddy.

So Mick went to pat the dog. The dog just about tore off Mick's arm.

"I thought you said your dog didn't bite!", screamed Mick.

"That's not my dog", replied Paddy.

***

An Irish girl was stopped for speeding and taken to the Police Station. The policeman stood up and unzipped his fly and the girl cried out, "Oh no, not another breathalyser test!"

***

One Sunday morning after Church, a pretty young church goer was knocked down by a truck as she crossed the road. She was hit with such force that by the time she hit the road, all her clothes had been stripped away.

The Parish Priest rushed to her assistance, and to preserve her modesty, removed his hat and placed it over her golden triangle.

O'Hara staggered out of the pub on hearing the commotion, pushed his way through the gathering crowd and stood beside the Priest. He stared down at the naked girl and pronounced, "Begorrah! May the saints preserve us! The first thing we've gotta do is get that man outta there!"

The Bishop moved out into the Remand Yard and came across three Irish inmates leaning against the wall.

"What are you in for?", he asked the first.

"Murder." he replied.

"And what did you get for that?"

"Life."

The Bishop asked the next man what he was in for.

"Fraud." he replied. "I got 15 years."

The Bishop asked the third man what was his crime.

"Pouring petrol over Protestants and setting them alight."

"And what did you get for that?", asked the Bishop.

"About fifteen to the gallon", replied the prisoner.

JEWISH

What sucks but doesn't swallow?
A Jewish girl.

***

What do you call an uncircumcised Jewish child?
A girl.

***

There's a new one hour Jewish porno movie just out.

There's 40 minutes of begging, 3 minutes of sex and seventeen minutes of guilt.

***

Jewish men are the most confident in the world.

They cut the end off their dick before they know how long it will grow.

***

The Israelis had no intention of getting involved in the Gulf War. The last time they got involved with a talking Bush, they wandered the desert for forty years.

***

Simon Solomon was at the funeral of a good friend when one of the mourners remembered he owed the deceased $100.

"I am a man of his word", he said putting ten $10 notes in the coffin.

This reminded another of the mourners. "I am also a man of my word", he said, coming forward and placing a $100 note in the coffin.

"I am also a man of conscience", said Simon. "I too owe our late friend $100." So he wrote a cheque for $300, put it in the coffin and took out the $200 change.

IRAQI

What did Saddam Hussein have in common with Little Miss Muffett?

They both had curds in their way.

ITALIAN

Mario gets a job on the farm. After a couple of days the other farmhands complain to the boss about him.

"He's weird" they tell the boss. "He sat down for lunch yesterday and produced a Coke bottle and proceeded to piss in it and then he sat there drinking it with his lunch! Then this morning he had hold of your wife's cat and was biting the back of its neck!"

The boss walked out into the field to talk to him. Mario had hold of one of the steers and was looking up its arse.

"Mario, what's the problem?" asked the boss. "Everyone's a bit worried about your behaviour."

"There's no problems," said Mario. "I justa wanna be one of da boys."

"What do ya mean?" questioned the boss.

"Well," said Mario, "I metta three Aussie guys in Italy anda they tolda me to be one of da boys ya gotta do three things. First, you gotta drinka da piss, next you gotta bite da pussy anda den you gotta listen to the bullshit."

***

Luigi's small fishing boat was sinking in a storm. He called the Coast Guard. "Helpa me, Helpa me, I'ma sinking" he cried.

"Where are you Luigi?" replied the Coast Guard.

"I'ma two miles froma da lighthouse, ina da north."

"Stay where you are Luigi, we'll send you our Fokker Friendship."

"I don't wanna your Fokker Friendship!" said Luigi "I wanna be fokker saved!"

***

How can you tell if an Italian woman is embarrassed about her long black hair?

Because she wears long black gloves to cover it up.

***

An Italian woman hailed a cab. She said to the cab driver, "I haven't gotta da money."

"How are you going to pay, then?", asked the driver.

"Widda dis", she said, lifting up her skirt.

The cab driver looked at it and replied, "Haven't you got anything smaller?"

***

118

Two racists are walking down the street in Rome when they pass an Italian organ grinder with a monkey. One throws a $5 note into the monkey's tin. His companion is surprised.

"Why did you do that? You've been telling me for years how much you hate Italians."

"Well, they're so cute when they're little."

***

An Italian and his 6 year old son Luigi go into a clothing shop. "May I help you?" asks the salesman.

"Yes" says the father, "I'd like a nice sweater for me and a pair of trousers for my son Luigi - WITH THE BIG FAT HEAD!" and he slaps little Luigi around the head. Shocked by this attack the salesman asks, "Will that be all sir?"

"No" says the father. "I'd like a pair of shoes for me and a pair for Luigi - WITH THE BIG FAT HEAD!" and he slaps little Luigi again.

"Now just wait a minute" protests the salesman. "You can't keep hitting that poor boy like that - why do you keep hitting him?"

"Why do I keep hitting Luigi - WITH THE BIG FAT HEAD?" yells the father, bashing Luigi again.

"Well, I'll tell you!" he says. "When I met his mother Maria she wassa eighteen years old, she had a perfecta body, the most beautiful breasts I ever saw - and a nice tighta pussy - until Luigi WITH THE BIG FAT HEAD!"

JAPANESE

What do Japanese men do when they have erections?

Vote.

***

A Japanese tourist goes into the bank to cash a travellers cheque. He is offered 85 yen to the dollar.

"85 yen!", cried the tourist, "That's robbery. Yesterday I get 80 yen to the dollar. Why do you do this?"

"Fluctuations", explains the Manager.

"Fluck you Australians!", says the tourist. "I'm not going to be ripped off by this bank!"

MEXICAN

"Where's ya bin?" the garbo asked Willy.

"I bin on holidays" answered Willy.

"No - where's ya Wheely Bin?" demanded the garbo.

"I weely bin in prison, but I tell me friends I've bin away."

***

Why is the Mexican Olympic team so lousy?

Because anyone who can run, jump or swim is in the United States by now.

***

The tourist driving through Mexico got the shock of his life when from behind a cactus, out jumped a Mexican brandishing a huge gun.

"Take my money! My car! Don't kill me!", he pleaded.

"You do as I say, I no kill you", replied the gringo. "Unzip your pants, start wanking yourself. Now!"

The shocked traveller did as he was ordered. On completion of the job, the Mexican stuffed the gun to his nose and said, "Do it again, now!"

With sweat running down his face and body, he managed another effort, before finally falling exhausted on the sand.

"Right!", said the gringo. "Now, you can give my sister a ride to the next village!"

***

A tourist went to a famous restaurant in Mexico City.

"What's the special tonight?", he asked.

"Poached gonads", said the waiter.

The waiter explained that they were the testicles of a bull that was slain in the ring that afternoon.

The tourist was adventurous, and had to agree that the poached gonads were tasty and satisfying.

Next evening he returned to the same restaurant and ordered baked gonads. On his way out, he complained to the manager about the two miserable testicles served up on his plate.

"Ah, senor!", said the manager, "sometimes the bull wins!"

NEW ZEALAND

Why do New Zealanders make love to sheep on their back?

So they can tongue kiss them.

***

Why do New Zealand race horses run so fast?

They heard about what happened to the sheep.

***

"You gonna shear that sheep?" the tourist asked the Kiwi farmer.

"No way mate!" said the farmer, "I'm not shearing her with anyone. Get your own!"

***

What's long and hard and fucks New Zealanders?

Third year in Primary School.

***

Why do New Zealand farmers fuck their sheep on the edge of a precipice?

So they will back up harder.

***

The farmer's wife gave him a plate of grass for dinner.

"What the hell's this?", he roared.

"If it's good enough for your girlfriend, it's good enough for you."

***

Little Bo Peep has lost her sheep and doesn't know where to find them, but a search revealed they were in the next field with a dirty big Kiwi behind them.

***

Toby had a little lamb.

His case comes up next Friday.

***

A New Zealander walked into a Sydney fish shop and asked for some "Fish 'n Chups."

"You're a Kiwi!", said the proprietor.

The New Zealander was crapped off about being picked on for the way he spoke, so he took some elocution lessons.

Six months later, he walked back into the same shop and asked, in perfect Oxford English, "Fish and Chips, please."

"You're a Kiwi!", pronounced the proprietor.

"How the hell could you tell that?", asked the surprised New Zealander.

"Because this has been a hardware shop for four months."

***

A New Zealander arrives in Australia and is over-awed by how big everything is. He goes to the biggest shopping mall he's ever seen, walks into a fruit shop and said to the owner "What sort of fruit do you have?".

"We have the largest range of fruit in Sydney." said the owner. Not to be outdone, the Kiwi replied "Is that all you have! Back home in New Zealand our stores are 3 or 4 times bigger than this - this is nothing!"

The fruit shop owner grabbed the Kiwi and threw him out.

The Kiwi went into a butcher shop. "What range of meat do you have?" he asked.

"We have the widest selection of meats available in this shopping centre." replied the butcher proudly.

"You mean this is **it**!!!" said the Kiwi sarcastically. "Back in New Zealand our butcher shops are much bigger, much more impressive than yours." So the butcher threw the Kiwi out. The Kiwi went into every shop, insulting each owner.

The fruit shop owner said to the butcher, "Let's fix this guy!"

So they went to a vacant shop and waited for the Kiwi to come in. Soon the Kiwi walked in and looked around. He saw nothing for sale - just the butcher and the fruiterer standing there.

"So, what do you sell?" asked the Kiwi arrogantly.

"Pricks!" replied the butcher.

"You're doing well..." said the Kiwi. "There's only two left."

***

Why do New Zealanders use velcro in their flys? Because sheep recognise the sound of zippers.

PALESTINIAN

The Palestinians were having their annual picnic when a bus load of Jewish tourists careered out of control through the middle of them. There were dead and injured laying everywhere.

"My God!", said the driver as he turned to his passengers, "give me a hand!", and they all stood up and applauded.

RUSSIAN

When the Russians were accused of being behind the assassination attempt on the Pope, the Russian Police said they'd thoroughly investigate the matter.

After exhaustive interviews and countless viewing of video tapes it became clear that the Pope opened fire first.

***

A Russian woman walked into an empty Moscow shop. "I see you have no vegetables today."

"No", said the shopkeeper, "this is a butcher shop. It's meat we haven't got. The shop with no vegetables is further down the street."

***

What do you call an attractive woman in Russia?
A tourist.

***

A Russian man and woman were in the same train carriage travelling across Russia. At the end of the first day he said to her "Are you going to Moscow?"

"Nyet." was her reply.

At the end of the second day he asked, "Are you going to Gorky?"

"Nyet." she said.

On the third day he said, "Enough of this lovetalk - off with your pants."

SCOTTISH

What's the difference between a Scotsman and a coconut?

You can get a drink out of a coconut.

***

McGregor was on his death bed and he gasped his last words to his old friend, McTavish.

"Jock", he said, "There's a bottle of Scotch under my bed. When I'm gone, will you sprinkle it on my grave? Promise me, Jock, that you'll do it."

"Och, aye, McGregor, but would ye mind if I passed it through my kidneys first?"

***

A Scotsman had a medical and was told he had sugar in his urine. So he went home and pissed on his cornflakes.

***

Have you heard the story about the Scotsman who gave an Englishman, an Irishman and a Welshman ten pounds each?

Neither has anyone else.

***

Dougal MacDonald stopped a young man in the street. "Aren't you the lad that saved my son from drowning in the loch yesterday?"

"Aye", said the young man. "Think nothing of it."

"Nothing indeed!", roared MacDonald. "Where's his bloody cap then?"

***

What's the difference between a Scotsman and a canoe?

A canoe sometimes tips.

***

Sergeant Major McIntosh of the Black Watch Regiment walked into the Edinburgh pharmacy. He placed a tattered old condom on the counter and asked the pharmacist how much it would cost to repair it.

The pharmacist held up the ragged condom and inspected it closely. "It needs a good rinse out and a few holes want patching. It's ripped down one side, but I suppose we could stick that together. But quite honestly, it would be just as cheap to buy a new one."

The Sergeant Major said that he would have to think it over. The next day he returned. "You've sold us", he said. "The Regiment have decided to invest in a new one."

***

How do you identify the clans in Scotland?

If you lift his kilt and he's got a quarter-pounder, he's a MacDonald.

***

The Irishman had just finished screwing the Scottish girl and she was far from satisfied.

"I thought Irishmen were supposed to be big and thick", she complained.

"And I thought the Scots were tight", he replied.

SWEDISH

Olaf and Inge were applying for a marriage licence.

"Name?", asked the clerk.

"Olaf Olssen."

"And yours, miss?"

"Inge Olssen."

"Any connection?"

Inge blushed. "Only vunce, when he yumped me."

U.K.

How does an Englishman know that his wife is dead?

Sex is still the same, but the dishes are piling up in the sink.

***

What's black and eats chips?

Forty seven percent of London.

***

When does a Pommy Bastard become a Briton?

When he marries your daughter.

***

Two Englishmen, two Scotsmen, two Welshmen and two Irishmen were stranded on a desert island. It wasn't long before the two Scotsmen started a Caledonian Club and were playing bagpipes, tossing the cabre and eating haggis.

The two Welshmen started an Eisteddford and were soon competing against each other in song and dance.

The two Irishmen set up a Branch of the I.R.A. and set out to bomb everything English.

The two Englishmen went to opposite ends of the island and would not speak to each other because they had never been properly introduced.

At the zoo, a lion lazed in the sun, licking his arse. A tourist said to a keeper, "Pretty quiet old thing, isn't it?"

"This lion is the most ferocious animal in the Zoo", said the keeper. "In fact, just an hour ago, it dragged an Englishman into its pen and completely devoured him."

"Gee!", said the astonished tourist, "why is it lying there licking his arse?"

"Trying to get the taste out of his mouth", said the keeper.

U.S.A.

If all American women were laid end to end, I wouldn't be surprised.

***

"Yahoo!" cried the Red Indian. He had just come across a pretty young tourist whose car had run out of petrol in the Nevada desert.

The handsome young brave offered to give her a lift to the nearest petrol station on the back of his horse. She climbed aboard and they set off. She was intrigued at his continual habit of letting out loud crazy "Whoopee!" It must be an Indian custom, she thought.

When they got to the gas station, she dismounted. "Whee!...yahoo!....whoopee!" yelled the Indian as he rode off into the desert.

"He seemed pretty happy", said the service station owner. "What did you do?"

"Nothing", she replied, "I simply rode behind him with my arms around his waist, hanging onto the saddle horn."

"Don't you know that Indians ride bareback?", queried the owner.

***

Two aerials meet on a roof, fall in love and get married.

The ceremony wasn't much but the reception was brilliant.

***

An Irish lad went to live in a small town in Alabama and soon associated with a local gang.

"What do we do for fun around here?", he asked.

"Usually we go to the bowling alley and beat up a few blacks", came the reply.

Off they went to the bowling alley and the Alabama boys started beating up the blacks. All excited and anxious to participate, the Irish lad grabbed a baseball bat and started smashing bowling balls.

"What the hell do you think you're doing?", asked one of the Alabama boys.

"You get the adults", yelled the excited Irish lad, "I'll take care of the eggs!"

***

The Godfather in Italy had found out that one of the Family members in America was fiddling the books. He decided to deal with the problem himself and, as he could not speak English, took an interpreter with him. He had three suspects and decided to put each through the third degree to find the guilty one.

The Godfather interrogated the first suspect, holding a gun to his head.

"I'm innocent!", he cried. "I swear on my mother's grave."

The interpreter said to the Godfather, "It wasn't him. He swears on his mother's grave."

The second suspect was interrogated. He also swore his innocence and swore on the heart of his wife and children. The interpreter repeated his denial to the Godfather.

The third suspect was brought in. He quickly broke down. "I did it!", he said, "but please, be merciful. Do not kill me. The million dollars I stole is in a suitcase under my bed."

"What did he say?", asked the Godfather.

The interpreter replied, "He said he did it, he spent all the money and he bets that you haven't got the balls to pull the trigger."

VATICAN

Don Corleone was paying his first visit to Italy. He had two appointments, one with the Pope and one with the head of the Mafia.

"Who shall I see first?", he asked his adviser.

"See the Pope first", he was advised, "You've only got to kiss his hand."

ART

Tattoos are becoming very popular these days, so the pretty young wife decided to surprise her husband and asked the tattoo artist to do a butterfly on each cheek of her bum.

"He calls me his little butterfly", she explained.

The tattoo artist looked at her little bum and said that it would take three or four visits and suggested that if she wanted the job done straight away, that he tatoo the letter 'B' on each cheek of her bum instead. The young wife was disappointed but agreed.

That night, she said to her husband, "I've got a surprise for you." She undressed, turned around and bent over.

"Who the hell is BoB?", he cried.

BACK CHAT

A woman walked into the butchers carrying a piss-pot.

"Pounda fillet" she said.

The butcher slapped a pound down on the counter and said, "Pound ya don't."

BAR TALK

Two guys were in an English pub. They called the publican over and asked him to settle an argument.

"Are there two pints in a quart or four?", asked one.

"There are two pints in a quart", confirmed the publican.

They moved back along the bar and soon the barmaid asked for their order.

"Two pints please, miss, and they are on the house."

The barmaid doubted that her boss would be so generous so one of the guys called out to the publican at the other end of the bar,

"You did say two pints, didn't you?"

"That's right", he called back, "two pints."

***

A drunk walked into the bar and ordered a beer. He gulped the beer down, banged the glass on the bar and said, "Piss."

The barmaid refilled the glass and again, the drunk gulped it down, slammed the glass on the bar and said, "Piss."

This angered the barmaid, so she went over to the drunk and said, "Piss off!"

"O.K.", said the drunk, "I'll have a double scotch then."

Two guys were having a quiet beer in the pub after work, when in walked a punk rocker with a multi-coloured hair style, his hair sticking straight up in the air and the sides shaved bald.

The guys stared at the punk rocker who, noticing them staring, promptly shirt-fronted one of them and toughly said, "What's the matter pal... you got a problem?"

Nervously the guy said "No... but I think we may be related."

"Why do you think that?" asked the punk.

"How old are you?" quivered the drinker.

"Twenty-two!" shouted the punk.

"Well", said the drinker "...twenty-two years ago I had sex with a parrot and I think you may be my son."

MOVIE STARS

Paul Simon was doing his first encore at the pop concert when a big breasted brunette screamed, tore off her clothes and streaked across the stage. She was thrown out by the bouncers.

***

Did you read Anna Nicole Smith's new book?

It's called, "How To Make $100 million With Just One Cunt Working For You."

Zsa Zsa Gabor was arrested at the international airport and charged with carrying drugs. Customs officers found six kilos of crack in her underwear.

BLONDES

What do blondes put behind their ears to attract men?
  Their knees.

***

What do peroxide blondes and a Jumbo jets have in common?
  Both have big black boxes.

***

Why did the blonde cross the road?
  Never mind that. What's she doing out of the bedroom?

***

What does a blonde get when she crosses Billy Ray Cyrus with a case of the Thrush?
  An Itchy Twitchy Twat.

How do you get a blonde's eyes to sparkle?
Shine a light in her ear.

***

What's the advantage of being married to a blonde?
You can park in the handicapped zone.

***

Why did the blonde have square boobs?
She forgot to take the tissues out of the box.

***

What does a blonde call a mushroom with a 9 inch stalk?
A Funghi to be with.

***

Why did the blonde stare at the frozen orange juice can for two hours?
Because it said "concentrate".

***

What is the first thing a blonde learns when she takes driving lessons?
You CAN sit upright in a car!

What do you get when you stand a blonde on her head?

A brunette with bad breath.

***

Did you hear about the blonde who swallowed a razor blade?

She gave herself a tonsillectomy, an appendectomy, a hysterectomy – circumcised her husband – gave the Vicar a hare lip – cut the end off the finger off a casual acquaintance – and it was still good for five shaves.

***

The blonde was visiting a friend in the hospital when she was approached by a member of the medical staff. "Will you buy a raffle ticket?" asked the nursing sister.

"What's the raffle for?", replied the blonde.

"One of our wardsmen died last week – it's for his poor widow and three children."

"No thanks," replied the blonde, "I won't have a ticket. What would I do with a widow and three children? I'm already supporting my defacto and his two kids."

***

"Not all blondes are stupid, and I can prove it!", said the blonde indignantly. "Give me the name of any American State and I'll tell you its capital."

"Missouri", called someone.

"M", said the blonde.

***

Did you hear about the man who poisoned his blonde girlfriend with a razor blade?

He gave her arsenic.

***

What do you give a blonde who has everything?
Penicillin.

***

Why do blondes wear panties?
To keep their ankles warm.

***

What's the difference between a blonde and a brick?

When you lay a brick, it doesn't follow you around for two weeks whining.

***

What's the difference between a group of blondes and a good magician?

A good magician has a cunning array of stunts.

***

What nursery rhyme did blondes learn at school?

Hump-me Dump-me.

***

The blonde walked into the hardware store and asked the young man behind the counter for a door hinge.

"How would you like a screw for that hinge?", he asked.

"No way!", said the blonde, "but I'll give you a blow job for that watering can over there."

***

Traffic cop: "Do you know you were doing over 100 kilometres an hour?"

Blonde: "But that's impossible, officer. I only left home twenty minutes ago!"

***

A leggy young blonde was on her way home. She was wearing a very tight leather mini skirt. It was so tight that she couldn't take the step up on the bus, so she reached behind and loosened the zip. It was to no avail – the skirt was too tight. She reached around and pulled the zip down a bit further but still could not make the first step. Suddenly she was lifted up by two strong hands on her bottom. She turned around and saw a young man smiling.

"How dare you!", she said.

"Well, I thought it'd be O.K. I thought by now we'd be friends, seeing you've already opened my fly twice."

***

The lovely young blonde was learning to swim and was being held afloat by a raunchy swimming instructor.

"Will I really sink if you take your finger out?", she asked.

***

How do you rebore a blonde prostitute?
Shove a leg of lamb up and pull out the bone.

***

The big breasted blonde always bought dresses to show off her boobs to their best advantage. Trying on a low cut dress, she checked with the sales assistant if she thought it was too low.

"Do you have hair on your chest?" queried the assistant.

"Of course not!", replied the blonde.

"Then this dress is too low."

***

The blonde walked into the butchers and said, "I'll have two kilos of those pissoles you've got on special."

The butcher pointed to the appropriate sign and said, "This is an R, not a P."

"That's O.K. then, give me two kilos of arsoles."

***

A blonde was browsing around the sex shop and stopped at the dildo counter.

"I'll have that one - the tartan one with the big white top", she said.

"Sorry", said the Manager, "that's not for sale. That's my thermos flask."

***

He went into the newsagency and started chatting up the beautiful blonde behind the counter.

"By the way, do you keep stationery?", he asked.

"I try to", replied the blonde, "right up to the last few seconds – then I really go crazy!"

***

The blonde walked into the hairdressing salon and insisted that the hairdresser cut around the earphones of the Walkman she was wearing. The stylist did as he was asked.

The blonde returned a month later, and again asked the hairdresser to cut around her earphones.

This happened regularly for ten months. Finally, the hairdresser couldn't contain his curiosity any longer, so, while giving the blonde a haircut, he pulled the earphones out. The blonde collapsed to the floor, gasping, and within minutes, died.

An ambulance was called, but she could not be rescusitated. The hairdresser picked up the headphones to hear what the blonde had been listening to. He put them on and heard, "Inhale, exhale, inhale, exhale..."

BUMS

Jimmy had been a jockey for thirty years and had suffered from painful piles for most of that time. This was an occupational hazard, and the remedy around the stables was a handful of cold tea leaves inserted every morning.

144

Eventually, Jimmy went to see a specialist, who got him to drop his trousers and bend over.

"Mmmm, yes, I see, I see it all", said the specialist, peering up Jimmy's bum.

"What is it?", cried Jimmy. "Is there some problem?"

"No", said the doctor, "Everything's O.K. You are going to meet a tall blonde, you will take a long trip and a lot of success is coming your way."

***

What did Adam say to Eve?
"Stand back, I don't know how big this thing gets."

BUSINESS IS BUSINESS

Solly had been in the clothing business with his partner, Izzy, for thirty years. He was giving advice to his son on business ethics.

"Ethics", said Solly, "is the most important thing you should consider. For instance, suppose a woman comes in and buys a dress for $90 and pays for it with a $100 note, I wrap it for her, and she is excited, and leaves the shop forgetting her $10 change. This is the big question of ethics. Do I tell my partner or not?"

***

Ruth and Rachel were walking through the park after attending a seminar on business opportunities when a large toad jumped out on the path in front of them.

"Please", pleaded the toad, "will one of you kiss me so that I can turn into a handsome Prince?"

Rachel picked up the toad and put it in her handbag.

"Aren't you going to kiss him and turn him into a Prince?", asked Ruth.

"No", replied Rachel, "Princes are a dime a dozen but a talking toad - now there's an opportunity for making big bucks!"

***

The Chairman stood to address the shareholders. "This time last year, we were poised on the edge of a precipice. Now, we are ready to take a great leap forward."

***

Solly suggested to Rachel that every time they made love, he would put a dollar into a jar. After they had been married for twenty years, Solly emptied the jar and found it contained not only one dollar coins but five, ten and twenty dollar notes.

"Where did all this money come from?", he asked Rachel. Every time I screwed you, I only put in a dollar."

"So, Solly", Rachel replied, "do you think everyone is as miserable as you?"

A busty woman gave a hundred dollar bill to pay for her purchase in the dress shop.

"I can't accept this", said the salesgirl. "This $100 note is counterfeit."

"Call the police", the woman cried out, "I've been raped!"

CONDOMS

BUMPER STICKERS FOR THE BASHFUL CONDOM USER

1 Cover your stump before you hump.
2 Before you attack her, wrap your whacker.
3 Don't be silly, protect your willy.
4 When in doubt, shroud your sprout.
5 Don't be a loner, cover your boner.
6 You can't go wrong if you shield your dong.
7 If you're not going to sack it, go home and whack it.
8 If you think she's spunky, cover your monkey.
9 If you slip between her thighs, be sure to condomize.
10 It will be sweeter if you wrap your peter.
11 She won't get sick if you wrap up your dick.
12 If you go into heat, package your meat.
13 While you're undressing Venus, dress up your penis.

"Don't you feel you're a little over-cautious?"

— from *Rude and Politically Incorrect Jokes* by Allan Pease

14 When you take off her pants and blouse, dress up your trouser mouse.

15 Especially in December, gift wrap your member.

16 Never deck her with an unwrapped pecker.

17 Don't be a fool, vulcanize your tool.

18 The right selection! Protect your erection.

19 Wrap it in foil before checking her oil.

20 A crank with armour will never harm her.

21 If you really love her, wear a cover.

22 Don't make a mistake, muzzle your snake.

23 If you can't shield your rocket leave it in your pocket.

24 Sex is cleaner with a packaged weiner.

***

An old couple went into the chemist and the old boy asked for a packet of condoms. "We're having a dirty weekend," he said.

The chemist said, "But you're both pensioners aren't you?"

He explained that a woman over 60 could not become pregnant.

"It's not that," said the old boy. "She just loves the smell of burning rubber."

***

Why is a condom like a coffin?

Both hold a stiff. One is for coming, one is for going.

***

The deaf mute needed condoms and nervously approached the pharmacist. He opened his fly, put his penis on the counter, pointed to it and laid a $10 bill next to it.

With an understanding nod, the pharmacist took his penis out, laid it beside the other man's, grinned in triumph, grabbed the money and walked away.

***

CONFESSIONS

Mildred lay on her deathbed. She wanted to confess to her husband. She beckoned him over and whispered in his ear, "I know that you were unfaithful to me, and many times I had to square off with you. I'm the one who informed the Taxation Office about your illegal business activities? Can you forgive me for that?"

"I was also responsible for having your Philippino girlfriend deported. Can you forgive me for that? And it was me that stole that $250,000 cash you had hidden in the safe. I spent it all on having an affair with your best friend. Will you forgive me for that before I die?"

"Of course I will, my darling", replied her husband tenderly. "But I must also confess and ask your forgiveness", he continued. "I'm the one who fed you the poisoned mushrooms."

***

Frank had smelly feet. They were so bad, and he was so embarrassed about them, that he thought he would never find a sweetheart and marry.

One day, he met Nellie. She had a chronic case of halitosis, and to disguise it she always held a handkerchief to her mouth.

Their courtship progressed without either knowing of the others' problem. Frank never took his shoes off. Nellie never took the handkerchief from her mouth.

Eventually they married. In the honeymoon suite on their wedding night, Frank was preparing for bed. He had taken Lysol, talcum powder, Nilodor and a scrubbing brush into the bathroom in an endeavour to overcome his foot problem.

When he had finished, it was Nellie's turn to use the bathroom. She had bought her double strength toothpaste, Listerine, Fisherman's Friend and chlorophyll tablets to try and sweeten her breath.

Meanwhile, Frank was panicking in the bedroom. He had left his socks on the basin! "What am I going to do!", he said to himself. "She'll know my secret! I must confess."

In the bathroom, Nellie was thinking the same way. "I must tell him now", she decided.

She opened the bathroom door, and there was Frank.

"I have something I must tell you!", she blurted out.

"I know", said Frank almost passing out from her breath, "you've eaten my socks!"

***

CONFUCIOUS SAY....

It is good for girl to meet boy in park, but better for boy to park meat in girl.

Man who drop watch in toilet have shitty time.

Man who fart in church must sit in own pew.

Man who go to bed with itchy bum wake up with smelly finger.

Man who grabs rooster and hen also grab cock and pullet.

Secretary not permanent unless screwed on desk.

Woman who fly upside down have crack up.

Woman who sleep in house with old man soon feel old age creeping on.

Wise men don't spit in strong wind – wise men don't fart in still wind.

Man who go out with flat-chested woman have right to feel low.

Man who take lady on camping trip have one intent.

Man who go through turnstile sideways is going to Bangkok.

COUNTDOWN

Jack and Jill had just been married and they were returning to Jack's farm up in the hills on his donkey. The donkey became stubborn. Jack swore and cursed, but the donkey wouldn't budge. He picked up a big stick and gave the donkey a hard thump behind the ear and said, "That's One."

The donkey started off up the hill. They hadn't gone too far when the donkey stopped again. Jack swore and kicked the donkey, but the donkey wouldn't move. Jack picked up a rock and gave the donkey a mighty whack between the eyes. "That's Two", he said.

A short time later, the donkey protested again at the weight of Jack and Jill on his back and dug his heels in and wouldn't continue. Jack got off, pulled out his shotgun and shot the donkey between the eyes. It fell down dead. "That's Three", said Jack.

This brutality was too much for Jill. "Why did you treat the poor beast like that?", she cried. "You're not only a cruel man but a stupid one. That donkey was worth $200. You're an idiot."

"That's One", said Jack.......

***

What does a ferocious lion and a one inch dick have in common?

You don't want to try to fuck with either of them.

COUNTRY LIFE

An old man and his son had eked out a living on their farm for 40 years. One day the son won the $900,000 in the lottery.

"Here's your share Dad" he said as he put a hundred dollar note in the old man's hand.

The old man went quiet and then said, "I've never had any money Son. I worked hard all my life to provide for you and your Mother. In fact, I never even had enough money to marry your Mother."

The son considered this. "Well that's just great!" he bitched. "You know what that makes me don't ya?"

"Yeah" said the old man "and a fuckin' mean one!"

***

The travelling salesman's car broke down in a lonely part of the country. He walked for miles before coming upon a farm house. He limped up to the front door and knocked. The farmer answered and told the salesman that he was welcome to stay the night and that dinner had just been put on the table.

"But", he said, " I must tell you that there's only two beds in the house. I sleep in one and my beautiful, blond haired twenty-one year old son sleeps in the other."

"Jesus!", said the salesman, " I'm in the wrong joke!"

***

The farmer's wife was feeling lonely and neglected. There was a knock on the door. When she answered, there stood a tramp asking for a handout. She noticed that the tramp had very large shoes and she remembered that men who have big feet also have big dicks. So she invited him in.

She gave him a feed and a couple of glasses of wine then took him to bed. When the tramp woke up the next morning, he found $60 on his pillow and a brief note which said, "Buy yourself a pair of shoes that fit."

***

Farmer Green missed the bend in the road and ended up in the river. He scrambled out of the car and sat on the roof, awaiting rescue. At last he heard a car stop. It was his neighbours, Mr and Mrs Ball. "We will go and get help", they said.

Then a second car stopped. It was another neighbour, Farmer Brown. "I'm glad you came along, George", said Farmer Green. "I'd hate to be pulled out by the Balls."

***

Clyde had just got back to his hometown after completing university.

"What sort of things did you study there?" asked his friend Mike.

"I studied Logic, for one", said Clyde.

"What's that?"

"Let me give you an example. Do you have a dog?"

"Yes", replied Mike.

"Well, it's logic that you have a backyard to keep him in."

"Well... yes."

"And if you have a backyard, you must have a house."

"Well...yes."

"And if you have a house, you would have a wife."

"Gee, yes", said Mike.

"Well", said Clyde, "if you've got a dog, a backyard, a house and a wife, then it's logical that you'd have children."

"Amazing!", said Mike.

"And if you have children", said Clyde, "you're not Gay."

Mike headed off to try his newfound knowledge on someone else.

In the bar, he bumped into Fred.

"Have you got a dog, Fred?"

"No", said Fred.

"Then you're a fuckin' faggot!"

***

The two country lads were visiting the big city.

"There's a great bar down the corner", said George. "For $5 you get this beaut cocktail called a screwdriver, then they take you out the back and you get a screw."

"Really?", replied Fred. "Have you been in there?"

"No, but my sister has."

***

A cattle station owner was having a drink at the bar in a pub in the Northern Territory. A Yank walked in and started bragging.

"Ah come from Texas", he said, "where everything's big. You call your stations big! In Texas, it takes a whole week to ride around my spread on a horse!"

"Shit!" exclaimed the station owner. "I had a horse like that so we shot the lazy bastard."

***

Col and Frank were two drovers. They had just come into town for a beer and Frank wanted to lodge his Income Tax Return. As they strolled down the main street, Col said, "Over there, Frank, that's where you go", and pointed to a sign which said 'Taxidermist'.

Frank went in and produced his income tax certificate. The taxidermist told him he was in the wrong place. "I stuff animals", he said.

"Do you stuff sheep?", asked Frank.

"Yes."

"Do you stuff kangaroos?"

"All the time."

"What about dogs?"

"Yes, often."

When Frank joined Col, he explained that the guy in the shop wasn't a Tax Agent.

"What is he then?", asked Col.

"He's just another drover like us", replied Frank.

***

Bill and Jean were sitting on the bench outside the country pub watching a bull humping a cow in the paddock across the road.

"Gee, I'd like to be doin' what that bull's doin", said Bill.

"Why don't you", said Jean, "it's your cow."

***

Farmer George thought that his prize bull was gay, so he called the vet to have a look at him.

"He's just not interested in the heifers", said the Farmer.

"Well", said the vet, "give him this mixture twice a day and see how he goes."

Farmer George was delighted at the change in his bull. He was humping everything that moved.

"What was the mixture that the vet prescribed?", asked his neighbour.

"Don't know what they call it", replied Farmer George with a big smile on his face, "but it's green in colour and tastes like vanilla."

***

A city guy was speeding along a country road and, as he passed a farm, a rooster ran in front of the car and was killed instantly. The guy got out, picked up the dead bird, took it over to the farmhouse and knocked on the door. The farmer's wife answered.

"I'm sorry, lady, I've just killed your rooster and I would like to replace it."

"Please yourself", said the farmer's wife, "the hens are around the back."

***

The primary school teacher was preparing the class for their annual concert. Some children were to sing songs, others recite poetry and some to play musical instruments. Little Alfie had just come down from the country and the teacher asked him if he would do some farmyard impressions.

On the night of the concert, Alfie nervously walked onto the stage.

"Farmyard noises", he announced. Then, cupping his hands to his mouth, he yelled at the top of his voice, "Get off that fuckin' tractor, "Shut the fuckin' gate." "Get that fuckin' calf out of the yard...!"

Two city blokes were watching Dave grooming his prize bull. One of them checked his watch and found that it had stopped, so he called to Dave, "Can you tell us the time?"

Dave squatted down and put his two hands under the bull's testicles, lifted them gently and said, "It's four thirty."

"That's incredible!", said one of the city guys. "You country fellas have really got a sixth sense about nature."

They wandered off, discussing what Dave had done, and just couldn't work it out. So they went back and Dave was still grooming his prize bull.

"Can you tell us the time again?", asked one of the city blokes.

"Sure", said Dave. Squatting down he carefully lifted the bull's testicles and said, "It's five past five."

"That's amazing! Do you reckon you could show us how to do that?"

"Sure", said Dave, "come over here."

"Now, squat down, gently lift the bull's balls, and you can see the Town Hall clock from here."

***

The new Priest was visiting Dennis and Doris out on their farm.

"And how many children have you got?", he asked.

"Six", replied Doris. "Three sets of twins."

"That's unusual", said the Priest. "Twins every time!"

"No! No!", said Doris. "Thousands of times - nothing!"

160

A farmer bought 6 sheep - 5 ewes and a ram. He asked the salesman "How will I know when the females are pregnant?"

"Simple" said the salesman. "At dawn, look out your window. If the sheep are standing around eating, they're not pregnant. When they become pregnant, they like to roll on the grass at the crack of dawn."

So every morning at the crack of dawn, the farmer looked out the window, and every morning the sheep were not rolling, they were eating. After a month of this he said to his wife "This ram's no good. He's not getting the females pregnant. What are we going to do?."

"Well", she replied, "a friend of mine told me that her husband had the same problem. He put the sheep in the back of the pick-up truck, took them out to the barn and did the job himself."

Being a New Zealander, the farmer liked the idea. "Do you think it would help?" he asked enthusiastically.

"I don't know but, it's worth a try", she said.

So he put the sheep in the back of the truck, drove them to the barn and did the job himself.

The next morning at dawn, he looked out the window but the sheep were still grazing on the grass. So he put them in the back of the truck again, drove them to the barn and did it again.

Next morning he looked eagerly out the window, but still the sheep were grazing. So he put them in the truck again, drove them to the barn and repeated the job.

This went on every day for ten days. On the eleventh day he woke up and said to his wife "I can't bear to look out that window and see those sheep grazing on the grass. Will you look out and see what they're doing?"

His wife looked out the window. "Well" she said "there's three in the back of the truck and one tooting the horn."

COURTSHIP

The young man was so nervous when he approached his highly formal prospective father-in-law that he blurted out the words,

"I am asking for your daughter's hole in handy matrimony!"

***

When the Transit Cop saw the young couple screwing away in the late night train compartment, he used his radio to notify the police, who boarded soon after.

The girl was let off with a warning, but her boyfriend was charged with mounting and dismounting while the train was in motion, and for having a first class ride while holding a second class ticket.

***

The young man was having his first sex experience, a quickie on the back seat of his car. After he had finished, he said, "If I'd have known you were a virgin I'd have taken more time."

"If I knew you had more time", she replied, "I would have taken off my pantyhose."

***

How do you stop a woman from giving you head?

Marry her.

***

They were both nervous on their first night together. He parked the car in Lovers Lane, put his arm around her and whispered in her ear, "Would you like to get in the back seat?"

"No", she replied, "I'd rather stay here in the front seat with you."

***

They were making love in the park. The session was getting really heavy. He was giving her oral sex. He looked up and said, "Gee, I wish I had a torch."

"So do I", she replied, "You've been eating grass for the last ten minutes."

***

The young guy was not proud of his small penis and was very shy about it. When he took his new girlfriend to bed for the first time he insisted that they turn out the lights. In the darkness, he put his erection in her hand.

"No thank you", she said, "I don't smoke."

***

"But this isn't an engagement ring. It's just a tiny, unset diamond", complained the petulant young woman.

"I know", said her boyfriend, "but it will be mounted the day after you are."

***

"What's the difference between a tram and a taxi?' he asked her.

"I give in. I don't know."

"Good. Then we'll take a tram."

ROYALTY

When Jock met Queen Elizabeth, he was overawed and didn't know how to behave. He'd only ever seen her on a postage stamp and didn't know whether to shake her hand or lick the back of her neck.

When Prince Andrew first got engaged to Fergie, he asked his father, "How will I know if she's a virgin?"

"It's simple, Son" replied Prince Phillip. "On your honeymoon night, when you get into bed, if she's clumsy, nervous, makes mistakes and is not sure what to do, then you can be fairly sure she's a virgin. But if she gives **you** instructions and tells **you** what to do, you'll know she's been around."

After the honeymoon, Phillip asked, "How was it, Son?"

"Just great, Father" said Andrew. "It was just the way you said... and she's definitely a virgin."

"Was she nervous, son?" asked Phillip.

"She sure was Father" Andrew replied. "In fact she was so nervous and confused that when we got into bed, instead of putting the pillow under her head, she stuck it under her bum!"

***

The true story of Michael Fagan breaking into Buckingham Palace and into the Queen's bedroom has never been told.

"Can I give you a kiss your Majesty?" Michael Fagan asked the Queen.

"No!", she replied sternly. "I'm the Queen of England!"

"Well, how about a little hug, then?", he asked.

"No!", she replied. "I'm the Queen of England!"

"Well, can I see your tits then?", asked Fagan.

"ABSOLUTELY NOT!", asserted Liz. "I shouldn't even be wanking you like this!"

What was Will Carling's favourite movie?
Poke-her-Highness.

***

Why did Camelot cum a lot? He played with his lance a lot.

***

Prince Charles was opening the Birdsville Racing Carnival. He looked dashing in his Saville Row suit, but on his head, he was wearing a fur cap with a bushy tail hanging down the back.

A reporter on the local paper approached His Royal Highness and asked him why he was wearing such a hat.

"Well", said the Prince, "I was talking to Mummy last night and telling her about the beastly flies, and when I told her that I was going to the Birdsville Races, she said, "Where the focks 'at?"

***

John Howard rang the Queen. "Make Australia a Kingdom", he said, "and I'll be the King."

The Queen replied, "I will make it a country and you can stay what you are..."

***

What's the difference between Prince Charles, Telly Savalas and a monkey?

Prince Charles is an heir apparent. Telly Savalas has no hair apparent, and a monkey is a hairy parent.

CUNNING LINGUISTS

Two Italian men get on a bus and take a seat behind a middle aged lady. An animated conversation takes place between the two Italians.

"Emma come first. Den I come. Den two asses, dey come together. Den I come again. Two asses, dey come together again. I come again and pee twice. Den I come once more."

The lady looked around and angrily said, "You filthy, foul mouthed swine! In this country, we don't talk about our sex lives in public!"

'You coola down, lady", said the Italian. "I'ma justa tellin my friend how to spella Mississippi."

***

Zoe was most concerned and went to see her local doctor.

"I've got green marks on the inside of my thighs", she complained to her doctor.

The doctor got her to remove her clothing and get on the couch for an examination.

"Hmm", he murmured. "I've seen this problem before."

"What is it?" cried Zoe.

"Have you had sex with a gypsy?" asked the doctor.

"Well, yes, I have", confessed Zoe.

"That's the problem", said the doctor. "Next time you see him, tell him his earrings aren't made of gold."

***

Cunnilingus: A real tongue twister.

***

A white guy is having a leak at a hotel urinal when two black guys walk in to take a leak. He glances down and notices that their dicks are no bigger that his and one of them has a white dick. "Hey, I'm disappointed with you guys," says the white fellow to one of the blacks. "You've got such a big reputation about your dicks but they're the same size as mine and your friend has a white one!"

"We're not black, we're white." says the first black man. "We work in the coal mines and he goes home for lunch."

***

ARMY

Private Maguire was in charge of the motor pool. The phone rang and an authoritative voice demanded to know how many vehicles were operational at that moment.

"We've got five trucks, a semi trailer, eight utilities, twelve staff cars and a Rolls Royce that that pompous alcoholic old Colonel swans around in."

"Do you know who you're speaking to?", demanded the voice.

"No", replied Private Maguire.

"It's that pompous alcoholic old Colonel you referred to."

"Well", said Private Maguire. "Do you know who you're talking to?"

"No!", roared the Colonel.

"Well, thank God for that", said Private Maguire as he hung up the phone.

***

At the Regimental Dinner, the Colonel ate too much and drank too much, got into a fight and was challenged to a duel. His friends quickly came to his rescue and sent him home in a taxi.

Next morning, he explained to his batman, "All that mess on my jacket – some drunken bounder bumped into me and vomited all over my tunic. I'll give the blighter a month's detention if I find him."

The batman gathered his clothes, saying, "I'd make it two months, sir. The bastard has shit in your pants too."

***

Representatives of the Armed Forces had got together for a meeting and were introducing themselves.

The first took a step forward, put out his hand and said, "George Smith, General, Australian Army, married, two sons, both lawyers."

The next stepped forward, put out his hand and said, "Bill Johnson, General, Australian Army, married, two sons, both surgeons."

There was an embarrassing silence until the third officer put out his hand and said, "Jack Collins, Petty Officer, Australian Navy, never married, two sons, both Generals."

***

A young Army officer arrived in the Falklands ready to face the enemy and defend the Empire.

"Where's the enemy?", he asked the Colonel.

"None of that stuff here!", said the Colonel, "we've kicked the Argies out. Today is Monday - we all play tennis."

"I don't play tennis."

"Well then, Tuesday we play polo."

"I don't play polo", said the young officer.

"That's O.K.", said the Colonel, "on Wednesday we have the Regimental dance."

"Sorry, sir, but I don't dance at all."

"Ah well, you'll certainly like Thursdays - that's wife swapping night. Lots of sex and fun."

"I'm sorry, sir, but I couldn't possibly take part in anything like that."

"God, Lieutenant!", said the Colonel, "you must be a homosexual!"

"I definitely am not homosexual!", replied the Officer.

"Oh dear", said the Colonel, "then you're definitely not going to like Friday nights either!"

***

Sergeant Dan was on patrol when he came across a quiet pool in the river. It was a hot, steamy night, so he stripped off for a swim. He was standing on the river bank when a shot rang out.

Next thing he knew, he was coming to in the recovery ward of the M.A.S.H. unit.

"What happened?", he asked.

"Well", said the surgeon, "a sniper's bullet shot your balls off. We've just repaired the damage."

Dan looked down to survey the wound. "Could have been worse", he said. "Luckily I was thinking about my wife's younger sister when it happened."

***

DEFINITIONS

What's Grosser than Gross?

1 Kissing your grandmother and she slips you the tongue.
2 Biting into a hot dog and it has veins.
3 When you throw your undies at the wall, they stick.
4 You're sitting on your grandfather's lap and he pops a boner.
5 Your little brother has lost his scab collection and you're eating corn flakes.
6 Finding a string in your Bloody Mary.

***

The Irish Guide to Medical Terms:

Artery	The study of paintings.
Bacteria	Back door to the cafeteria.
Barium	What undertakers do.
Caesarian section	A district of Rome
CAT scan	Searching for pussy.
Cauterise	Making eye contact with a woman.

Dilate	To live to a very old age.
Enema	Somebody who's got it in for you.
Labour pain	Off on Workers Compensation.
Morbid	A higher offer at auction.
Nitrate	Cheaper than day rate.
Post operative	A person who carries the mail.
Recovery room	Where they do upholstery.
Rectum	Damn near killed 'em!
Secretive	Hiding something.
Tablet	A little table.
Terminal illness	Getting sick at the bus depot.
Tumour	More than one more.
Urine	Opposite to "you're out!"

***

DICKS

A man went into jewellers shop and flopped his dick on the counter.

Unperturbed, the blonde saleswoman looked him straight in the eye and said: "This is a clock shop, not a cock shop."

Calmly he replied, "Then put two hands on this!"

***

What's the difference between white onions, brown onions and a 30 centimetre dick?

Nothing. They all make your eyes water.

***

A man went into the Body Parts shop and asked to see the latest range of penises for sale. The salesman produced one from under the counter and said, "This six inch model is our most popular, sir."

"Very nice," said the customer. "Do you have one a bit bigger?"

"How about this?" smiled the assistant, producing a seven inch circumcised model.

"Yes, it's not bad," agreed the customer. "Would you have a bigger one, preferably uncircumcised?"

"Then look at this!" said the assistant, triumphantly laying a huge cock on the counter.
"That's exactly what I want!" cried the customer. "Can I get it in white?"

***

It was the first time they had made love. They were fondling each other intimately. She had his donger in her hand.

"What do you call it?", she asked. "Some guys call theirs Dick or Peter, John Thomas or Willie. What do you call yours?"

"I don't have to call mine anything", he replied. "It usually comes without being called."

***

Most men give their penis a name because they don't want a stranger making 99% of their decisions for them.

***

Sam and Geoff were standing at the urinal together. Sam peered over at Geoff and notice how well endowed he was.

"Gee, you've got a beauty!", Sam remarked.

"Not bad, is it", replied Geoff, "but it wasn't always as big as this. I had a transplant done a couple of years ago by a cosmetic surgeon. It cost a thousand dollars."

Sam was envious and asked for the surgeon's address.

Twelve months later, Sam bumped into Geoff and could hardly wait to tell him that he'd had a penis transplant too and was thrilled with the result.

"And what's more", said Sam, "I got mine for only $500."

Geoff was shocked, and felt that he had been ripped off. He asked Sam if he could have a look. Sam dropped his strides and Geoff studied the transplant. He looked up and smiled.

"No wonder it was only $500", he said, "that's my old one!"

***

Fred was standing at the urinal when in rushed a black man who whipped out a twelve incher and said, "Phew, I just made it!"

Wide eyed, Fred looked over and said, "Gee, can you make me one too?"

***

What does a man with a nine inch prick have for breakfast?

Well, this morning I had fried eggs on toast......

***

What did Pavarotti give his girlfriend for Xmas?
  An antique organ.

***

My wife calls me 'Computer Man', because I've got a three and a half inch floppy.

***

What's the difference between Hard and Light?
  You can go to sleep with a light on.

***

He was 6'6" tall and was wearing high heeled boots and a ten gallon hat. Soon, he was approached by a woman.

"I'll bet you're from Texas", she said. "Is it true that everything is big in Texas?"

"It sure is, m'am." said the Texan.

One thing led to another, and the Texan was invited back to her apartment. He took off his big Texas hat, and his big Texas boots, and his big Texas pants and lo and behold, proved that everything from Texas was very big.

Later, having a post-coital cigarette, the Texan asked, "By the way ma'am, what part of Texas are you from?"

***

MEDICAL PROBLEMS

I sent my wife in for plastic surgery - they cut her credit cards in half.

***

The registrar of the local hospital stopped the Irish intern as he was about the enter the ward with a jug of boiling water.

"No! No! I told you to prick his boil", shouted the agitated registrar.

***

How do you get herpes in hospital?
On crutches.

***

After much soul-searching and having determined the husband was infertile, the childless couple decided to try artificial insemination.

So the woman made an appointment at the clinic, where she was told to undress from the waist down, get on the table and place her feet in the gynaecological stirrups.

She was feeling rather awkward about the whole procedure, and when the doctor came in, her anxiety was not diminished by the sight of him pulling down his pants.

Wait a minute! What's going on here!", she yelped, pulling herself up to a sitting position.

"You want to get pregnant?" asked the doctor breezily.

The patient nodded, wide-eyed.

"Well, we're out of the bottled stuff, so you'll have to settle for draught."

***

There's a new operation where they can change a woman into a man. It's called Addadictome.

***

The nurse at the Pathology Clinic was getting a bit beyond it. She was approaching retirement and was continually getting things mixed up.

One day, a young man came to the laboratory for a blood test. After half an hour, the pathologist looked in on the nurse and his patient. There she was, stroking the young man's erection.

"No!", shouted the pathologist. "Stop it! I said, prick his finger!"

***

Woman: "Quickly! I need to see an Outern."

Doctor: "You mean an Intern?"

Woman: "Have it your way, but I need a contamination."

Doctor: "You mean an examination?"

Woman: "Yes, quick, I want to go to the Fraternity Ward."

Doctor: "You mean the Maternity Ward, don't you?"

Woman: "What the hell. Outern - Intern, Contamination - Examination, Fraternity - Maternity. All I know is that I haven't demonstrated for nine months, so I must be stagnant."

***

The young country doctor thought his wife might be embarrassed if he had told her that the lecture he was giving to the Young Country Women's Club was on sex in marriage, so he told her he would be speaking on sailing.

The following day, a bright young lady who was at the meeting stopped his wife in the street and congratulated her on the doctor's lecture.

"You're lucky having such an expert for a husband", she said.

"An expert!", replied the doctor's wife. "He's only done it twice. First time he got seasick and the second time blew his hat off!"

***

There was a nurse who liked boating so much that she spent most of her time going down on the docs.

***

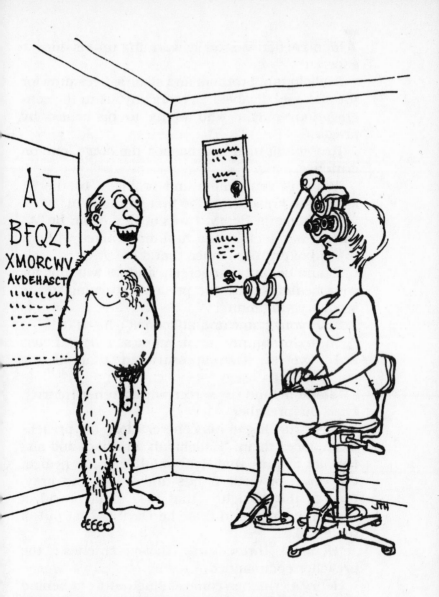

"Mrs Suter, I guarantee that you will know immediately when the correct lenses are in!"

— from *Rude and Politically Incorrect Jokes* by Allan Pease

The preacher was really warming up his audience.

"Hallelujiah, brothers and sisters. Let's pray for the sick and disabled. Is there anyone in the congregation tonight who wants to be healed by prayer?"

Two young men approached the stage, one on crutches.

"What is your name and problem, brother?", asked the preacher of the first young man.

"My name is Henry. I was struck down by MS when I was a child and have not walked without the aid of crutches since that day."

"Stand behind that screen, and we will pray for your healing", said the preacher, turning to the second young man.

"And your name and affliction?", he asked.

"M..m..m..m..my na.n..name's P..P..P..Peter. I...I....I've st..st..st..st..stuttered a..a..all my l..l..l..life."

"Stand behind the screen with brother Henry!", cried the preacher.

Then, turning to his congregation, the preacher implored them, "Hallelujiah, brothers and sisters, let us pray that Henry and Peter are healed. Get down on your hands and knees and pray, pray to the Almighty, that they shall be rid of their afflictions and that the Devil is cast out of their bodies."

"Henry - throw away those crutches", the preacher commanded.

Henry's crutches came sailing out from behind the screen.

"Peter - speak to us!"

"H..H..H..Henry's f..f..f..fallen o..o..over."

The old sailor had a wooden leg, a hook on his right arm and a black patch over one eye. "Aye, matey. These be old war wounds", he said. "I lost me leg to a cannon ball and me right hand in a sword fight."

"And how did you lose your eye?"

"I was up in the riggin' when a seagull shit in me eye. I was hangin' on with me good hand and I wasn't use to havin' the hook in the other..."

***

Why was the leper caught speeding?

Because he couldn't take his foot off the accelerator.

***

Dr Jim had just informed his patient that he had only three more minutes to live. The patient looked up wistfully and said. "There must be something you can do for me!"

"Well", replied the doctor, "I could boil you an egg..."

***

"I've got good news and bad news. What do you want first?"

"The bad news, doc."

"You have three weeks to live."

"What's the hell's the good news?"

"See that blonde nurse over there with the big tits? I'm screwing the arse off her tonight."

***

The doctor was doing his ward rounds.

"I've got some good news and some bad news for you, Mike. What do you want first?"

"Give me the bad news", replied Mike.

"I had to amputate both your legs."

"My God! What's the good news?"

"The man in the next bed wants to buy your slippers."

***

"Well, Mr Smith. I've got good news and bad news."

"What's the bad news?"

"Well, we've amputated the wrong leg."

"What! What's the good news?"

"Your bad leg is getting better."

***

DISAPPOINTMENT

The loneliness of a middle aged widow and widower eventually blossomed into love and then marriage, but the wedding night turned out to be a real disaster.

"You just don't fulfil my sexual expectations", the bride commented next morning.

"You're right about that", replied her new husband, "but when I promised to fill the void in your life, I had no idea it would be so large."

***

"Doctor, doctor. I need some pills. I've become a kleptomaniac."

"Try these", said the doctor, "and if they don't work, get me a C.D. player."

***

"Doctor, doctor. Every time I sit down, I see visions of Mickey Mouse and Pluto. And when I stand up, I see Donald Duck."

"How long have you been having these Disney spells?"

***

A couple went to the doctor's surgery. The man said, "Will you watch us have sexual intercourse and give us some advice?"

"Go ahead." said the doctor.

When the couple had finished, the doctor said, "There's nothing wrong with the way you do it", and charged them $35.

This happened several weeks in a row. The couple would make an appointment, have intercourse a different way each time, pay the doctor and leave.

After a couple of months, the doctor asked, "What exactly are you trying to find out?"

"Well", said the man, "she's married, so we can't go to her house. I'm married, so we can't go to my house. The Holiday Inn charges $180 for a room. The Hilton charges $195. Here, we can do it for $35 and get back $30 from medical insurance!"

***

She was beautiful, blonde and buxom, with a baby in her arms. He was in his first day in private practice.

"What's the problem?", he asked.

"It's the baby", she said, "He seems undernourished."

Eagerly the doctor carried out an extensive examination of the baby and asked, "Is he breast fed?"

"Yes", she replied.

"Then I'd better check you. Strip off to the waist."

Embarrassed, she took off her blouse and bra, revealing a perfect pair of firm breasts. The young doctor eagerly weighed each one in his hand, stroked the nipples and lightly squeezed them.

Ah!", he said, "that's the problem, you haven't got any milk!"

"That's not a problem", she replied, "I'm just the babysitter, but it's been very nice to meet you."

"**D**octor, doctor, where will I put my clothes?"
"Put them over there, next to mine."

***

I've got a gastric problem, doc."
"Do you use your bowels regularly?"
"Yes, every morning at eight o'clock."
"Well, what's your problem?"
"I don't get up till nine."

***

The doctor was caught in bed with the farmer's wife and explained to the shocked husband that he was only taking her temperature.

The farmer took his shotgun off the wall, primed it and said grimly, "I guess you know what you're doing, doc, but that thing had better have numbers on it when you take it out."

DRUNKS

The drunk staggered up the driveway of his home, where his son was working under the bonnet of his car.

"What's wrong, Son?", he asked.

"Piston broke", came the reply.

"So am I", muttered his father as he stumbled off.

A cab driver picked up a drunk. The drunk climbed into the back seat. "Do you have room for a crayfish and six bottles in the front?", he asked.

"Sure", said the cab driver.

So the drunk leaned over and threw up.

***

The punter had been in the bar too long. As he staggered out, he saw a sign that said, "Lunch. 12 to 1."

"Not bad odds!", he thought.

He staggered over to the barman and muttered, "Shcush me, I wanna putsch a bet on lunch."

"You're drunk", said the barman, "Get out of here before I throw you out."

The drunk staggered down the street to the next pub, where he saw another sign. "Lunch. 11 to 2". He panicked. "The odds are falling! I'd better get my bet on." He staggered up to the barman and muttered, "I wanna back lunch at 11 to 2."

"You're drunk", yelled the barman. "Get out of here!"

He staggered further down the street till he came to another pub where he saw another sign which read, "Lunch. 1 to 2".

"Odds on favourite!", he thought. "No value in that. But I'll go in and see how the race finishes."

As he walked through the bar door, the barman yelled out to the cook, "Hamburger, one."

"Shit!", said the drunk. "Just as well I didn't back lunch!"

First drunk: "I'll never forget the day I turned to the bottle as a substitute for a woman."

Second drunk: "Why, what happened?"

First drunk: "I got my prick stuck in the neck."

***

The drunk was standing in the carpark with his car keys in his hand.

"Someone's stolen my car", he slurred to a passing Police Constable.

"Where did you leave it?" asked the Constable.

"At the end of this key", said the drunk.

"You're a drunken mess", said the policeman. "Why is your fly open?"

The drunk looked down. "And they've stolen my girlfriend too", he muttered.

***

First drunk: "I didn't have sex with my wife before I got married. Did you?"

Second drunk: "I can't remember. What was her maiden name?"

***

George went into the bar for a drink one night after work and he noticed a man in the corner passed out over his beer. He went over to check him out. The man was drunk and incoherent. George decided to do his good deed for the day, checked the man's wallet and found his address. George kept trying to help the man stand up, but he kept falling to the floor. Dragging and heaving, he finally carried the drunk outside and put him in his car. When George reached the drunk's house, he pulled him out of the car and tried to help him to the front door but the drunk kept collapsing in a heap.

George sought help from a passerby and knocked on the drunk's door, which was answered by a pleasant looking woman. George explained that he had bought her husband home.

"Thank you", she said, "but where's his wheelchair?"

ECONOMIES OF SCALE

A plumber knocked at the door. "I've come to fix your blocked toilet", he said to the man who answered the door.

"But we haven't got a blocked toilet."

"Are you Mr. Collis?"

"No. He moved away six months ago."

"There are some real bastards in the world," said the plumber. "They ring for a plumber saying it's an emergency, then piss off to another address."

FACTS OF LIFE

Maurice arrived home unexpectedly. He went up the stairs and burst into the bedroom, to find a strange man laying naked in bed with his wife.

"I'll kill the bastard", said Maurie, reaching for his gun.

"No darling!", pleaded his wife. "You see the red sports car in the drive? This man gave me the money to buy it. Those golf clubs I gave you for your birthday last week? This man gave me the money. And you know how we paid off the mortgage last month? The money came from this man."

"For Christsake's woman - cover him up so he doesn't get a cold."

***

When Vietnamese Nuygen rolled a big win at the Casino, he looked around town for the finest house on the choicest piece of real estate. He found that the Vanderbilts, great industrialists and financiers, had the finest of all homes. He proceeded to build an identical mansion beside it.

On completion of the building, Mr Vanderbilt congratulated Nuygen on the fact that the properties were identical. "An amazing feat in every respect."

"But it's worth more than yours", said Nuygen.

"How come? I don't see that", replied Mr Vanderbilt.

Nuygen replied, "The properties are identical in every respect, until you try to sell them. My prospective buyers would be told that my neighbours are the famous Vanderbilts. But when they ask you about your neighbours, you'll have to admit they are Vietnamese boat people!"

***

Husband comes home and finds a man bonking his wife in bed. She pleads with him. "He's been unemployed for months. He looked so miserable. He knocked on the door and asked for something to eat so I gave him the quiche that you didn't want. He had no shoes, so I gave him a pair that you wouldn't wear. Then he asked if there was anything else my husband didn't use...."

FAIRY TALES

Red Riding Hood is tripping merrily through the forest when out jumps the big bad wolf and says, "Aha, Red Riding Hood. I'm going to gobble you up ... gobble, gobble, gobble!"

Red Riding Hood replies, "Gobble gobble gobble, that's all they think about around here. Doesn't anybody fuck anymore?"

What did Cinderella do when she got to the ball?
She choked.

FAITH

The boat was slowly sinking, and one passenger remained on the deck praying. A lifeboat came past.

"Quickly! Jump in!", called the boatman.

"No, I have faith in the Lord. God will save me."

The boat continue to sink and the passenger continue to pray, when a helicopter flew past.

"Grab the rope!", called the pilot.

"No", said the passenger. "I have faith in the Lord. God will save me."

The chopper moved off.

The boat continued to sink and the passenger continued to pray, when a speedboat came by.

"Quickly! Jump in! The ship is just about to go down!"

"No", said the passenger, "I have trust in the Lord. God will save me."

So the speedboat moved off.

Eventually the ship sunk and the passenger drowned.

When the passenger arrived at the Pearly Gates, he asked St Peter if he could use the intercom.

"Lord", he said, "I trusted you all my life, but you let me drown. I just can't believe it."

"You can't believe it?", said the Lord. "And I sent you two fucking boats and a chopper!"

FAMILY PLANNING

A group of women from the fertility clinic were having a get-together to catch up on each others' progress.

"Look at you!", said one. "You must be eight months gone!"

"Yes", said the expectant mother, "but I finally went to a hypnotherapist."

"We tried that", said the first woman. "My husband and I went for six or seven sessions but it was no good."

"You've got to go alone", whispered the pregnant one.

***

A journalist for 'Womans Day' was interviewing a mother who had fifteen children.

"And what are their names?", she asked.

"George", she said. "They're all named George."

"But what if you want to call one in particular?"

"That's easy", replied the mother, "I use their surnames."

***

Have you heared about the latest male contraceptive pill? You put it in your shoe and it makes you limp.

FARTS

A man goes to the doctors with a serious farting problem. The doctor listens to a few that rattle the windows and then asks him to lay on the couch.

The doctor reaches for a long pole with a large metal hook on the end of it and walks menacingly towards the patient.

"What are you going to do with that?" said the terrified patient.

"I'm going to open the window" gasped the doctor.

***

Why do farts smell so bad?
So the deaf can enjoy them too.

***

Geoff went to the doctors.

"Doctor, I've got a very embarrassing problem. Every time I stand up after I've been sitting down, I fart something awful. Funny thing is, you can't hear it and you can't smell it."

"Give me a demonstration, Geoff", said the doctor.

Geoff stood up, and on cue, let go a thunderclap. He sat down and stood up four or five times, each time letting go an enormous fart.

"I'll book you in for surgery straight away", said the doctor.

"What's wrong?" asked Geoff, panic stricken. "What are you going to do?"

"I'll operate on your nose first, and we'll get around to your ears when we've fixed that up", replied the doctor.

***

Arthur had been in the Old Folks Home for twelve months. He was sitting in his chair, dozing on the verandah. Every time he leaned to one side, a nurse would run over and gently push him upright. This happened constantly.

Arthur's son had come to visit and ask him how he liked the home, just as the nurse raced over and pushed him upright again. "It's a nice place", replied Arthur, "but they won't let you fart!"

***

Two old ladies were discussing the merits of pantyhose.

"I don't like them", said the first. "Everytime I fart, I blow my slippers off."

***

FINAL DESTINATION

A young man took his date to the movies to see Madonna's most shocking film. They noticed a guy a couple of rows in front, stretched out over four seats, laying there, moaning and groaning.

"Ooooohhh...Aahhhh..........Oooooohh...Aahhhhh...."

The couple complained to the Manager, who returned with a flashlight, where he asked the man, "What are you doing? Where are you from?"

"Ooooohhh......Aahhhhhh...from the balcony", he replied.

FINANCIAL PLANNING

Horrie had just pulled a $100,000 jackpot on the poker machine. When the club manager was presenting him with the cheque, he asked Horrie how he was going to spend the money.

"Well", said Horrie, "first I'll spend $25,000 at the racecourse, and I'll spend $25,000 on wine and whisky and another $25,000 on women."

"Wow!", said the manager. "What are you going to spend the other $25,000 on?"

"I'll probably just squander that", replied Horrie.

An elegant woman walked into the bank to deposit a large bag of cash. The bank manager was called over.

"Did you hoard all this money yourself?", he asked.

"No", she replied, "of course not. My sister whored half of it."

***

Zeek, the bank manager, was dismissing his accountant.

"I don't know what the world is coming to. Isn't anybody honest these days?", he asked.

"Where were you educated?"

"Yale", replied the young accountant.

"Such a grand university - what is your name?"

"Yim Yohansen", replied the accountant.

***

FISHY STORIES

A guy went past a seafood restaurant and saw a sign on the Specials Board which read, "Big Red Lobster Tails, $1 each." Amazed at the value, he said to the waitress, "$1 each for lobster tails! Is that correct?"

"Yes", she said, "it's a special just for today."

"Well", he said, "they must be little lobsters!"

"No", she replied, "it's the big lobster."

"Are you sure they aren't green lobsters - a little tough?"

"No", she said, "it's the big red lobster."

"Big red lobster tails, $1 each?", he said, amazed. "They must be old!"

"No, they're today's."

"Today's big red lobster tails - $1 each?", he said, astounded.

"Yes", she insisted.

"Well, here's my dollar," he said, "I'll take one."

She took the dollar and led him to a table where he sat down. She sat down next to him, put her hand on his shoulder and said, "Once upon a time there was a big red lobster...."

GAMBLERS

Sue was playing hard to get, so Jerry played his last card.

"I'll bet you I can keep my eye on my beer whilst I go out to my car", he challenged her.

Sue knew that this was impossible so she put down $5 and said, "You're on."

Jerry took out his glass eye, placed it on the bar beside his glass, went out to his car, came back and claimed the bet.

"I'll give you a chance to win your money back", he said. "I bet you $5 I can bite my own ear."

"You're on", said Sue.

He took out his false teeth and bit his ear lobe with them, and picked up the money once again.

"I'll give you another chance", he said. "Double or nothing. I bet you I can poke my head through this hole", he said, holding up his hand and making a circle with his thumb and forefinger. She checked the size of the hole and said, "You're on." He poked the forefinger of his other hand through the hole and touched his forehead.

"You're down $20", said Jerry, "I'll give you one last chance to get your money back. I bet I can make love to you so tenderly that you won't even feel it."

Sue knew that this was impossible, so she threw down $20 and said, "You're on!"

Jerry took Sue to the back seat of his car where he proceeded to screw her, hard and fast

"I can feel it! I can feel it!", she cried. "You've lost!"

"Ah well", said Jerry as he continued to hump away, "you win some, you lose some."

***

The drunk was busy feeding coins into the condom vending machine and laughing as he took the packets and put them into his already bulging pockets. A young man waiting impatiently behind him asked if he could use the machine.

"No way!", replied the drunk, "I'm on a winning streak!"

***

Dennis the drunk was broke as usual but needed a drink. He knew the barman was a sporting man so he offered him a bet.

"I'll bet you the price of a glass of beer that my prick is longer than your cat's tail", he said to the barman.

The barman couldn't resist a winning bet and laid down his money. He grabbed the tape measure and measured both items.

"You lose by 3 inches Dennis, so pay up."

"Not yet", said Dennis. "Where did you measure the cat's tail from?"

"From its arse to its tip", replied the barman.

"Well", said Dennis, "would you mind giving me the same courtesy?"

***

Quentin and Wally were arguing about who had the ugliest dog. Finally, a $20 bet was made. Off they went to Quentin's house to look at his dog.

"My God!", said Wally, "that's an ugly dog, but it's not as ugly as mine."

Next, they went to Wally's house. There was a paling missing from Wally's back fence, and obviously Wally's dog had taken off, so he devised a plan.

"Wait here Quentin. I'll check in the house and see if the dog's there."

He got his wife to strip off, get down on her hands and knees, threw the kangaroo rug over her and got the feather duster and shoved it up her glory hole, then asked Quentin to come in the house.

"Here she is", said Wally, "the Feather-Tailed Flock Hound."

"You win!", said Quentin. "Here's your $20. It's not the ugliest dog I've ever seen, but it's the only one whose arsehole's on top of it's tail."

***

Lionel the licensee of the country pub was known to bet on anything, even two flies crawling up the wall. One day, one of his regular customers offered him a bet.

"I'll bet you $10 I can piss in the neck of a beer bottle while it rolls along your bar", he challenged.

Lionel couldn't resist such a sure thing. "Put your money down", he said, and placed a beer bottle on the bar. His customer unzipped his fly, took out his prick, aimed with both hands, and said, "O.K., let 'er roll."

Lionel gave the bottle a push and as it rolled down the bar, his customer shuffled sideways, keeping pace with it. His aim was hopeless. Not a single drop found its way into the bottle.

"I've won!", said Lionel.

"Yes", said his customer, "you have. But I'm gonna collect $50 from each of those four guys over there who bet I couldn't piss all over your bar and get away with it!"

***

The smart young college boy was heading home on the train on his holiday from boarding school. His only companion in the compartment was an elderly farmer.

"Let's play a game", suggested the college boy.

"What kind of game?", asked the farmer.

"General knowledge. We ask each other questions and if one of us can't answer the other, then he pays a dollar."

"I like a quiz", said the old fellow, "but I don't know about the betting."

"What do you mean?"

"Well, I've spent most of my life on the farm. I'm just a simple country man and you're an educated college boy. It doesn't seem fair to me. How about if I can't answer your questions, I pay you fifty cents, and if you can't answer mine, you pay me a dollar."

The college boy was sure that he could make a few dollars here.

"I'll go first", said the farmer. "What's got five legs and flies backwards?"

"I don't know", said the college boy, slapping down his dollar."What **does** have five legs and fly backwards?"

"Beats me too", said the farmer, "but here's your fifty cents."

***

GAYS

Two gays went to the fairground. Danny said he wanted to go on the ferris wheel but Bruce was too scared, so Danny went on his own. The wheel went round and round. Suddenly Danny's seat was thrown off the wheel and he landed in a heap at Bruce's feet. "Are you hurt, Danny?", he asked.

"Of course I'm hurt! Three times around and you didn't wave once."

***

Now that gays can join the Armed Forces, what is their motto?

"Never leave your mates behind."

***

A gay said to his doctor, "I think I've got AIDS."

"Who did you get it from?", quizzed the doctor.

"How should I know- do you think I've got eyes in the back of my head?"

***

Four gays were sitting in the hot tub when a blob of semen rose to the surface.

"All right........who farted?"

What do you call a gay dinosaur?
Megasaurus.

***

What do you call a gay with diarrhoea?
A juicy fruit.

***

If the answer is "cockrobin", what's the question?
"What's that up my bum, Batman?"

***

When Brooth told Thethil that his penis was twelve inches long, Thethil thed, "That's a hard one to thwallow."

***

Jeffrey: "I think my flat mate is becoming a queer."
Johnnie: "Why do you say that?"
Jeffrey: "He shuts his eyes when I kiss him goodnight."

***

Jeffrey: "Are you gay, Johnnie?"

Johnnie: "No, but I once slept with a guy who was."

***

Bruce went to the doctor complaining about a pain in the arse. The doctor examined him and said, "No wonder, you've got a bunch of roses shoved up there."

"Have I really?", said Bruce excitedly. "Who are they from? Can you read the card?"

***

The epitaph on Elton John's headstone:

He was great on the piano but he sucked on the organ...

***

Cyril the interior decorator was telling his flat-mate about his exciting day.

"This gorgeous woman in a Saab convertible picked me up and drove me to her apartment", he explained. "Then she took off all her clothes and said I could have anything I wanted."

"How exciting! What did you do?", asked his flatmate.

"I took the car but none of her clothes fitted me", said Cyril.

What's three things a man should never say in a gay bar?

1 Bottoms up!
2 Well fuck me!
3 Can I push your stool in for you?

***

How do two gays settle a dispute?
They go outside and exchange blows.

***

John Lennon, James Dean and Liberace were sitting around Heaven, bored out of their brains. They wandered down to the Pearly Gates and asked St Peter if there was any way they could get out for a while. St Peter said he would let them go for the afternoon, but if they committed any sin during their short earthly stay, they would go straight to hell. They accepted, and with a flash of lightning and a clap of thunder, they materialised in the Red Light District in Los Angeles.

James Dean spotted a bar and headed in and ordered a bottle of bourbon. Poof! In a flash, he disappeared the moment he touched it.

A little while later, John Lennon saw a little packet of white powder laying on the footpath. He considered St Peter's warning, hesitated, then bent over to pick it up. Poof! Liberace disappeared.

Two gays are walking past the morgue on a very hot day. One turns to the other and says, "Let's go in and suck a cold one."

***

What's the difference between a homo and a hobo?

A hobo's got no mates and a homo's got mates coming out of his arse.

***

A gay masochist is a sucker for punishment.

***

Gay poker is a new card game played in gay bars. Queens are wild and straights don't count.

GENEROUS GESTURES

A homeless deadbeat approached the well dressed businessman and begged money for a meal.

"Have a cigarette", said the businessman.

"No, I don't smoke."

"Then come in the bar and let me buy you a drink."

"No, I don't drink."

"Here, then, let me give you this lottery ticket."

"No thanks, I don't gamble. All I want is some money for a meal."

The businessman thought for a moment. "I can do better than that. Come home with me and my wife will cook you the best meal you've ever had."

"Wouldn't it be easier if you gave me the money?", said the derelict.

"Yes", replied the businessman, "but I want to show my wife what happens to a man who doesn't smoke, drink or gamble."

***

Three old boys were discussing their families at the high school reunion.

"My son is a top computer salesman", said the first. "He topped the sales for the year last year and they gave him a brand new Jaguar", said the proud father. "But he gave it away. A very generous chap."

"That's interesting", said the second old boy. "My son's an insurance salesman. He won the sales competition last year. He won a penthouse on the Gold Coast. And he gave that away. A very generous man, also."

"And what about your son?", they both asked the third old boy.

"I'm really disappointed in him", he replied. "He

turned out rather badly. He's a raving poofter and lives at Kings Cross and won't work. But I suppose he's managing quite well. Only last week one of his best friends gave him a Jaguar and another gave him a penthouse on the Gold Coast."

GET IT RIGHT

The new English teacher took her first class.

"Give me a word beginning with A," she said.

"Arseholes!" said little Johnny proudly.

Ignoring his remark, she continued, "Now a word beginning with B."

"Bastard," came the answer from Freddy.

She gave C a miss and moved on to D.

"Dwarf," said little Cameron.

With a sigh of relief she asked him to explain what a dwarf was.

"A little cunt about thirty centimetres tall!" said Cameron.

***

A husband called home at noon one day and a five year old boy answered. "Put your mother on the phone, Son," he said.

"She's in the bedroom with her boyfriend." said the boy.

"Right!" said the husband "Get my rifle from the closet and shoot the both of them in the head!"

The boy put the phone down. He heard footsteps going down the hallway, then two shots rang out. The boy picked up the phone and said, "Okay, I did it. What will I do now?"

"Push the bodies under the bed out of sight", he instructed.

Minutes later, the boy returned. "I did what you said and now I'm all covered in blood!" he protested.

"Go out to the pool and wash the blood off", said the man.

"What pool?" the boy asked.

After a moment of silence, the man said, "Is this 479 5821?"

***

Jack was hurrying to get dressed, and looking forward to taking a girl from work out for the first time. His braces had broken. He couldn't find a belt. So he grabbed a pair of jumper leads from the garage to keep his trousers up.

His date looked at him curiously. "Well", said Jack, "my braces broke."

"That's O.K. then", replied his date, "just don't try and start anything!"

***

Jacko and Joe, two big brawny bouncers, were walking home from a late night out when Jacko said, "When I get home, I'm gunna rip my wife's undies off."

"Why's that?", asked Joe.

"Cos the elastic is killing me", he replied.

***

A guy walked into the chemist shop.

"I'd like some deodorant please."

"Aerosol?"

"No, under-arm."

***

The young American businessman visiting Tokyo knew no Japanese, but he nevertheless managed to persuade an attractive girl who spoke no English to accompany him to his hotel room. He felt proud of his prowess as the girl kept exclaiming "Nachigai ana!" with considerable feeling during the sex act.

The following afternoon, he played golf with a prominent Japanese industrialist. When the latter happened to score a hole in one, the American decided to make some intercultural brownie points by shouting, "Nachigai ana! Nachigai ana!" at the top of his voice.

The industrialist turned slowly, and fixed him with a penetrating stare. "What do you mean - wrong hole?"

TRANSLATIONS

Advertisement: Something that makes you think you've wanted for it for years, but you've never heard of it.

Bigamist: A fog over Italy.

Condom: An item to be worn on every conceivable occasion.

Copulate: What an Italian police chief says to a constable who doesn't get to work on time.

Mine shaft: What a German calls his penis.

Pornography: Cliterature.

Red Riding Hood: A Russian condom.

Sitting pretty: Sitting Bull's gay brother.

Specimen: An Italian spaceman.

Tear jerker: A guy who cries while masturbating.

Vice squad: A pussy posse.

Vice versa: Dirty poetry from Italy.

A Virgin:	Any Tasmanian girl who can run faster than her brothers.
Incest:	Relatively boring.
Self deception:	Faking orgasm during masturbation.
Sex:	The most fun you can without laughing.
Mistress:	Something between a mister and a mattress.
Economist:	A person who marries Elle MacPherson for her money.
Dancing:	The perpendicular expression of a horizontal desire.
Adamant:	The very first insect.
Detest:	A West Indies cricket game.
Parents:	Couples who practice the rhythm method.
Snuff:	I'm finished for the day.
Stalemate:	A husband whose lost his get-up-and-go.

***

GET YOUR OWN BACK

The statues of the male and female nudes had stood in the park for ages. One day they were struck by lightning and a booming voice called from the sky, "You can come alive for one hour."

The statues jumped off their pedestals and ran into the bushes where, for the next hour, came sounds of moaning, groaning and grunting of pleasure.

"Shall we do it one more time?", said the male statue to the female statue?

"Yes, oh yes!", she cried. "This time I will hold the pigeon and you can shit on it."

***

"Enough was enough!", said Bill the butcher to himself. It was fifteen years since the pretty, shy young girl had come into his shop with the news that the baby she was carrying was his. Bill had agreed to provide her with free meat until the child was fifteen.

When the child, who was now fifteen, came to collect the next lot of meat, he said, "You'll be fifteen tomorrow. You can tell your mother that this is the last lot of free meat she'll get from me. Then watch the expression on her face!"

When the boy relayed the message to his mother, she replied, "Son, go back to the butcher and tell him that I've had free groceries and free fruit and vegetables for the last fifteen years, and watch the expression on his face!"

"Another low blow like that and you're disqualified!"

— from *Rude and Politically Incorrect Jokes* by Allan Pease

"I bet I can tell you how many sheep are in your field." said the hitchhiker to the farmer.

"I bet you can't!" said the farmer

"If I can guess correctly, will you give me an animal?"

"Sure!" said the farmer.

"There are 5,619 sheep" said the hitchhiker.

"Christ...How did you do that?"

"I can't tell you, but can I have my animal please?"

The hitchhiker picks up an animal and walks off.

"Just a minute" called the farmer. "If I can tell you where you're from, will you give me back my animal?"

"Sure" sniggered the hitchhiker.

"You're from Dublin."

"Christ...how did you know that?"

"I can't tell you," said the farmer, "but can I have my dog back?"

GOLFERS

Before sex, what does a woman do with her arsehole?

She drops him at the golf course.

***

I don't play golf. It ruins a nice walk.

Maurie was not having a good day on the golf course. After he missed a twelve inch putt, his partner asked him what the problem was.

"It's the wife", said Maurie dejectedly. "As you know, she's taken up golf, and since she's been playing, she's cut my sex down to once a week."

"Well, you should think yourself lucky", said his partner. "She's cut some of us out altogether!"

***

A pretty young lass had just joined the golf club, and Mike offered to give her some instruction. He stood behind her and showed her how to grip the club and how to swing back and forward. Their moving bodies caused the zipper on his fly to get caught in the zipper of her skirt. They were stuck. Slowly they moved towards the club house to get assistance, when a big brown dog jumped out from behind a bush and threw a bucket of water over them.

***

Arguing about the score is not the done thing on a golf course, but here were three members going at it hammer and tongs while the fourth lay dead in a bunker. A club official was called.

"What's the problem here?", he demanded.

"Well", said one player, "my partner's had a stroke, and these two bastards want to add it to my score."

It was Disabled Day at the golf club, and they were playing mixed fours. Wally's partner hadn't turned up, so he wandered through the club house looking for a partner. There, sitting in the coffee lounge, was a beautiful blonde.

"I wouldn't mind playing around with her", he thought as he approached.

"I would be only too happy to join you", she said.

Wally was showing off on the first hole, and hit a beautiful wood straight down the middle.

"That's wonderful", said the blonde, "considering you're disabled. What is your problem?"

Wally took his jacket off and screwed off a false arm.

On the next hole, the blonde noticed that Wally was favouring his left leg.

"What's the problem?", she asked.

Wally rolled up his trousers and screwed off his false leg.

On the third hole, Wally hit one into the rough and his blonde partner went in with him to find his ball.

Some ten minutes later, one of the other members of the foursome headed into the rough looking for them. When he returned, his partner asked him where they were and he replied, "Wally's in there, screwing his heart out."

***

GOLF: An infuriating game that brings out the worst in people. Why was it called golf? Because all the other four letter words were taken.

Question on golf etiquette:

What do you do when your opponent claims to have found his ball in the rough and you know that he hasn't because you've got it in your pocket?

***

A husband and wife were playing golf together when the wife got severely stung by a bee. Panic-stricken, the husband ran to the club house, looking for a doctor.

"Come quickly!", he said, "My wife's been stung by a bee."

"Where was she stung?" asked the doctor.

"Between the first and second holes", gasped the husband.

"Gee", replied the doctor, "she must have a wide stance."

***

Keith, a sales representative, was taking his client, Ron, for a day out on the golf course for a quick round. After playing a couple of holes, they were slowed down by two women players in front of them.

"I'll go and ask if we can play through", said Keith.

Keith returned, visibly shaken.

"You won't believe this, Ron, but the two women in front – one is my wife and one is my mistress!"

Ron looked at his watch impatiently and said, "You keep out of sight. I'll go and talk to them."

A few minutes later, Ron returned.

"You're not going to believe this, Keith", he started.......

***

"**F**orgive me, Father, for I have sinned. I used the F word this morning on the golf course."

"Tell me, my son, what were the circumstances that put you under such extreme provocation?"

"I drove my tee shot three hundred metres, but the wind suddenly caught it and it landed in the rough."

"I can appreciate your disappointment. I am a golfer myself."

"No, that's not it, Father. I hit a beautiful shot out of the rough. It dropped about ten metres short and rolled into a sand trap."

"Now", said the Priest, "I can really understand you using the F word."

"No, Father. I pulled out my sand wedge and hit a perfect shot, In fact, the ball hit the pin and bounced two inches from the hole."

"Is that where you used the F word?"

"No, Father."

"Don't tell me you missed the fucking putt!"

***

George was walking towards the green, and had just pulled out his putter when he heard the call,

'Fore'. He turned to see what was happening, was hit by a golf ball and doubled over in pain.

A very attractive lady golfer who had hit the ball came rushing to his assistance. "I'm terribly sorry", she said to George, who was clasping his hands in his crotch. "Let me help you."

The woman unzipped his fly and began to stroke his balls and dick. After a few minutes, she asked, "Does that feel better?"

"Yes", replied George, "that feels really great, but my thumb still hurts like hell."

***

A professional golfer driving his Porsche, picked up an Irish girl hitchhiker. He had his golfing gear on the back seat. The Irish girl picked up something and asked, "What are these?"

"Those are tees", he said. "I rest my balls on them when I drive."

"Wow!", said the girl, "what will those car makers think of next!"

***

GOOD ADVICE

Every man should have a woman for love, companionship and sympathy, preferably living at three different addresses.

Brian had just caught his wife in bed with another man. His friend Wally was consoling him.

"Come on, Brian", he said, "its not the end of the world."

"That's alright for you to say, Wally. How would you feel if you came home one night and caught your wife in bed with another man?"

Wally thought for a moment and replied, "I'd break his white cane and kick his guide dog in the arse."

***

If a bird craps on your car, never take her out again.

***

Pete's blood tests had been mixed up with those of another patient. The doctor scratched his head and said, "Either you've got Alzheimers or Aids."

"God!" said the patient. "What'll I do?"

"For the time being, if you can find your way home, don't screw your wife."

***

"Doctor, doctor, what's the best thing to take when you are run down?"

"The registration number of the bastard that hit you."

Gerry was seeking sex counselling from his doctor. His wife was losing interest in sex.

"Next time you get home from work, bring home a box of chocolates, kiss her passionately, sweep her off her feet, give her one on the lounge room rug and you will be surprised at her reaction."

When Gerry next visited the doctor, he was asked how it worked.

"Yes, she was certainly surprised", said Gerry, "and so were all the members of her bridge club."

DIETS

Gordon was overweight. He weighed 130 kilos. He had tried every diet and weight reduction course available. One day he picked up the week-end paper and saw an ad for the Sex Diet - "The Most Enjoyable Way To Lose Weight". He rang the number and was told that the course would cost $10 per kilogram of weight lost.

"How much do you want to lose?", they asked.

"Ten kilos", replied Gordon.

So the transaction was completed on his credit card.

"At eight o'clock tonight", said the weight loss counsellor, "one of our beautiful hostesses will knock on your door."

Gordon couldn't wait.

At eight o'clock, sure enough, there was a knock on his door. There stood the most beautiful, ravishing blonde.

"You can screw me if you can catch me", she said, and off she ran, with Gordon in hot pursuit. He didn't catch her, but by the time he got home, he'd lost ten kilos.

Next weekend, he rang the Sex Diet again. "I'd like to lose another ten kilos", he said.

"The more you lose, the more it costs", the counsellor advised him. "This will cost you $200", she continued.

"I'll take it!", said Gordon.

So a time was set for a hostess to drop by.

This time it was the most beautiful redhead Gordon had ever seen. "If you can catch me, you can screw me", she said, and off she ran, with Gordon in hot pursuit. He didn't catch her, but sure enough, he lost another ten kilos in the effort.

The following weekend, Gordon called the Sex Diet line again. "I want to lose another ten kilos", he said.

"You're getting into a very difficult area now", said the counsellor. "It will cost you $300 this time."

Forever hopeful, Gordon completed the transaction.

At the appointed time, the tallest, incredibly attractive brunette arrived. "If you can catch me, you can screw me", she said, and off she went. And she ran and ran, with Gordon hot on her heels. He nearly caught her and he lost another ten kilos.

Next weekend, Gordon again rang the Sex Diet line and said he wanted to lose another ten kilos.

"You are getting into an impossible area", said

the counsellor. "This would take drastic measures."

But Gordon had plans. He was not going to let the next hostess get away. He completed the transaction for $500.

At the appointed time, there was a knock on the door. Gordon opened the door, ready to lunge, but there, was the fattest, ugliest, smelliest woman he had ever seen. She said "The Diet Clinic told me that if I can catch you I can screw the arse off you."

***

Laurie had just returned from a tour of the brothels in Asia. He was feeling poorly and had broken out with terrible skin eruptions.

"This is serious", said his doctor sternly. "We're going to have to put you on a special diet of pancakes and pizzas."

"Pancakes and pizzas?", exclaimed Laurie.

"Yes", replied the doctor. "That's the only food that can be shoved under your door."

GYNOS

Two gynaecologists meet at golf. They discuss what cases they've had during the past month.

"Well, I had a patient with tits as big as water-melons."

"Wow! That big?"

"Yes... that big."

"Well, I had a patient with a clitoris like a lemon."

"Yeah? That big?

"No, that sour."

***

Most other specialists are very wary of gynae-cologists. They say that they're always spreading old wives tails.

***

Have you heard about the gynaecologist who always looked up his old girlfriends when on hol-idays?

***

Then there was the specialist who was so good at gynaecology that he could wallpaper his bed-room through the keyhole.

***

The fat woman complained to her gynaecologist. "I'm just not enjoying sex any more."

"Well", he said, "why don't you diet?"

"Oh, will that do any good? What colour do you suggest?"

***

Patient: "Are you the gynaecologist?"

Gynaecologist: "Yes. At your cervix, madam."

Patient: "I am dilated to meet you".

***

"There's something wrong with my aviaries", she complained.

"You mean your ovaries?", said the gynaecologist.

"No", she insisted, "it's my aviaries."

"OK, have it your way. Take off your clothes, lie on the table and put your feet up here."

"You're right", he said, "It is your avaries! There's been a cockatoo in there!"

***

She went to the gynaecologist with her problem.

"Can you stop having sex with your husband for a month?" he suggested.

"Sure", she said, "I've got a couple of boyfriends who could stand in for that long."

***

HEADLINES

The journalist from 'Womans Day' was interviewing an elderly lady in the retirement home on her 100th birthday. She was still in excellent health.

"Have you ever been bedridden?", asked the journalist.

"Many times!", she beamed. "But don't put that in the magazine!"

***

Then there was the newspaper story about the four foot tall fortune teller who escaped from jail and the headlines ran:

"Small medium at large."

***

Leo the Lion was drinking from a stream with his bum pointing skyward just as a big gorilla was passing. The gorilla was intoxicated after eating fermenting fruit. The gorilla crept up on the lion and sunk his sausage into him. The lion let out a mighty roar and the gorilla sped off. The gorilla found a deserted hunter's camp and quickly put on a safari suit and helmet, donned a pair of sunglasses, jumped into a chair and grabbed a newspaper, hiding behind it as though he was reading. The ferocious lion dashed into the camp and asked the 'hunter' – "Did a gorilla come through here?"

"Not the gorilla that fucked the lion down by the stream?" said the 'hunter'.

"Hell!", said the lion, "don't tell me it's in the newspapers already!"

MORE IRISH

An Irishman is walking along the beach in Sydney. There are many beautiful women lying in the sun and he'd love to meet one but they don't seem interested in him. So he says to a bronzed Lifesaver, "I've been trying to meet one of these beauties and I can't seem to get anywhere. You're an Aussie, you know them. What do they want?" he asks.

"Go and buy some swimming briefs that are too small for you and then walk up and down the beach until they notice you" says the Aussie.

"Thanks," says the Irish guy and goes off to the shops. He buys some tiny blue swimmers, puts them on, goes back to the beach. He parades up and down but still has no luck. So he says to the Lifesaver, "I still haven't been able to meet a girl."

"OK, I'll tell you what you do." says the Aussie. "Go to the store and buy a large potato. Put potato in your swimmers and then walk up and down the beach. Then you'll meet girls very, very quickly."

"Thanks", says the Irishman. He goes to the store and buys a potato, puts it in the swimmers. But after walking up and down for an hour, the women are still avoiding him. So he goes back to the Aussie. "I got the swimmers and put the potato in. I walked up and down the beach. Still nothing. What more can I do?"

"Well," says the Aussie "try putting the potato to the front of your swimmers - not the back!"

***

An Irishman goes on "Sale of the Century" and chooses Irish history as his category.

"In what year was the Easter rising?"

"Pass." he replies.

"What's the famous stone in Ireland that you can kiss?"

"Pass." he replies.

"What's the difference between the Orange and the Green?"

"Pass." he replies.

"Good man Patrick!" says a voice from the audience, "tell 'em nothing!"

***

The time keeper was checking the bus driver's running sheet. "What time did you pull out this morning, Paddy?"

"I didn't", said Paddy, "and I've been worrying about it all day."

An Irishman went into a hardware store and asked for a chainsaw that would cut six trees in one hour. The salesman recommended a top of the line model. The Irishman was impressed and bought it.

A couple of days later, the Irishman bought the chainsaw back, complaining that it took all day to cut down one tree.

"All day?", queried the salesman. "There must be something wrong with it."

He started up the saw to see if he could find the problem, and the Irishman said, "What's that noise?"

***

Paddy was having a Guinness with his mate Kevin.

"If you don't mind me saying, Paddy", said Kevin, "you should draw your bedroom blind at night. I walked past your place last night and saw you in bed screwing your wife."

"Ha ha ha", said Paddy, "the joke's on you. I wasn't even home last night!"

***

Francis O'Connor had the flu.

"Why don't you take the day off?", said one of his workmates. "But the boss wouldn't like it", said Francis, coughing and sneezing.

"Don't worry, he's never here on Wednesdays anyway."

So Francis took his friend's advice and went home. As he passed his bedroom window, he saw his boss in bed with his wife. He rushed back to the office and said to his mate, "That was a close one, to be sure. I nearly got caught!"

***

Three builder's labourers, an Australian, an Englishman and an Irishman, were working on Sydney's highest skyscraper. It was lunchtime, and they sat down together for a friendly chat.

"Not bloody Vegemite again!", said the Australian, opening his lunch. "Bloody Vegemite! Day in and day out. If I have Vegemite sandwiches tomorrow, I'll jump off this bloody building!"

The Englishman opened his lunch. "Jam sandwiches again. If I get jam sandwiches again tomorrow, I'll jump off with you!"

Paddy opened his lunch. "Cheese sandwiches again! If I get cheese sandwiches again tomorrow, I'll jump too!"

Next day the three friends sat down for lunch. The Australian took one look at his Vegemite sandwich and said, "Shit!", and jumped off the building.

The Englishman opened his lunch and said, "Jam!", and followed the Australian down.

The Irishman peered into his lunchbox and said, "Cheese again!", and he jumped.

Being friends, there was a triple funeral and the widows got together at the Wake. The Australian widow sobbed, "If only I'd have known he hated Vegemite!"

The English widow cried, "If only I'd have known that he hated jam!"

The Irish widow added, "Begosh and begorrah, it's beyond me. Paddy always made his own sandwiches!"

***

Paddy rushed into the bank and pointed a banana at the teller and shouted, "This is a cock up!"

"Don't you mean a stick up?", said the terrified teller.

"No", replied Paddy, "it's a cock up. I left my bloody gun at home."

***

Pat and Mick were walking along the street when Pat grabbed Mick by the arm.

"Look out, Mick", he said, "mind where you're stepping. That looks like dog shit."

Mick bent down and pushed it with his finger. "It feels like dog shit", he said.

Mick then put his fingers to his lips. "It smells like dog shit and tastes like dog shit. Pat, I think you're right. Lucky we didn't step in it."

***

Pat walked into the house with a handful of dog shit and said to his wife, "Look what I nearly trod in."

How do Irish count bank notes?

"One, two, tree, four, foive, another, another, another..."

***

The headstone read "Here lies the body of Sir Thomas Parker, an Englishman and a gentleman".

"Not likely", said Paddy, "No gentleman would ever be buried with a pommy."

***

How does an Irishman know if his girlfriend is wearing panty hose?

Her toes curl up when he's screwing her.

***

Paddy went to the doctors. He had two burnt ears.

"I was doing the ironing when the phone rang", said Paddy.

"But what about the other ear?", queried the doctor.

"Well, I had to phone you for an appointment, didn't I?" replied Paddy.

***

Dr Roberts was explaining to Michael O'Regan about how nature adjusted for some physical disabilities.

"For example", said the doctor, "if a man is blind, he develops a keen sense of touch. If he is deaf, he develops other senses."

"I know exactly what you mean", said Michael. "I've noticed that if a bloke has one short leg, then the other one is always a bit longer."

HIGHER EDUCATION

A university lecturer was discussing the anatomy of the male genitalia of various African tribes. He went on, "The Zulu tribe is known to have the longest penis."

It was starting to get embarrassing for the female students. One girl at the back of the lecture hall decided she'd had enough and walked out. She had just reached the door when the lecturer called out, "There's no hurry, madam. The next plane to Johannesberg doesn't leave until 9.30 Saturday morning."

***

A University graduate had just arrived for his first day's work. The manager gave him a broom and asked him to tidy up the office.

"But I'm a University graduate!", protested the young man.

"I'm so sorry. I just wasn't thinking", apologised the manager and added, "I'll call someone to show you how to do it."

HIRED HELP

The wealthy socialite had a night out with her friends. She woke up the morning after, totally naked and with a terrible hangover. She rang for the butler and asked for a cup of strong coffee.

"Giles", she said, "I can't remember a thing about last night. How did I get to bed?"

"Well, madam, I carried you upstairs and put you to bed."

"But my dress?"

"It seemed a pity to crumple it, so I took it off and hung it up."

"But what about my underwear?"

"I thought the elastic might stop the circulation, so I took the liberty of removing them."

"What a night!", she said. "I must have been tight!"

"Only the first time, Madam."

***

*"There will be no second warnings Jeeves.
Disobey me and I'll fart again."*

— from *Rude and Politically Incorrect Jokes* by Allan Pease

The butler had been reprimanded frequently for his behaviour with the female servants, and was given one last chance for atonement. He promised to reform. One night, however, he was not to be found when needed and after a search, was discovered in the basement buggering the pageboy.

The butler was paraded in front of the master. "I thought you had promised to reform", said the master.

"It's true, My Lord, I have turned over a new leaf – it's just that I started at the bottom of the page."

***

Charles knocked at Her Ladyship's door and entered.

"You rang, Your Ladyship?"

"Charles, please unzip my dress."

With a great deal of embarrassment, he did so.

"Now Charles, take off my stockings."

He was really embarrassed.

"Now Charles, take off my underwear.....and if I ever catch you wearing my clothes again, you will be instantly dismissed."

***

Charles was again summoned to the bedroom by Her Ladyship. She was lying on the bed, naked.

"Charles", she asked, "do you think I've got a beautiful body?"

"Yes, Your Ladyship. I think you've got a fantastic body."

"Good, Charles", she said, "are you a good fuck?"

"Indeed I am, Madam!", replied Charles excitedly.

"Then fuck off. It's April Fools Day."

***

Giles the butler was summoned by the Lord of the manor.

"Giles, the Vicar is coming for tea this afternoon. Would you go down to the village and buy a bottle of whisky, a box of cigars and two ounces of snuff."

It was a long walk to the village and when halfway back, Giles realised that he had forgotten the snuff. It was too far to walk back to the village, so he needed to improvise. On the side of the road were three sun dried dog turds. Giles picked these up and crushed them to a powder.

When he returned to the manor, the Lord of the house checked Giles' purchases. When he got to the snuff, he asked, "Do you smell dog shit, Giles?"

"No, My Lord."

The Vicar arrived soon afterwards and immediately got stuck into the scotch.

"Can you smell dog shit, Vicar?", asked the Lord.

"Can't say I can, old chap", replied the Vicar, "but then, I do happen to have a heavy cold."

"In that case, take a pinch of snuff", said the Lord.

The Vicar reached out and took a sniff up each nostril.

"By jove!", said the Vicar, "you do get the best snuff. That's cleared my head completely and I can smell the dog shit now."

***

Bass and Flinders circumcised Australia with a forty foot cutter.

HYGIENE

It was a rough looking cafe but the motorist was hungry and decided to give it a try.

"What will ya have Sweetie?" asked a waitress who looked like a wrestler.

"Two hamburgers and a hot dog," he ordered.

She went to the fridge, got two meat patties and stuck them up under her armpits.

"What's that for?" asked the motorist.

"Everything's deep frozen and the microwave's busted," she explained, "this is the only way I can thaw them out."

"Well okay," said the disillusioned motorist, "but forget the hot dog."

The pastry cook was sealing the edges of his pasties with his false teeth when the Health Inspector walked in.

"Haven't you got a tool for that?", he asked.

"Yes, but I save it for putting holes in donuts."

***

"We Specialise In Hygiene", said the sign at the bread shop.

The customer was delighted when she saw the baker pick up her rolls with a pair of tongs and put them in a bag.

"Untouched by human hands!", said the baker.

"Very good!", said the customer, "but tell me, what is that piece of string hanging out of your fly?"

"Hygiene!", said the baker. "When I have a piss I pull it out with the string. My hand never touches my dick."

"How do you put it back?", asked the customer.

With the tongs", replied the baker.

***

COUPLES

After fifteen years, they had separated amicably, and after the court case, decided to go out and have a celebration dinner together.

"There's something I've wanted to ask you for years", he said, "and now that we're divorced, you can tell me. Why is it that five of our six children have black hair and our youngest, Billy, is blonde? Come on, it's O.K. you can tell me now. Whose child is Billy?"

"Well", replied his ex-wife, "if you really want to know, he's your child. The rest aren't."

***

Fred had just arrived home after a couple of hours in the bar. He was feeling pretty cocky. His wife was washing her bra.

"I don't know why you worry about those", he said. "You've got nothing to put in them."

She looked at him and said, "I think the same thing when I'm ironing your underpants."

***

INCEST

Dave was a country lad. Kicking the dirt and looking at the ground he said "Dad I'm gettin' married to Mabel. Is that OK? She's a good girl, Dad - she's still a virgin."

"Well Dave", said Dad, "if she's not good enough for her family, she's not good enough for ours!"

***

"**C**lean up your bedroom!", said the Tasmanian father to his teenage daughter.

"I'll do it when I finish watching T.V.", she replied.

"Immediately!", her father demanded.

"When I'm finished watching TV!" retorted his daughter.

"That's it!", said the father, turning off the TV set. "Now you'll pay the penalty for your disobedience!"

"Oh no! Not **the** penalty!", replied the girl.

"Yes, **the** penalty", said father, unzipping his fly.

Reluctantly, she gave her father a blow job.

"Yuk! Your dick tastes like shit!", she said, spitting and spluttering.

"Well, your brother wouldn't wash the car!"

RACISM

Three Tongans are in a car going down the freeway. Who's driving?

The police.

***

Why did God give black men such big dicks?

Because he was so ashamed of what he did to their hair.

What's a slope?
A Vietnamese person who just left the room.

ITS A HARD LIFE

There was a young fella called Skinner
who took a young lady to dinner
At half past nine
They sat down to dine
And by quarter to ten it was in her.
(The dinner, not Skinner).

Another young fella called Tupper
Took the same young lady to supper
At half past nine
They sat down to dine
And by a quarter to ten it was up her.
(Not Tupper, some bastard called Skinner).

***

Mick landed a job on an oil rig. One month on, one month off. Half way through the first month on, Mick was getting lonely for female company. Nervously, he asked one of the other workers, "What do you do for sexual relief when you're out on the rig?"

"Try the hole in the barrel down in the shower room. Most of the men say it's great."

Mick cautiously tried it out and came back to his co-worker and said, "The hole in the barrel is fantastic. I'm going to use it every day."

"Not on Wednesdays", replied the co-worker, "that's going to be your day in the barrel."

***

Kevin dropped into the local bar for a drink on his way home. He met a very attractive redhead who later suggested that they go back to her flat. After a few more drinks at the flat, they jumped into bed and were having a wonderful time.

Kevin lost track of time, and before he knew it, it was 2 a.m.

"God!", said Kevin, "what am I gonna tell the wife?"

"Put a piece of chalk behind your ear and tell her the truth", said the redhead. "I guarantee it'll work."

Kevin was creeping into his bedroom when suddenly the lights came on and there was his wife, with her arms folded on her chest.

"Where have you been 'til this hour of the morning?", she demanded.

"I've been in bed with a beautiful redhead that I picked up in the bar."

"You liar!", roared his wife. "You've been playing snooker all night with your deadbeat mates. Do you think I'm stupid or something? You've left the chalk behind your ear."

***

Two crayfish were in the fish tank in the seafood restaurant. The male crayfish put the hard word on the female crayfish.

"Yes", she said, "but will you still respect me in the mornay?"

***

There was a brave Dutch lad who stuck his finger in a dyke. So she punched the shit out of him.

***

A driver returned to his parked car and found his front mud guard damaged. Under the windscreen wiper he found a note which said, "Sorry I backed into your car. The crowd who saw me do it were most impressed when they saw me writing down my name and other particulars, but I'm not..."

***

It was after midnight when the veterinarian answered the phone. The call was from a little old lady seeking advice about separating two dogs that were love-locked on her back lawn.

"Try using a broom handle", he suggested.

Not long after, the little old lady called back to report that the broom handle hadn't worked.

"Try throwing a bucket of water over them", advised the vet.

Ten minutes later, the little old lady was back on the line to say that that hadn't helped either.

"As a last resort", grumbled the vet, "go out and tell the male dog that the telephone's ringing for him."

"Do you think that'll work?", asked the little old lady.

"Well", roared the vet, "it's worked three times tonight with me."

JINX

Old Harry was on his deathbed. He raised himself on one elbow and beckoned his wife.

"Doris", he whispered, "you were with me through the Great Depression."

"Yes, Harry."

"Doris, you were with me through the worst droughts in the fifties and the eighties."

"Yes, Harry."

"And you were with me when the farm got burned out by the bushfires in the nineties. And last year, you were still hanging in there with me when the bank foreclosed on our mortgage and we lost the farm."

"Yes, Harry."

"And now, here you are with me today, when I'm just about to die."

Doris nodded.

"You know, Doris", he whispered, "I'm beginning to think that you're nothin' but fuckin' bad luck!"

JUST DESERTS

Breakfast was late and husband and wife were badly hung over from a particularly wild party the night before. Bleary eyed, he said to his wife, "Was it you I made love to in the garden last night?"

"About what time?" she replied.

***

When King Arthur took off on his search for the Holy Grail, he fitted his Queen, Guinevere, with a novel chastity belt. It contained a little guillotine. If anybody tried to push past it, it sprung down with a mighty whack.

On his return from the Holy Land, King Arthur commanded that all the Knights that had stayed behind remove their trousers, and there was hardly a cock in sight. All except Sir Lancelot had lost their manhood.

"Lancelot, you are the only one I can trust", said King Arthur. "What will we do with these traitors? What will their punishment be? Come, Sir Lancelot, speak up. Have you lost your tongue............?"

***

The blind man was standing on the corner with his trusty labrador guide dog. Suddenly, the dog cocked its leg and pissed on the blind man's trousers. As the warm piss ran into his shoe, the blind man pulled out a dog biscuit and offered it to the dog. A casual observer remarked, "Why are you rewarding that dog? He just pissed on your leg."

"I know", said the blind man, "I just want to find which end his head is, then I'm going to give him a good kick in the arse."

LAST RITES

Roland had been the meanest husband that ever lived, but now he was dead and his wife had got her hands on his life savings and insurance policy. His wife's friends and relatives were most surprised when she asked that his ashes be bought back to their home.

After the ashes had been delivered, she removed the lid from the urn and said, "Look at this beautiful big diamond ring, Roland. It's the ring that I always wanted."

She then took the urn into her bedroom where all her new clothes hung. "Look at my new clothes and that fur coat. It's the one that I always wanted."

She then went to the window and held the urn outside and said, "See that Jaguar in the driveway, Roland? That's the car I always wanted."

"And Roland", she said, "you know that blow job that you always wanted, well here it is." Whooooosh !

LESBIANS

What sort of timber is a lesbian's bed made of?
All tongue and groove.

***

The guy wandered up to her and began chatting her up.

"Look", she said, "will you piss off? I'm a lesbian."

"What's that?", he frowned.

"Well, see that beautiful blonde over there? I could go for her. In fact I've love to get into her pants."

"Really?", he replied. "I must be a lesbian too."

***

"Everything's neat and tidy in there", said the gynaecologist after the examination.

"So it should be", said the lesbian. "I have a woman in twice a week."

What do you call a lesbian dinosaur?
Lickalottapus.

LIARS

Zeke came home early one day to find Mary Lou lying on the bed naked, except for a small wet towel on her thigh.

"What's happening?" he asked suspiciously.

"Nothing," replied Mary Lou, "I been doin' aerobics and I'm restin'."

"What's that towel doing there?"

"I wet it in water to put on my forehead, 'cause I was hot, that's all," she said.

Zeke went to the bathroom, got out his razor and began sharpening it.

"What ya gonna do with the razor, Zeke?" she asked.

"If that towel dries soft," said Zeke, "I'm gonna shave."

***

The husband came home early to find his wife completely nude on the bed and the plumber standing beside her, also nude.

The plumber immediately went into a squatting position and said, "I was just telling your wife Mr. Varney, that if she doesn't pay the the plumbing bill straight away, I'm going to shit on this floor."

Ivan was the smoothest talker in the world. He even made his wife feel sorry for the hitchhiker who had lost her bra and panties in his car.

***

Merv the Perv was sitting in the tram fantasising about a young nurse sitting at the other end of the carriage. The conductor came along collecting fares. He said to Merv, "I can see you're lusting after that nurse, I'll let you in on a secret. She loves to have sex with tram conductors. Every Friday night she comes down to the back of the tram depot and lets one of the conductors have his way with her."

This excited Merv. He borrowed a tram conductors uniform and went to the back of the tram depot on Friday night. It was quite dark but there she was.

As he came up behind her, he realised that she must have heard him coming for she hitched up her skirt and bared the creamy white cheeks of her bum. The excitement was too much. He rushed at her, plunged in and humped away like a jackhammer.

Late, during a post-coital cigarette, Merv laughed. "I'm not really a tram conductor", he confessed. "That's O.K.", came her reply, "I'm not really a nurse – I'm the tram conductor."

***

LIMELIGHTERS

There was a drum roll, and the lion tamer cracked his whip. The largest, most savage looking lion opened his mouth, and to everyone's amazement, the lion tamer unzipped his fly and stuck his dick in the lion's mouth. The applause was tumultuous. There were cheers and calls for an encore.

The lion tamer went to the microphone and announced, "That act was not difficult. Anyone can do it! The owners of this circus offer $1,000 to anyone from the audience who can emulate that feat right here and now. Do we have any volunteers?"

"Here!", called a squeaky voice from the back row, and the spotlight picked up a skinny little man with a droopy moustache. He was called down into the ring and the Ringmaster asked him if he was ready. "Yes", said the timid little fellow. "I don't think I can open my mouth as wide as the lion, but I'll give it a go."

LOVERS

It was their first date and she was giving him a lingering kiss goodnight.

"Is there anything else I can do for you?", he asked.

She whispered in his ear, "I want you to weigh me."

Anxious to impress, he drove her back to the local railway station where he knew there was a set of scales.

When she got back home, her mother asked if she had a good time.

"Absowutewy wousy", she replied.

***

"**D**ad", said eight year old Danny, "I'm gonna get married."

Dad smiled indulgently. "Who to, Son?"

"My girlfriend Kathy next door. She's eight too."

"Found a place to live?"

"Well", said Danny seriously, "she gets fifty cents pocket money, and you give me a dollar, so if she moves in with me, we can manage."

Dad nodded. "You might be able to get by on a dollar fifty a week now, but what will you do when the children start to arrive?'

"No worries", said Danny confidently, "we've been lucky so far."

***

The errant wife was in the middle of a very passionate session with her lover when the phone rang. She picked up the phone and listened for a few minutes, and told her lover that it was her husband on the phone.

The boyfriend panicked and started to dress.

"Calm down", she said, "we've got plenty of time. He's playing cards with you and the rest of his mates."

***

"I don't know how I'm going to look my parents in the face after being made love to three times by a total stranger," said the French girl.

"What do you mean, three times? We've only done it once."

"Yes, but you're not going home yet, are you?"

LUCK

Simon Solomon was drinking in a bar in Belfast when he suddenly felt a pistol in his back.

"Catholic or Protestant?" demanded a voice behind him.

"Jewish" replied Simon.

"Well, I must be the luckiest Arab in the whole of Ireland."

***

Wally had never won a prize in his life. Not even a chook raffle. So one day he'd decided to buy a lottery ticket. He bought a $5 ticket and two days later he won $500,000. He couldn't believe it!

Overjoyed, he decided to spend a week in the Las Vegas Hilton. When he walked through the door of the Hilton, the Manager approached him and said "Congratulations! You are our five-millionth customer this year! You've just won $100,000 in gambling tokens and a month's free holiday here at the Hilton."

Wally couldn't believe it. He was on a winning streak! He went to the bar to celebrate. In the bar he noticed the most beautiful Indian woman he'd ever seen. She smiled softly at him, approached him and asked if he would come up to her room for a while. He couldn't believe his luck. He went to her room and had the wildest night of sex and passion he'd ever imagined.

Later, he was lying there exhausted, having a post-coital cigarette when he noticed she had a red spot in the middle of her forehead. He leaned across, scratched it and won a colour TV!

MANNERS

Colin was a bachelor. He lived in an apartment and was in the pet shop looking for a suitable pet.

"This African grey parrot would be perfect for you." said the pet shop owner. "It's the most intelligent bird in the world. It can do tricks and has a huge vocabulary. In fact, it's quite talkative."

A week later, Colin bought a girl friend home. The parrot looked at her and screeched, "Boy! You look like a good screw!"

Colin apologised to his girlfriend and cautioned the parrot. "Do anything like that again and I'll lock you in the fridge!"

The following week, Colin bought home another date. "Wow!", screeched the parrot. "Great tits!"

Colin grabbed the parrot and said, "I warned you!" and locked him in the fridge.

Five minutes later, Colin opened the fridge door. The parrot looked subdued, his beak chattering, and squawked, "What the hell did that chook in here say?"

***

John and Joanne were arguing with their next door neighbours, Ray and Ruth about their late night parties, when Ray let go an enormous fart. It could only be described as a triple thunderclap.

"How dare you fart in front of my wife!", yelled John.

"I didn't know it was her turn", replied Ray.

***

MAN'S BEST FRIEND

Steve took his dog for a walk down to the local pub on Saturday night. He was having a quiet drink when the footy results came up on the television set. Steve's team had won and the dog started running in circles and yelping with delight.

"What does he do when your team loses?", asked the barman.

"Somersaults", said Steve.

"How many?", asked the barman.

"Depends on how far I kick him."

***

Little Jimmy was sitting on the floor pulling the wings off flies, dripping liquid on them and watching them sizzle.

Father O'Flaherty was walking past and asked, "What's in that bottle, Jimmy?"

"Sulphuric acid, Father", replied the boy.

The priest was shocked. "You mustn't do that, Jimmy. You must use holy water. Here. I have some in a bottle."

"What's the good of that?", asked Jimmy.

"Well", said the priest, "just this morning I poured some on a woman's stomach and she passed a baby."

"So what!", said Jimmy, "This morning I poured some of this on a dog's arse and it passed a motorbike!"

An accountant, a scientist, a draftsman and a union organiser were standing at the bar having a drink and bragging about their dogs.

The accountant bragged that his dog, Calculator, could solve mathematical problems. He put twelve biscuits on the floor and called his dog over.

"Calculator", he commanded, "divide this pile of biscuits into four equal heaps." The dog did so.

The scientist bragged that his dog, Test Tube, could take a litre of milk and divide it equally into four parts. He called the dog over and the dog completed the task.

The draftsman said, "My dog, T-Square, can draw geometric figures. He commanded the dog to get a piece of paper and draw a square and a circle on it. The dog performed this task.

"What does your dog do?", the three of them asked the union organiser. He called his dog over. "Show 'em your stuff, Coffee Break", he said.

The dog crapped on the sheet of paper, drank the milk, ate the biscuits, screwed the arse off the other three dogs, then claimed he strained his back on the job and went home to make an insurance claim.

***

Why do dogs lick their balls.
Because they can't make a fist.

***

George came home one day and found his wife in bed with his best friend. He shot his wife but gave the dog a reprieve.

***

An Alsatian went into the Post Office to send a telegram. He wrote down, "Woof woof. Woof woof. Woof woof woof. Woof woof." He handed it over the counter and the clerk studied it.

"You can have ten words for the same price."

"So?", said the Alsatian. "It wouldn't make any sense if I added another woof, would it?"

***

It was Pets Show and Tell Day at school. Melissa showed her poodle and said that it was called Fifi because poodles are French and Fifi was a French name.

Jackie showed her pomeranian who was called Fluffy because pomeranians had fluffy hair.

Young Fred called his dog Porky because he fucks pigs.

***

MICK: My dog's called Carpenter. He's always doing little jobs around the house."

PHIL: "I call my dog Mechanic. I give him a kick in the nuts and he makes a bolt for the door."

***

All the regulars were sitting around the fire in the country pub when Roy walked in with his mangy dog Ralph. Roy bragged to all and sundry that Ralph was a very intelligent dog.

"Never gets it wrong", he said. "Reacts instantly."

All the farmers and drovers in the bar were sceptical.

"I'm not just talking about simple commands like 'sit', 'stay' and 'heel'," said Roy. "I'm talking about six word sentences and instant obedience."

So a bet was laid - $100 to prove that Ralph wasn't capable of passing such a test. Roy matched it, picked up Ralph and threw him on the blazing fire and yelled, "Ralph! Get off that bloody fire!"

***

Roxy, a large black labrador, was sitting up in the seat at the movies, wagging his tail, growling at the villain and barking excitedly at the hero's escapades.

The man in the seat behind was intrigued. "Excuse me", he said, tapping Roxy's owner on the shoulder. "That dog is extraordinary. I've never seen anything like it."

"He surprised me too", said the owner, "He hated the book."

***

Max usually took his kelpie for a walk down to the local pub. Max was enjoying a few drinks when the results of the football games appeared on the television set. The kelpie rolled over onto his back and started whining mournfully.

"What's wrong with your dog?", asked the barman.

"He always behaves like that when my team loses", replied Max.

"What does he do when they win?", asked the barman.

"I don't know. I've only had him two years."

***

Jane went to her doctor complaining of a bad back. After trying every remedy that he knew, her doctor finally said, "Tell me, Jane, how do you have sex?"

"I always have it doggy fashion", she said.

"Ah, that's it!" said the doctor. "Why don't you try having it on your back?"

"Have you ever smelled a labrador's breath?" said Jane.

***

ALLAN: "Hey Terry, I saw a guy screwing a big Alsation yesterday!"

TERRY: "Really?"

ALLAN: "Yeah, and you know how the tail gets in the way ...?

TERRY: "Yeah..."

ALLAN: "I thought so..."

MARKETING

A Sydney prostitute decided to take a novel approach to marketing her wares. Inside her right thigh, she had the face of Elvis Presley tattooed, and inside her left thigh, the face of Mick Jagger. She then offered a 50% discount if a client could identify one of the tattoos, or a freebie if they could identify both.

One day Hugh Grant wandered in. He gazed at the tattoos for some time before blurting out excitedly, "I don't know the one on the left, and I can't pick the one on the right, but the one in the middle - that's Rolf Harris!"

MATES

Jerry and Jack are hiking through the mountains when Jack is bitten on the prick by a snake. Jerry panics, "What can I do?" he cries.

"Get my mobile phone and dial Emergency" instructed Jack.

"My friend's been bitten by a snake", screamed Jerry into the phone, "What'll I do?"

"Was it a poisonous snake?" asked the operator.

"Yes, a tiger snake!" said Jerry.

"You must **immediately** suck the poison out, otherwise your friend will be dead within an hour", instructed the operator.

Jerry hangs up and says to Jack, "I'm sorry, pal, you'll be dead within an hour."

***

"**D**id you know my wife is a wrestler?"

"No. Why do you ask?"

"I thought you might've seen her wrestle."

"I haven't, but I've seen her box three or four times."

***

Wally and Joe were having a few drinks and discussing old times. Joe's wife suggested that Wally had had too many drinks and maybe he should stay the night. There was no spare bed, so Wally bunked in with the married couple.

As soon as Joe was snoring, his wife tapped Wally on the shoulder and suggested he might like to make love to her.

"No way!", said Wally. "If Joe woke up, he'd kill me!"

"Don't worry", said Joe's wife. "When Joe's had a few beers, he sleeps like a log." Wally wasn't too sure.

"Pull a hair out of Joe's bum, and I bet he doesn't move", suggested Joe's wife.

Wally plucked a hair, and sure enough, Joe didn't move.

So he got on the job and they had a delightful screw.

Not long after, she tapped Wally on the shoulder again. Carefully he leaned over and plucked another hair out of Joe's bum. Again, Joe didn't stir, so they continued on for a second round of screwing.

Next morning, when they awoke, Wally asked Joe how he'd slept.

"Not bad", replied Joe, "and I don't mind you screwing my wife Wally, but I don't like you using my arse as a scoreboard."

***

Fred was giving his bald mate Jim a bit of a stir.

"Your head reminds me of my wife's bum", he said, rubbing Jim's nude nut.

"By golly, you're right", said Jim, putting his hand on his head, "it sure does."

***

Frank and Harry had been partners for many years. They had just employed a new secretary and Frank had taken her out.

"How was it?", enquired Harry.

"Fantastic! And I don't mind saying, that she's far better in the cot than my wife."

A couple of weeks later, Harry took the secretary out, and the following morning, he said, "You're right Frank, she is better in the cot that your wife!"

***

The new slave had just joined the oarsmen in the Phoenician war ship, when one of the rowers collapsed and died over his oar. The dead slave was duly released from his chains and thrown overboard. The Slave Master strode up and down the aisle, separating the rowers, lashing each viciously with his whip. When he had finished, all the slaves laid on their backs and pissed into the air.

"What's going on?", asked the new slave.

"It's an old Phoenician tradition", came the reply. "Every time someone dies, there is a quick whip around and a piss-up."

***

MIXED FEELINGS

She had been left on the shelf and was resigned to a life on her own.

One afternoon as she was strolling through the park, a man jumped out from behind a tree and said, "This is a stick-up."

"I haven't got any money", she said, giving the would-be robber her handbag.

"I'm going to search you", growled the robber.

He put his hand inside her blouse and felt inside her bra – then ran his hands up and down her legs and his fingers searched inside her knickers. Finding nothing, he turned to walk away.

"Don't stop searching", she said. "I can write you a cheque."

***

She came screaming into the Police Station. "This guy broke into my apartment", she said. "He ripped off my clothes and threw me onto the floor. When I laid there, naked, he grabbed my purse and ran off."

"Did you scream?", asked the Sergeant.

"Of course not!", she replied. "How did I know he was going to rob me?"

***

ETHNIC

What's the difference between a Jewish woman and an Italian woman?

The Jew has fake orgasms and real diamonds.

***

A Frenchman, an Italian and an Australian were arguing about who was the best lover.

"When I make love", said the Frenchman, "I use my tongue with such expertise in foreplay that my wife rises one foot off the bed."

"You thinka that'sa good?", said the Italian. "I whisper sucha love talk to da wife and I stroke her so sensuously, that she a moans and a groans and she rises two a feet offa da bed!"

"That's nothing!", said the Australian. "After I've finished making love to my missus, I wipe my cock on the curtains and she hits the roof!"

***

The Australian politician was attending his first United Nations function in New York. He approached a group of diplomats and, in an attempt to make small talk with them, said, "Excuse me, what is your opinion of the meat shortage?"

The American frowned and said, "What's a shortage?"

The Bosnian slapped his forehead and said, "What's meat?"

The Russian shrugged and said, "What's an opinion?"

And the Dutchman asked, "What's 'excuse me'?"

***

An Arab, an Englishman and an Australian were boasting about their families.

The Englishman said, "I've got eleven sons. If I had one more, I'd have my own cricket team."

The Australian bragged, "I've got nine daughters. If I had one more, I'd have my own basketball team."

The Arab said, "I've got seventeen wives. If I get one more, I'll have my own golf course."

***

Mr Woo often went to Phil's Greek restaurant and always ordered fried rice. Phil and his friends thought it a great joke to hear Mr Woo order "flied lice".

Mr Woo was sick of the taunts and asked his friend, an Oxford graduate, to teach him to speak English properly.

When he next went back to the Greek restaurant, Phil and his friends were waiting with their taunts.

"I'll have a large serve of fried rice, old chap", said Mr Woo.

"What did you say?", asked a surprised Phil.
"I said fried rice, you flucking Gleek plick."

***

How do you know when a Vietnamese has robbed your house?

Because the dog is missing and your homework's done.

MUSICIANS

Why are trombones like elderly parents?

Both are unforgiving and hard to get in and out of cars.

***

The piano player in the Casablanca bar leant across and put his hand on Rick the American's leg.

"Didn't I tell you I could make you forget that girl Rick?"

"Yes…", sighed Rick. "Play with it again, Sam."

***

Why are girls like pianos?
When they're not upright, they're grand.

***

The couple were sitting in the front row of the box just above the stage. During interval, he was feeling a bit horny and asked her to give him a hand job.

After he was relieved, she threw the handful over the balcony, where it hit the second violinist on his bald head.

"Christ!", he said, "I've just been hit by a flying fuck!"

"That's justice", said the first violinist. "You've been playing like a cunt all night."

NUDISTS

The young man was showing off his new sports car to his girlfriend. She was thrilled at the speed.

"If I do 150kph, will you take off your clothes?", he smirked.

"Yes!", said his adventurous girlfriend.

And as he gets up to 150, she peeled off all her clothes. Unable to keep his eyes on the road, the car skidded onto the gravel and flipped over. The naked girl was thrown clear, but he was jammed between the back of the seat and the steering wheel.

"Go and get help!", he cried.

"But I can't! I'm naked and my clothes are gone!"

"Take my shoe", he said, "and cover yourself."

Holding the shoe over her pubes, the girl ran down the road and found a service station. Still holding the shoe between her legs, she pleaded to the service station proprietor, "Please help me! My boyfriend's stuck!"

The proprietor looked at the shoe and said, "There's nothing I can do. He's in too far."

***

Colin was always sent for coffee in the nudist colony. He was the only man who could carry two cups of coffee and ten donuts.

***

Dwarves are banned from joining nudist colonies - they're always poking their nose into other peoples' affairs.

NEIGHBOURS

The charges were being read against the man in the dock.

"You are charged that on the 25th February you murdered your wife with an axe."

From the back of the Court someone yelled, "You bastard!"

The Judge brought down his gavel and sternly demanded that there be silence in the Court.

The Clerk of Courts continued. "You are further charged that on the same day you murdered your mother-in-law with an axe."

"You rotten bastard!", came a shout from the back.

Again the Judge brought down his gavel and ordered that the interjector be bought before him.

"What's the meaning of this outburst?", he demanded.

"I'm his next door neighbour, Your Honour. Only a month ago, I asked him for a lend of his axe and the swine said that he didn't have one."

***

An Irishman drives into his neighbourhood garage in Dublin.

"Can you fill up the petrol?" he asked.

"No—we don't sell petrol." replied the attendant.

"Can you check my oil?" he asked.

"No—we don't have any oil." said the attendant.

"Well, what do you do?" asked the puzzled Irishman.

"We're a front for the I.R.A.!"

"Well—can you blow up my tyres?"

***

POLITICAL CORRECTNESS

It has been brought to our attention that some individuals have been using politically incorrect and bad language during the execution of their duties. Due to complaints from some employees and customers who are more easily offended, this type of language will no longer be tolerated.

However, we do realise the importance of staff being able to properly express their feelings when communicating with others. With this in mind, the Personnel Section has compiled a list of code phrase replacements so the proper exchange of ideas and information can continue in an effective manner without risking offence to our more sensitive co-workers.

OLD PHRASE   NEW PHRASE

No fucking way
       I'm fairly sure that's not feasible

You're fucking kidding
       Really?

Who the fuck are you?
       Hi - we haven't met....

Tell someone who gives a fuck
>> *Have you run that by ....*

No cunt told me
>> *I wasn't involved with that project*

You know fuck all about it
>> *You seem perplexed*

I don't have the fucking time
>> *Perhaps I can work late*

Who fucking cares
>> *Are you sure that's a problem?*

Eat shit and die
>> *You don't say!*

What the fuck do you want?
>> *Hello - can I help you?*

Kiss my arse
>> *So, you'd like me to help you*

He's a fucking prick
>> *He's somewhat insensitive*

She's a ball-busting bitch
>> *She's assertive and goal-
orientated*

You wouldn't have a fucking clue
>> *You could use some more training*

This place is fucked
We're a little disorganised today

Stick it up your arse
No, thanks very much

What sort of fuck-wit are you?
You're new here aren't you?

Fuck off shit-head
Well, there you go!

You're a fucking wanker
*You're my supervisor and I
respect you*
He's a dumb cunt
He drives a Volvo

Ha - suck eggs
I wasn't here that day

You're fucking paranoid
So, you're from Adelaide

You're as thick as two planks
So, you're a Queenslander

You're fucking useless
So, you're English

Fuck off
I'll look into it and get back to you

Fuck off dickhead
I no longer require your assistance

How'd ya get this piece of shit to work?
> *Well done!*

You fucking loser
> *Gee, that was unfortunate*

I don't give a shit
> *I'll certainly think it over*

Well, fuck me!
> *Golly!*

NEWLY WEDS

"**F**orgive me, Father, for I have sinned. Yesterday I made love to my wife."

The priest explained that there was nothing wrong with that.

"But Father, I did it with lust."

"That's alright", said the priest, "that was no sin."

"But Father, it was in the middle of the day."

"That's quite natural", replied the priest.

But Father, I couldn't help myself. She leant over the deep freeze and I jumped on her. We made love on the floor. Am I banned from church?"

"Of course not!."

"What a relief. We've both been banned from Woolworths."

***

The new bride was a little confused about what to do with her husband's constant erection.

"Don't worry about it", advised her husband. "When you want to make love, tug it three times. When you don't want to, tug it three hundred times."

***

On their first night of wedded bliss, the groom took off his trousers and asked his new bride to try them on.

"They don't fit", she said.

"And never forget it!", said the husband. "In this house I wear the trousers."

She continued to disrobe. She threw him her frilly knickers and said, "Put those on."

He looked at the scanty briefs and said, "I'll never get into these!"

"You're right", she said. "And if you don't change your attitude, you never will!"

***

It was the young couple's first night of wedded bliss. They undressed each other tentatively, he admiring her beautiful body and she his fine physique. When she removed his sock, the last item of clothing, she saw that he had no toes on his left foot.

Shocked at this terrible deformity, she ran sobbing into the night, back to her mother.

"I told you what to expect", said her mother. "I've given you good sex education. What's the problem?"

"It's not that", she cried. "When he stripped off, he only had three quarters of a foot."

"Oh!", said mother. "Why don't you finish the dishes and go off to bed. I'll be back in the morning."

***

The honeymooners approached the reception desk of a posh hotel.

"Bridal suite?", asked the clerk discretely.

"No", giggled the bride. "I'll just hang onto his ears."

***

The eighty year old man had gone to see his doctor for pre-marriage tests.

"I'm marrying a twenty year old", he said.

"Why are you doing that?", asked the doctor.

"I want a son and heir. Can you give me any advice?"

"Yes, get a lodger", said the doctor, smirking.

A few months later, the old fellow returned to the doctor.

"Is your wife pregnant yet?", queried the doctor.

"Yes."

"So you did take in a lodger?"

"Oh yes", replied the old man, "and she's pregnant too!"

A FREE LUNCH

The blonde at the next table was devouring an enormous meal.

"I'll bet her boyfriend's a taxidermist", said Bert to his wife.

"What makes you think that?", she replied.

"Well, can't you see he's stuffing the bird before mounting her?"

STUNTMEN

The famous filmstar wanted a stunt man to do his dangerous and dirty jobs on film. He went to see an eminent medical scientist and arranged to have a clone made.

When the clone came around to his apartment on the twenty-fifth floor, the filmstar was amazed at the likeness. When the clone stripped off to go to bed, the filmstar was shocked to see that the clone was far better developed in the nether regions than anyone he had ever seen before.

When the clone noticed the difference, he became excited, ran out on the balcony and started exposing himself. The filmstar panicked. Everyone would think it was him out on the balcony, so he went out and tried to push the clone back into the apartment. A struggle developed and the clone fell off the balcony to his death.

When the Police arrived, the filmstar was charged with murder.

"Why are you charging me with murder?", he shouted.

"It's obvious", said the Police sergeant. "It was you who made the obscene clone fall."

OBVIOUSLY...

What's round and hard and sticks so far out of a man's pyjamas that he can hang his hat on it?
His head.

***

What's pink and wrinkly and hangs out your pants?
Your Grandma.

Why do so many brides get crows feet as soon as they're married?

From squinting and saying, "Suck what?"

***

What's got seventy five balls and screws old ladies?

Bingo.

***

What does it take to circumcise a whale?

Foreskin divers.

***

Why is a joke like pussy?

Neither's any good if you don't get it.

***

Dr Watson and Sherlock Holmes were walking through the park when they passed three women eating bananas.

"Ah", said Holmes, "I see a spinster, a prostitute and a newlywed."

"Amazing, Holmes!", said Dr Watson, "How did you deduce that?"

"Elementary, my dear Watson. "See how the

spinster breaks the banana into small pieces before popping them into her mouth? Whilst the prostitute in the middle holds the banana in both hands."

"Yes, Holmes, but how do you know the other one is a newlywed?"

"Well", said Holmes," she's holding the banana with one hand and thumping herself on the back of the head with the other."

***

OH SHIT !

The studious looking young man in horn rimmed glasses approached the young lady sitting on her own in the singles bar. After introducing himself, she said, "Tell me about yourself."

"I'm a nuclear physicist", he said, "and I've been working on a top secret job for the last five years. Would you like me to tell you all about it?"

"Let me ask you a few questions first", said the young lady.

She continued, "When a rabbit poops, why does it come out in hard little round balls?" "I've got no idea", said the nuclear physicist.

"Well, here's another one", said the young lady. "How can elephants drop square turds out of a round arsehole?"

"I can't answer that", repeated the physicist.

"Well, why do dog turds drop like a coil of rope?", she asked.

"You've got me again!", he said.

— from *Rude and Politically Incorrect Jokes* by Allan Pease

"Well", she said, "it seems to me, you don't know shit! And you want to talk to me about nuclear physics!"

OLDIES

Charlie was a very sprightly 80 year old. He thought he'd give the ladies at the Old Folks Home a bit of excitement and ran across the lawn naked. As he passed a couple of elderly spinsters, one said to the other, "My goodness, Annie, what was that that just passed?"

"I don't know what it was", said her companion", but it certainly needed ironing."

***

The sweet old couple in the Old Folks Home were suffering from Alzheimers.

"Darling", she said, "would you get something for me from the kitchen?"

"Certainly, sweetheart", he replied. "What would you like?"

"Get me a pen and paper and I'll write it down", she said.

"No, you tell me. I'll remember", he said proudly.

"But you always forget. I'll write it down."

"No, I won't forget!", he protested.

She gave in.

"Alright... I want two scoops of vanilla icecream with chocolate sauce and crushed nuts sprinkled on top, and a wafer biscuit. Have you got that?"

"Yes", he replied.

"Well, repeat it to me", she demanded.

So he repeated the order.

About two hours later, he returned from the kitchen with a large plate of bacon and eggs.

"You silly old fool", she growled. "You've forgotten the toast!"

***

A couple of old boys went down to the pub.

"I've heard that stout will put lead in your pencil. Why don't we try some?", said one.

"You can", replied the other, "but I don't have anybody to write to."

***

Poor old Norm had had no visitors that day. He was in the Geriatric Ward of the Old Folks Hospital. A social worker went over to wipe the dribble off his chin and noticed a bowl of almonds on his tray.

"They were given to me as a present", he spluttered, "but I don't want them. You can have them."

The social worker thanked him, and began nibbling away on them. After she'd eaten most of them, she remarked, "It's a funny thing, giving nuts to a man who has no teeth."

"Oh, no", replied Norm, "they had chocolate around them when I first got them."

***

The old couple were sitting in their rocking chairs on the verandah of the Old Folks Home. They had had designs on each other for some time. He looked over and said to her, "Fuck you", and she looked back wistfully and said, "Fuck you too."

Then they rocked away for another thirty minutes and he looked over to her and said, "I don't think much of this oral sex, do you?"

***

The old bloke was a bit embarrassed, but he had to see the doctor.

"I'm worried, doc", he said. "I met this twenty five year old woman last night and she made passionate love to me. Since then, my old fella has swollen to twice its normal size, its become red and itchy and there's a discharge beginning to appear."

The doctor examined him.

"You'd better sit down", he said. "You're about to cum."

Grandpa had just told them the news - he was getting engaged to a twenty five year old nymphomaniac. The family was very concerned. His eldest daughter spoke confidentially to him.

"Dad, we're most concerned that sex with a girl like that could prove fatal."

"So what?", said Grandpa. "If she dies, she dies."

***

The old couple had fallen in love at the retirement village. Eventually, he put the hard word on her.

"Oh, yes!", she said, as she hurriedly started undressing. "But I must tell you, I have acute angina."

"Well that's good 'cause you've got lousy tits", he replied.

***

Justin, the hotel check-in clerk, told the couple that the only room available was the bridal suite.

"But we've been married for twenty five years! It would be wasted on us", said the husband.

"But if I put you in the ballroom, we wouldn't expect you to dance all night!" replied Justin.

***

Mary Maloney was a healthy, vigorous, octogenarian. She was being interviewed about her secret for such a long and happy life.

"I have seven gentlemen a day", she said. "I get out of bed with Will Power, then I go to my John. I follow this up with breakfast with Uncle Toby, then I have Billy T. The rest of the day is spent with Arthur Ritis, then I have a bit of Al Zymer. Then I go to bed with Johnny Walker."

ONE UP-MAN-SHIP

Pat and Mick were being shaved by the barber in the barber shop. The barber started to put aftershave on Pat's face.

"Don't put that stinkin' stuff on me!" exclaimed Pat. "My wife will think I smell like a brothel!"

Then it was Mick's turn. "You can put as much aftershave on me as you like. My wife doesn't know what a brothel smells like!"

***

Nigel bumped into Steve and his friend Paul at the bar where the lawyers meet on Friday night for a drink. It was always a big night for one-up-man-ship.

Whilst having a drink together, a phone started to ring and Nigel stuck his thumb in his ear and started talking into his little finger. "It's the latest technology", he explained. "I've had a silicon chip inserted into my thumb and another into my little finger, and I've got a little amplifier in my ear. It's better than screwing around with one of those cumbersome mobile phones."

The next time they met, a phone rang again whilst they were having a drink. This time Paul answered, merely by talking . "It's the latest technology", he said. "It's the tooth phone. Not as intrusive as sticking your thumb in your ear and talking into your little finger. I've had a silicon chip inserted into a hollow tooth and another inserted into my ear."

About half an hour later, Steve bent forward, flexed his knees and let go a roaring fart.

"Are you O.K.?", asked Nigel.

"Don't worry," Steve replied, "it's just a fax coming through."

***

A pompous Englishman arrived to pick up his Australian visitor in a Rolls Royce. The Australian sat next to him in the front seat.

"I suppose, being a Colonial, you've never ridden in a Rolls Royce?", said the puffed up Pom.

"Sure I have", replied the Aussie, "but never in the front!"

***

OPPORTUNITY

Two men were sitting in Macdonalds having a hamburger when the town's fire alarm started to ring. One jumped up and headed for the door, the other called out "I didn't know you were a fireman."

"I'm not", he replied, "but my girlfriend's husband is."

***

Dougal was a typical Scot. His wife Janet had just died and he wanted to place the least expensive death notice. He went to the newspaper office and wrote on the lodgement form, "Janet died".

The clerk explained that there was a minimum charge and he could have six words. Dougal added three more words: "Janet died, Toyota for sale".

ORAL HYGIENE

Gerry was half way through his meal when he called the manager. "There's a hair in this spaghetti so I'm not paying for it."

Later that night the manager found Gerry giving one of the waitresses oral sex and said, "You don't seem to mind a bit of hair now."

Gerry looked up and replied "No... But if I find any spaghetti down here I'm not paying for it either."

***

A woman was in a serious car accident and ended up in hospital in a coma. One day, while bathing her, the nurse noticed that when she washed near the woman's pubic region, her vital signs increase.

Surprised, the nurse called the woman's husband and explained that, maybe if the husband came down to the hospital and engaged in oral sex with his wife, she might come out of the coma.

The husband rushed down to the hospital and locked himself in his wife's hospital room. About twenty minutes later, he came running out of the room, all flustered. "Nurse! My wife's vital signs have stopped!"

The doctors and nurses rushed into the room and revived her. Later, the nurse was discussing with the husband what had gone wrong.

"I don't know", he said, "I think she was choking."

***

OUTBACK

The dingoes around the sheep stations in the Outback were causing a serious problem. A meeting was held in the local hall. The pastoralists wanted to poison the dingoes whilst the environmentalists wanted to castrate them. Finally, one of the station owners lost his patience and shouted, "Listen, you Greenies, the dingoes are killing our sheep, not fucking them!"

***

A guy walked into the pub with an ostrich and a cat. He walked up to bar and ordered three beers,they sat at a table and began drinking.

When they'd finished, the ostrich went to the bar and ordered three more beers. This happened several times. First the man, then the ostrich, but never the cat.

"Why isn't the cat buying?", asked the curious barman.

"It's a strange story", replied the man, "I was walking along the beach one day and found a lamp. I gave it a rub and a genie appeared and said, "You have one wish - anything you like". I thought for a moment and asked for a big bird with long legs and a tight pussy."

PARENTHOOD

Three kids are smoking in the school toilets.

"My dad can blow smoke through his nose," said one.

"Mine can blow smoke through his ears," said the second.

"Mine can blow smoke through his arse," said the third, "Here's his underpants ... see the nicotine stains?"

***

Little Harold was hopping on one foot then the other.

"I gotta piss! I gotta piss!", he cried to his mother in front of her friends.

Mother took him to the toilet and explained to him that next time he wanted to go to the toilet, he should not use those words. She said he should come in and talk quietly - "That's a whisper" she said.

Two hours later, Harold came rushing in again.

"I wanna whisper! I wanna whisper!", he said.

His mother knew what he wanted and took him to the toilet, after which he was rewarded with a candy bar.

That night the urge came on again. Harold jumped out of bed and ran to his father.

"What is it, son?", his father asked.

"I wanna whisper, Daddy. I wanna whisper."

"O.K. son, come here and whisper in my ear."

PATIENTS

A man was in a serious car accident and was so badly burned he had to be bandaged from head to toe and could only be fed rectally, through a tube.

A nurse had just served his afternoon coffee when he began waving his arms around.

"What's the matter?" she asked, "is it too hot?"

Through his head bandages she heard his muffled response: "Too much sugar!"

Later, his wife called in to see how he was going and asked, "How is his appetite?"

"Excellent," said the nurse. "It would have done your heart good, to see his arse snap at a piece of toast this morning."

***

Vic went to the doctors. His hands were trembling. He thought he had Parkinsons Disease. The doctor checked him over and asked, "Do you drink much?"

"No", said Vic, "I spill most of it."

***

A university student went to her doctor for a general check-up. When she removed her blouse, the doctor noticed the letter "H" imprinted on her chest.

"What's that?", he asked.

"My boyfriend goes to Harvard, and he's so proud of it that he never takes his Harvard tee-shirt off, even when we make love."

The next day, another student came for a check-up and the doctor noticed that she had a "Y" imprinted on her chest.

"What's that?", he asked.

"My boyfriend is a student at Yale University, and he's so proud of it he never takes his Yale tee-shirt off, even when we make love."

A few days later, he examined another young student and she had an "M" on her chest.

"Oh", said the doctor, "I see your boyfriend must go to Michigan University, because you've got an "M" on your chest."

"Oh no", replied the student, "my boyfriend's a French exchange student, and he's going to Wisconsin."

PEARLY GATES

St Peter was checking entrants to Heaven at the Pearly Gates. "You must answer three religious questions", said St Peter, "to prove that you have been devout."

"Shoot", said the first applicant.

"Who spoke to God in the burning bush?", asked St Peter.

"Moses", came the reply.

"Well done. Now tell me, who was God's only son?"

"Jesus", came the answer.

"Good. The third and last question", said St Peter. "What is God's first name?"

"Andy."

"Andy?", queried St Peter.

"Yes. It's in the song.....Andy walks with me, Andy talks with me, Andy tells me I'm his own."

***

The doctor asked Luigi for a faeces specimen, a urine specimen and a sperm specimen, so he left his underpants.

***

POLITICIANS

The Prime Minister was sick and tired of all the bad press coverage. He decided to do something about it, and held a press conference under the Sydney Harbour Bridge. He then proceeded to walk on the water across the harbour.

The next morning, he opened the Sydney Telegraph where the headlines read:

"Prime Minister Can't Swim!"
The Sydney Morning Herald proclaimed,
"Government Rorts: Prime Minister Avoids Payment Of Bridge Tolls".

***

How can you tell when a politician is lying?
His lips are moving.

***

John Howard was visiting America and had a meeting with George Bush. He was very impressed with George Bush's staffers and associates.

"You certainly keep everybody on the ball, George", Howard said. "How do you do it?"

"Easy John", replied Bush. "Every morning I ask everyone a trick question which they know they're expected to answer."

George Bush called Dick Cheney into his office.

"Watch this", Bush said.

"Dick, answer this... Brothers and sisters have I none, but that man's father is my father's son. Who am I?"

"That's simple, George. It's you."

"Well done, Dick!", said the President.

Howard was suitably impressed.

On his return to Canberra, he decided to introduce this system into his office. He immediately called John Anderson and said, "John answer this... Brothers and sisters have I none, but that man's father is my father's son. Who am I?"

"You'll have to give me time to think about that, John", said Anderson, as he wandered back to his office.

On the way, Anderson bumped into Bronwyn Bishop and said, "Bronwyn... Brothers and sisters have I none, but that man's father is my father's son. Who am I?"

"John, you moron, it's you", she replied.

"Great!", exclaimed Tim, and he ran back to Howard's office. "I know the answer to your question, Johnnie. I know who it is. It's me! John Anderson!"

John looked at Anderson and said, "Don't be so bloody stupid, John. It's George Bush!"

***

At a political rally, the Labor Party man was claiming that the Hawke Government was the best Government Australia ever had.

"Hawke should be bloody well hung!", shouted a heckler.

"He is! He is!" shouted his wife.

***

She was a Liberal, he was a Left Wing Labor, but it was only politics, so they decided to live together and enjoy friendly but spirited differences of opinion.

300

When they went to bed, she slept on the far right and he remained on the left.

One night, she was feeling a bit randy, so she came a little to the left and whispered, "There is a split in the Liberal movement and it's quite likely that if a Labor member stood, he could slip in unopposed."

"It's too late", he replied. "There's been much stimulation in the private sector and he's blown his deposit."

***

There's a story around the White House that Richard Nixon hired a Playboy centrefold as his Adviser on Women's Affairs. There was such a fuss that he decided he had to fire her.

He searched every room of the White House and finally asked one of the White House aides if he had seen her.

"Yes", the aide replied, "I found her in one of the bedrooms, lying naked on the bed. And lying naked next to her was the Secretary of State, Henry......"

"Kissinger?"

"No.....fucking her!"

PUSSIES

A woman rushed up to the manager of the movie theatre and complained that she had been molested in the front stalls.

The manager calmed her down and was ushering her to another seat when another woman complained to him that she had been molested in the front stalls too.

The manager went down to the front and shone his torch along the floor where he saw a bald man crawling along on his hands and knees.

"What are you doing?" demanded the manager.

The bald man looked up. "I've lost my toupee. It fell off in the dark. I had my hand on it twice but it got away!"

***

What did one ovary say to the other?

They must be going to have a party downstairs. Two nuts are trying to push an organ up the passage.

***

Little Johnnie was learning new words.

"Mum, what's a pussy?"

Mother pointed at the cat and said, "That's a pussy."

"Mum, what's a bitch?"

Mother pointed to their female dog and said,

"That's a bitch."

Johnnie wanted to confirm this information with his father.

"Daddy!", he said excitedly, "What's a pussy?"

Father pulled out the centrefold of the Playboy magazine and drew a circle around the appropriate part.

"Son", he said, "that's a pussy."

"Well, Dad, what's a bitch?"

"Everything outside the circle", replied his father.

***

Dennis: "How many legs has a rooster got, Dean?"

Dean: "Two?"

Dennis: "Correct. How many ribs has a cat got?"

Dean: "I've got no idea."

Dennis: "So... You know all about cocks and nothing about pussy."

***

Sixteen year old Johnny asks his father "Dad, what does a vagina look like?"

"Well" said the father knowingly, "It has two looks. Before sex it looks like a beautiful rose with folds."

"What about after sex?" asked the son.

"Well" said the father "Have you ever seen a bulldog eating porridge?"

A dwarf walked up to the tall blonde at the bar and said, "Can I smell your fanny?"

"Absolutely not!", she replied.

"Then it must be your feet", he said.

***

It was their first time in bed together.

"That's a little organ!", she said disappointedly.

"Sorry", he replied, "I didn't know I'd be playing in the Town Hall!"

DONALD DUCK

Donald Duck had split with Daisy Duck, and soon found himself going to a brothel.

"I'm here for a good time", he told the Madam.

"You must have a condom", she replied. "That'll be $1. Can I stick it on your bill?"

"What sort of duck do you think I am?"

***

Donald Duck wanted a divorce from Daisy.

"But Daisy's not insane", said Donald's lawyer.

"I didn't say she was insane", protested Donald. "I said she was fucking Goofy."

R.I.P.

Terri the tart was such a good-time girl that when she died they had to bury her in a Y-shaped coffin.

***

A guy and his wife were playing 18 holes of golf. It was a beautiful sunny day and they had the entire course to themselves.

When he was about to hit off at the 13th hole, he collapsed to the ground, clutching his chest, having a heart attack. Despite the fact that he was 6'2" and weighed 18 stone, she picked him up, put him on her shoulders and headed for the clubhouse.

She eventually arrived at the clubhouse still carrying her huge husband on her shoulders. Two other club members arrived and helped carry him inside, called an ambulance and sent him to the hospital.

"How could you carry such a huge man on your shoulders from the 13th hole?" the Club President asked the wife in amazement. "Wasn't it difficult?"

"Yes", said the wife, "but carrying him wasn't the hard part. It was picking him up and putting him down after each shot that was difficult."

***

Every seat in the football stadium was sold except one. It was Grand Final day. A television reporter noticed the empty seat and thought there might be a story.

"Why is this seat empty?", he asked a man sitting beside it.

"That's my wife's seat", came the reply.

"Then why isn't she here?"

"She died last week", replied the man.

"I'm so sorry to hear that", said the reporter, "but surely you could have found a friend to come with you today."

"No", replied the man, "they're all at the funeral."

***

Jesus was relieving St Peter at the Pearly Gates. An old man asked for admission.

"Name?", said Jesus.

"Joseph."

"Occupation?"

"Carpenter."

Jesus became excited. "Did you have a son?", asked Jesus.

"Yes."

"Did he have holes in his wrists and ankles?"

"Yes!" said the old man.

Jesus looked at the old man with a tear in his eye, put his arms out and said, "Father! Father! It's me! It's me!"

The old man looked puzzled, then beamed - "Pinocchio!"

***

Private Smith's mother had died unexpectedly and the Sergeant Major had to break the news to him.

"Break it gently to him", advised his Lieutenant.

It was parade time, and the Sergeant Major was giving his troops a quick inspection.

"Brown! Straighten your hat! Jones! Your shoes are filthy. Johnson! Button up your jacket. Smith! Your mother's dead."

Smith's knees buckled, and he was carted off to Sick Bay.

A few weeks later, Private Smith's father died, and the Sergeant Major again had to pass on the bad news.

"Break it to him gently", said the Lieutenant. "You saw what happened last time."

Out on the parade ground, the Sergeant Major called his men to attention.

"All those who have a father take one step forward!", he roared. "And where do you think you're going, Private Smith?"

***

REAL GOERS

The dancing school barred Dave from the hokey pokey class.

He kept putting it in when you're supposed to shake it all about.

The cabaret dancer said her left leg was pretty good, her right was even better, and between the two she could make a fortune.

***

Phil was also banned from the dance class because of the way he did the fandango. He had his fan in one hand and his dango in the other.

***

The Rifle Club invited Jack to a small bore shooting competition. When he arrived they stood him on a box and started firing at him.

***

Did you hear about the English nympho maniac?

She had to have a man every six months, no matter what.

***

A Jewish nymphomaniac is one who will let her husband make love to her after she's just returned from the beauty parlour.

RED LIGHT

What do you get when you cross a computer with a prostitute?
A fucking know-it-all.

***

What did the leper say to the prostitute?
You can keep the tip.

***

Two young women met for a cup of coffee after being out of touch for many years. They asked each other what sort of work they were doing.

"I'm a receptionist at a hotel. I'm getting half my board", said one.

"Gee", chided the other, "I work in a massage parlour and get my hole bored."

***

A dejected used car salesman was sitting in the corner drowning his problems.

"What's up?" asked the local harlot.

"Things aren't going too well. If I don't sell more cars, I'll lose my arse."

"I know how you feel", said the harlot. "If I don't sell more arse this month, I'll lose my car."

He was eight feet tall and asked the Madam if she had a girl his height.

"No", she replied. "In fact, the only two girls available are about four feet tall."

"That's O.K.", he said. "I'll screw them together."

***

A man is driving down a deserted stretch of highway, when he notices a sign out of the corner of his eye. It reads, "Sisters Of Mercy House Of Prostitution - 10 Miles".

He thinks it is just a figment of his imagination, and drives on without a second thought. Soon, he sees another sign which says, "Sisters of Mercy House Of Prostitution - 5 Miles", and realises that these signs are real.

When he drives past a third sign saying, "Sisters of Mercy House Of Prostitution - Next Right", his curiosity gets the best of him and he pulls into the driveway. On the far side of the parking lot is a sombre stone building with a small sign next to the door reading "Sisters of Mercy".

He climbs the steps and rings the bell. The door is answered by a nun in a long black habit who asks, "What may we do for you, my son?"

He answers, "I saw your signs along the highway and am very interested in doing business."

"Very well, my son. Please follow me."

He is led through many winding passages and is soon disoriented. The nun stops at a closed door and tells the man, "Please knock on this door."

He does as he is told and the door is answered by another nun in a long habit who is holding a tin cup. This nun instructs, "Please place $50 in the cup, then go through the large wooden door at the end of this hallway."

He gets $50 out of his wallet and places it in the second nun's cup. He trots eagerly down the hall and slips through the door, pulling it shut. As the door locks behind him, he finds himself back in the parking lot, facing another sign which read, "Go In Peace. You Have Just Been Screwed By The Sisters Of Mercy".

***

What's the difference between a counterfeit note and a skinny prostitute?

One's a phoney buck.

***

The prostitute was visiting her psychoanalyst. One intimate question led to another, and before he knew it, the shrink was on the couch, bonking his patient.

When it was all over, they looked at each other for a moment and then exchanged $100 bills.

REINCARNATION

Rex the labrador knocked a paling off the back garden fence, came back home and deposited the neighbour's now-dead rabbit at the back door. Rex's owner, Barney, was very upset, for he knew how much his neighbour's children loved the rabbit.

He decided that the best thing to do was to clean the rabbit up, put it back in its cage, and everyone would think that it died from some disease. He shampooed the rabbit in the bath, brushed off the dirt and blood and blow-dried its fur. It looked as good as new again. He carefully placed it back in the rabbit cage.

That night, Barney's neighbour came hammering on his door. Barney flew into a panic. His neighbour had found the rabbit dead. Tentatively he opened the door and saw his neighbour's stunned face.

"What's wrong?", asked Barney.

"Come and have a look at this!", replied the neighbour. He took Barney to the rabbit's cage. "This morning", said the neighbour, "I ran over the rabbit and killed it. I buried it in the garden, and now it's back in its cage!"

REPARTEE

It took time, but Len eventually developed an attachment for his mother-in-law. It fitted over her mouth.

"You're a typical hen-pecked spineless husband!" the drinker told Bill.

"You wouldn't have the guts to say that if my missus was here!" replied Bill.

***

"I think you should know before we go too far that I am a lesbian."

"That's O.K., I've got a cousin in Beirut."

***

"Are you a virgin?"

"Yes, but I'm not a fanatic about it."

***

"How would you like a Harvey Wallbanger."

"I'd love one, but let's have a drink first."

***

"I'm yours for the asking."

"I'm asking $50."

***

RESEARCH

Research proves that 22% of men like girls with big legs, 34% of men like girls with slender legs, and the rest said they liked something in between.

RESOURCEFULNESS

How can we solve the world's problems?
Get the hungry to eat the homeless.

***

Irene was stark naked when she arrived at the fancy dress ball.
"You must be dressed as something!", said the doorman.
So Irene put on a pair of black gloves, put on a pair of black shoes, and announced, "I'm the Five of Spades."

***

A honeymoon couple booked into a quiet seaside hotel. All the staff exchanged knowing glances. At three o'clock on the first morning, the desk clerk noticed the groom heading out laden with fishing gear. Amazed, the clerk asked, "You're going fishing? Why aren't you making love to your lovely new wife?"

"No way!", answered the groom, "she's got gonorrhoea."

"Well, why don't you try anal sex?"

"No way! She's got diarrhoea."

"Well, what about oral sex?"

"No way! she's got pyorrhoea."

"Gonorrhoea, diarrhoea, pyorrhoea...why the hell did you marry her and come to a place like this?"

"Because she's got worms, and I just love to fish."

***

He was obviously trying to impress her as they walked into the jewellery shop on Friday night.

"Choose any diamond ring you'd like, darling", he said, gesturing flamboyantly.

She chose a five carat setting worth $40,000.

"Can I pay by cheque?", he asked the manager.

"Certainly, sir, but of course you understand that we will have to keep the ring until the cheque is cleared."

A few days later, he returned to the jewellers. The concerned manager said, "I'm afraid your cheque has bounced."

"Yes, I know," he said, "I just dropped by to thank you and say that I had a really great weekend."

Leo went to the doctor for his annual check-up. The doctor checked his heart and blood pressure and frowned.

"You've got ten hours to live", he said.

"I demand a second opinion", said Leo, and rushed off to a heart specialist.

The heart specialist checked him out immediately and said, "Leo, you've got nine hours to live."

Leo jumped into his car and raced home to his wife.

"Darling", he said, "I have only eight hours to live."

"What do you want to do in your final hours, Leo?"

"I want to make love", said Leo.

So they jumped into bed.

During their post coital cigarette, Leo said, "I've got seven hours to live. Can we make love again?"

"Of course", said his loving wife.

After another hour, and another post coital cigarette, he said, "Darling, I have only six hours to live. Let's do it again."

"For Christ's sake, Leo", she said, "It's O.K. for you! You don't have to get up early in the morning."

***

The cab broke down in a lonely part of town. The driver got out and lifted the hood. His pretty young passenger called out, "Do you want a screwdriver?"

"Yes, Miss", he replied, "but wait till I've fixed the motor."

BONKS

What's the difference between a goldfish and a mountain goat?

One mucks around the fountain.

***

A tortoise had been raped by two snails.

"Describe them", demanded the Police.

"I can't", said the tortoise, "it happened too fast."

***

The Irish girl had never been into a bar before, and she asked the barman to recommend a drink.

"Try this", he suggested, and mixed her up a dry martini.

She thought it was great, but an hour and six martinis later, she was asleep on the floor, dead drunk.

The barman asked a couple of regulars to help him carry her out to the back room, where one of them suggested that they give her a quickie while she was out cold.

"I just remembered - we've got to buy some
seafood dip for the party."

— from *Rude and Politically Incorrect Jokes* by Allan Pease

Next night, she returned to the bar and got stuck into the martinis again. As before, she finished up dead drunk. The same three carried her out the back and bonked her again. This went on for a week.

When she came back on the eighth night, the barman started mixing the martinis as soon as she walked through the door.

"I'll have a scotch tonight!", she said. "Those martinis make my cunt sore!"

***

"**D**octor I'm getting married tomorrow and I don't know much about men. Can I ask you a question?"

"Certainly Miss, go ahead."

"I saw my fiancé with his pants off last night and hanging between his legs he's got a great big dic..."

"Organ, miss! It's called an Organ!"

"Call it what you like Doc, it looks like a clarinet to me."

S.T.D.s

What has a woman with gonorrhoea got in common with a woman married to a midget con man?

Well, the one married to the midget has a cunning runt.

Green fungus was growing all over his balls and he anxiously rushed to the hospital to remedy the problem. A specimen was taken and investigated by the hospital scientists. Finally the report came back.

"You've heard of cauliflower ears?" said the doctor.

"Well you've got brothel sprouts."

***

Patrick picked Maureen up at the local Rave Party. Later he took her home and she asked him to go to bed with her.

"I've got no protection", said Patrick.

"That's O.K", said Maureen, "but be careful."

Patrick was just working up a full head of steam when he stopped dead and looked at her and said, "You don't have AIDS, do you?"

"No", said Maureen, "of course not!"

"That's a relief", said Patrick, "I don't want to catch it twice."

***

SHAGGY DOGS

A teenager in jeans, braces and Doc Marten boots was travelling on a late night train. In the carriage with him was an old lady, an attractive young woman and a policeman.

As they entered the subway, the lights went out. In the darkness a kiss and a heavy blow could be heard. When the lights came on, the policeman was rubbing a swollen eye.

The old lady thought, "That young lady must know self defence and she hit the policeman for his unwelcome attention".

The young woman thought, "Why would that policeman want to kiss that old lady instead of an attractive young woman like me?"

The policeman thought, "That vandal in the Doc Martens must have made advances on the young lady. In the darkness she went to punch him, missed and hit me!"

But here's what really happened. The teenager kissed the back of his own hand and punched the policeman.

***

Eric was a keen bear hunter. One day whilst out hunting he spotted a huge brown bear on the edge of a clearing. Aiming his rifle, he fired a couple of shots. He rushed to the edge of the clearing, expecting to find the dead bear. To his horror, he found the bear very much alive.

"I'm sick to death of you hunters shooting at me all the time", said the bear, "and I'm going to teach you a lesson. Get down on knees and give me a blow job. Now!"

Eric obeyed.

The next day, Eric returned to the spot with a buffalo gun. He was going to get even with this bear. Sure enough, there was the bear on the edge of the clearing. Eric lined him up and pulled the trigger. He dashed to the edge of the clearing, expecting to see the dead bear. But again, there was the bear, waiting for him.

"You'll never learn", said the bear. "Down on your hands and knees and give me another blow job."

Eric obeyed again.

Next day, he returned with an elephant gun. He was going to get this bear for sure this time. There was the bear, standing on the edge of the clearing. He crept closer, took aim and fired. He rushed over to the spot where the bear had been standing, and there was the bear, waiting for him.

"O.K.", said the bear, "let's have the truth - you're not in this for the hunting at all, are you?"

**

There was a fly buzzing about one foot above the river. A trout saw the fly and thought, "If that fly comes down six inches I can jump out of the water and catch it."

What the trout didn't see was a bear hiding behind a bush who also saw the fly and realised what the trout was up to and thought, "If I wait until the fly drops six inches, the trout will jump and I'll catch the trout."

There was a hunter watching the bear watching the trout watching the fly. He thought, "When the fly drops six inches and the trout jumps and the bear grabs the trout, I'll be able to shoot the bear."

It was a long wait, so the hunter munched on a cheese sandwich.

There was a mouse watching the hunter watching the bear watching the trout watching the fly. The mouse thought, "When the hunter shoots the bear he'll put down his sandwich and I'll steal the cheese."

There was a cat who was watching the mouse watching the hunter who was watching the bear who was watching the trout who was watching the fly. The cat figured that if the fly dropped six inches, the trout would jump out of the water, the bear would grab the trout, the hunter would shoot the bear, the mouse would grab the cheese and he would grab the mouse.

All of a sudden the fly dropped six inches, the trout jumped out of the water, the bear grabbed the trout, the hunter shot the bear, the mouse ran for the cheese and the cat went for the mouse........ but missed and fell into the river.

The moral of the story? When the fly drops six inches the pussy gets wet.

***

An old farmer decided it was time to get a new rooster for his hens. The rooster he had was doing a poor job and was getting old. The farmer figured a new rooster could do a better job.

So he buys a new one and turns him loose in the barnyard. The old rooster sees the young one strutting around amongst the hens and gets a bit worried.

They're trying to replace me", he thinks. "I've got to do something about this."

So he walks up to the new bird and says, "So

you're the new stud around here. I bet you think you're pretty good! Well, let me tell you, I'm not ready for the chopping block. And to prove it, I'll challenge you to a race around the barn. Ten times around, and whoever finishes first has all the hens to himself and the loser takes off."

The young rooster thought he was more than a match, and said, "You're on!"

The old rooster said, "I'm so great, I'll give you half a lap start and still beat you!"

So the two roosters go over to the barn and start the race. After the first lap the old rooster was gaining on the young one. After the second lap he had made up more ground, and still more after the third. But the old rooster tired and started to slip back each time round. By the eighth lap, he was just barely in front of the young rooster.

The farmer had heard all the commotion in the chook yard. He ran into the house, got his shotgun and ran out to the barn, figuring a fox was after his hens. When he gets there he sees two roosters running round the barn, the old rooster still slightly in front. He immediately takes aim, fires and shoots the young rooster dead.

As he walked away he mumbled to himself, "I'll be damned - that's the third gay rooster I've had this month."

***

Brown Eagle had proved himself to be a very brave warrior and was now entitled to take a wife. He chose the most beautiful squaw in his village.

Before the wedding he jumped on his horse and rode to the Trading Post. He said to the trader, "I am marrying the most beautiful squaw in my village. I want a very special wedding gift for her."

The trader suggested a large soft buffalo hide, and every night he rolled up in the hide with his beautiful squaw.

Brown Eagle became the most heroic warrior of his Indian tribe and was able to take another wife. He chose the most beautiful squaw of his whole tribe. Again he hopped on his horse and rode to the Trading Post, telling the Trader "I am marrying the most beautiful squaw of my whole tribe. I want a very special wedding gift for her."

The trader suggested a beautiful bear hide that would keep her very warm on the cold winter nights.

Brown Eagle went on to become the Chief of the whole Indian nation and could now take a third wife. He chose the most beautiful squaw in the whole Indian nation and again, jumped on his horse, galloped to the Trading Post and said to the trader, "I am now a big Chief. I am marrying the most beautiful squaw in the whole of the Indian nation. I want a very special wedding gift for her."

The trader said, "I have on my shelf a hippopotamus hide. It's the only hide like it in the country. It is thick, soft leather. It's huge. It will never wear out. Your squaw can wrap herself in it in the long winter nights and never be cold."

Brown Eagle decided that it was time to settle down and raise a family. His three squaws got pregnant at the same time. When they gave birth, the squaw on the buffalo hide had a baby girl, while the squaw on the bear hide had a baby boy, but the squaw on the hippopotamus hide had twins - a boy and a girl. This proves that:

the Squaw on the Hippopotamus is Equal to the Sum of the Squaws on the other Two Hides.

***

A man was lost bush walking. It was getting dark and it was raining. He had nowhere to stay so he ran up to a farmhouse and knocked on the door.

"Can you please give me a room for the night?" he asked the woman owner.

"Yes, you can sleep in the barn." she said sympathetically.

The man walked to the barn in the dark and got tangled in the clothes lines, tearing some clothes and dropping others on the ground.

He sat down in the barn and began to shave. There was a loud thunder clap and the man dropped his razor. It landed on the cat and shaved some cat hair off. The cat jumped up, giving the man a fright and he fell backwards hitting a shelf of paints. The paints fell onto a donkey and the donkey squealed.

The woman came running.

"I'm calling the cops." she yelled, picking up the phone.

"Hello Officer?" she said, "a man just ran into my house, ripped off my clothes, shaved my pussy and painted my ass!"

***

Texas is the biggest State of North America and Texans reckons they have the biggest of everything. There was a Texan girl who met a Texan cowboy in the world's biggest bar in Texas.

He bragged, "I've got the biggest feet in the world, size 20."

She went one better, "I've got the biggest cunt in the world."

"I'd have to see that", said the cowboy, so they went around to his motel. He took his size 20 boots off and said, "I'll bet you can't even get the big toe of one of these up there."

She just smiled and said, "Try me, cowboy."

She spread her legs high in the air and the Texan slid the whole boot in and said, "Wow!"

He then took his other boot and slid the whole boot in.

She said, "I didn't even feel that, cowboy."

So the cowboy said, "I must have a look at this", bent over and stuck his whole head in. Before he knew it, he tripped over the carpet and fell right inside.

Groping around, he brought out his flashlight and, to his amazement, saw another guy in there.

"What are you doing here?", the cowboy asked.

"Same thing as you", was the reply.

"Well, it's a good thing I've got this flashlight so we can find our way out of here", the cowboy said.

But the other guy replied, "Let's use it to look around first. If we can find my horse, we can ride out of here."

**

Maureen had her eye on Cameron for a long time. But Cameron was oblivious to her romantic overtures. He was obsessed with his Harley motor cycle, for which he had a deep passion.

One day he was lubricating his bike with vaseline when Maureen called in and asked if he would like to come to tea on Saturday night.

"Can I bring my bike?", Cameron asked.

"I guess so", said Maureen.

On Saturday night, Cameron turned up on his Harley, the tank and the chromework sparkling.

"Can I bring my bike inside?", he asked Maureen's mother.

"No, leave it on the porch", Mother said.

"Alright", said Cameron, "but if it's staying out here in the moist air, I need to give it another rub of vaseline to keep the rust away. I do this every night", he said, pulling out the jar and a cloth.

It was a most enjoyable meal and as everyone was about to leave the table, Maureen's mother said, "Hold on a bit, where are you all going? I'm not going to wash the dishes."

"Well, I'm not," said Maureen.

"And I'm not", said Maureen's father.

"And I'm certainly not", said Cameron. "It looks like rain and I want to polish my bike."

"Well", said Mother, "I cooked the meal and I'm not doing the dishes."

"Enough!", roared Father. "No more arguments. Not another word. In fact, whoever says the next word will do the dishes!"

They all sat there in silence. Outside there was a flash of lightning and a roll of thunder, and Cameron was becoming most anxious about the possible rain on his bike. He desperately wanted the jar of vaseline to rub over the frame and the tank, but silence persisted.

Another clap of thunder, and Cameron decided that he would force somebody else to speak. He got up, pushed Maureen to the floor, tore off her clothes and had his way with her. Mother and Father were horrified, but not a word was spoken.

Cameron decided his actions must be more drastic. He jumped on Mother, threw her to the floor and had his way with her too.

Father gritted his teeth, but not a word passed his lips.

What else could Cameron do? He was defeated. As he heard the rain falling on the roof, he got up from the table and said, "O.K., I'm going to get the vaseline."

"I'll do the dishes! I'll do the dishes!" yelled Father, jumping up and dashing into the kitchen.

***

Quasimodo, the Hunchback of Notre Dame, had a unique way of ringing the Church bells. He would stand on the parapet, calculate the wind speed, swing off towards the bell and kick it with his feet.

Unfortunately for Quasi, he misjudged the wind one stormy day, twisted in mid air, hit the bell with his head and fell to the ground, dead. A crowd quickly gathered and a policeman was called.

"Does anybody know this man?", the policeman asked of the crowd.

One man came forward, looked at Quasi and said, "No, but his face rings a bell."

***

Quasimodo's twin brother was hired to replace Quasi after he died. Quasi had taught him how to swing on the rope and kick the bell with his feet. The brother misjudged the wind one day also and fell dead on the pavement.

A crowd quickly gathered and a policeman was called.

"Can anyone identify this man?", asked the policeman of the crowd.

"Yes", said someone, "he's a dead ringer for his brother."

***

One sunny Sunday, Superman was flying around with nothing to do, so he decided to drop in on Batman.

"Hi, Bat", said Superman, "let's go down the pub and have a beer."

"Not today, Super. My Batmobile's broken down and I've got to fix it. Can't fight crime without it, you know."

Disappointed, Superman went over to Spiderman's place.

"Let's go down the pub for a drink, Spider."

"Sorry Super. I've got a problem with my web gun. Can't fight crime without it, you know."

Dejectedly, Superman took to the air again,

and decided to drop by on Wonder Woman. There she was, laying on her back out on her balcony, stark naked and writhing around. Superman conceived a cunning idea. "Everyone says I'm faster than a speeding bullet, and I've always wondered what sort of screw she'd be".

So he zoomed down, did her in a flash and zoomed off.

"What the hell was that!", cried Wonder Woman.

"I don't know, but it hurt like hell!" said the Invisible Man.

***

St Peter was doing market research with the applicants at the Pearly Gates. Three men were awaiting entry.

"Cause of death?", St Peter asked the first.

"I suspected my wife was cheating on me", the first man replied, "so I came home early and burst into my apartment on the twenty-first floor. I ran into the bedroom and my wife was lying naked on the bed. I searched the apartment but found no-one. I went out on the balcony, and sure enough, there was a man hanging by his fingers. I went inside and got a hammer and started beating his fingers. He let go and fell, but hit the awning across the pavement. I could see that he was still alive, so I rushed back into the apartment, grabbed the refrigerator, pushed it over the balcony and let it fall. The effort was too much for me and I had a heart attack and fell down dead."

"Next?", said St Peter. "Cause of death?"

"I lived on the twenty-second floor of an apartment building. I always do my exercises out on the balcony and today I fell, but I was lucky. I grabbed hold of the railing on the balcony below, when suddenly, this guy came out and started beating my fingers with a hammer. I had to let go, but I dropped onto an awning beneath. Next thing, a refrigerator dropped out of the sky and crushed me. That's why I'm here."

"Next?", said St Peter. "Cause of death?"

"Well.. I was hiding in this refrigerator....."

***

Jesus, nailed to the cross, sees Peter in the crowd.

"Peter", he calls. "Peter."

Peter hears his name and calls, "I hear you, My Lord. I'm coming."

Peter begins to walk up the hill to the cross but is challenged by a Roman Centurion.

"Stop!", said the Centurion, "or I'll cut off your arm."

"But I must go. My Lord is calling."

The Centurion swung his sword and severed Peter's arm.

"Peter, Peter", called Jesus.

Peter staggered up the hill, only to be confronted by another Centurion.

"Stop! Or I will cut off your other arm", said the Centurion.

"But I must continue. My Lord is calling me."

The Centurion swung his sword and cut off Peter's other arm.

Peter staggered on up the hill, becoming weak from loss of blood and still he heard Jesus calling, "Peter, Peter."

Again, he was confronted by a Centurion.

"Stop! Or I'll cut off your leg!"

"But My Lord is calling me", replied Peter, as he attempted to climb the hill. The Centurion swung his mighty sword and cut off Peter's leg.

"Peter, Peter", called Jesus.

In great pain, Peter began to hop up the hill, and as he neared the bottom of the cross, he was confronted by yet another Centurion who said, "Stop, or I will cut off your other leg."

"Peter, Peter", cried Jesus.

"Can't you hear? My Lord is calling me."

"I don't care", said the Centurion, and cut off Peter's other leg.

Peter dragged his mutilated body to the bottom of the cross, his eyes focused on Jesus. "I am here, Lord. I have answered your call."

Jesus looked down at Peter and said, "Peter... I can see your house from up here!"

SHOPPING SPREES

A woman walked into a sex shop and asked to buy a vibrator. The shop assistant beckoned with his finger and said, "Can you come this way."

The woman replied, "If I could come that way, I wouldn't need a vibrator."

She was gazing in the window of the shoe shop, admiring a beautiful pair of black Italian stiletto heeled shoes, priced far beyond her capacity to pay.

The shoe salesman in the shop beckoned her in. "You can have those shoes if you come to bed with me", he said.

"O.K.", she replied, "but I should tell you, I don't like sex very much."

He gave her the shoes and they booked into a motel room. They took off their clothes and jumped into bed. He humped away while she lay passively, missionary style. Suddenly, she threw her legs up into the air and cried, "Wonderful!.....Beautiful!.....Oh my God, so lovely!......"

"I thought you didn't like sex", he panted.

"I don't", she replied, "I'm just admiring my beautiful new shoes."

***

Diana and Barbara were in the shopping centre.

"There's my husband, coming out of the florist with a dozen roses. That means I'm going to have to keep my legs up in the air for three days", said Diana.

"Why?" said Barbara. "Don't you have a vase?"

***

Pete had an embarrassing twitch in his eye. He had tried everything to get rid of it. At last he found a Chinese doctor who told him that a regular dose of aspirin would fix his problem.

When he returned, Dr Woo asked him how he was progressing.

"No good", said Pete. "Every time I go into the drug store and ask for a packet of aspirin, they give me these!", and he threw down fifty packets of condoms.

***

A blind man went into a department store, picked up his guide dog by the tail and began swinging him around.

A sales clerk came over and said, "Can I be of assistance?"

"No", said the blind man, "I'm just looking around."

SHRINKS

The pressure was too much for the Stock Exchange executive. He had a breakdown and was committed to a mental hospital. During therapy time, he said he was having sex with biscuits.

"Are they chocolate biscuits?"

"No", he said.

"Are they shortbreads?"

"No."

"Are they those dry biscuits with pepper and salt on them?"

"Yes, yes, that's the sort!"

"Then you're fuckin' crackers!"

***

The blonde patient pleaded with her psychiatrist. "Kiss me! Please, kiss me!"

"No", said the psychiatrist, "that's unethical Miss. I shouldn't even be screwing you."

***

"Doctor, doctor, can you help me? I'm suffering from a premature ejaculation problem."

"I can't cure you of your problem", said the doctor, "but I can put you in touch with a woman who has a short attention span."

***

A beautiful young thing goes to see a psychotherapist.

"Take off your clothes and lie on the couch", he instructed.

He then jumped on the couch with her and ravished her.

When he finished, he put his clothes on and said, "Well, that's my problem solved - what's yours?"

A soldier was having a psychiatric test prior to discharge. The psychiatrist asked, "Tell me, Private, what would happen if I cut off one of your ears?"

"It would be hard to hear", replied the soldier.

"Good", said the psychiatrist. "What would happen if I cut off your other ear?"

"I wouldn't be able to see."

"That's interesting, why do you say that?"

"Because my cap would fall over my eyes."

***

A public speaker had an appointment with his psychiatrist who ran his private practice at a mental hospital. Whilst in the waiting room, the psychiatrist came out and said, "You're a public speaker, aren't you? Would you do me a favour? I've got a group of hospital patients in the lecture room and the speaker hasn't turned up. Could you fill in for an hour or so?"

"Certainly", said the public speaker.

The speaker stood behind the lectern and looked down at the group of patients, who stared blankly back at him. But being a pro, he gave forth his most motivational talk. He was constantly being interrupted, however, by a patient at the back of the room, who kept calling out, "Bullshit."

When he had finished speaking, the speaker said to his psychiatrist that he didn't think the man at the back of the room was very impressed with his motivational talk.

"No!", said the psychiatrist, "you were fantastic!

That's the first intelligent thing that patient has said in three years!"

***

"**D**octor, I keep thinking I'm a wheelbarrow."

"Well, you must stop people pushing you around."

***

A young man went to the psychiatrist complaining that he was getting married and he was worried about the small size of his penis. The psychiatrist advised him to go and stay on a dairy farm, and every morning, dip his penis in milk and get it sucked by a calf.

Some time later, the young man met the psychiatrist in the street.

"How's the marriage going?", asked the psychiatrist.

"I never got married", said the young man. "I cancelled it and bought the calf."

***

Garry was depressed, he told his psychiatrist, because he thought he was gay.

"Why do you feel that way?"

"Because my father was a gay."

"Being a poof is not hereditary", said the psychiatrist.

"My brother is gay."

"That still doesn't mean that you are."

"My Uncle Bruce is gay. And my cousin Jeffrey is gay."

The psychiatrist gave a concerned look and frowned.

"Does anyone in your family have sexual contact with women?", he asked.

"Yes", said Garry, "my sister does."

***

It was the end of the football season and many football fans were suffering from withdrawal symptoms. One psychiatrist had a thriving business helping them get through it.

One day he had a patient on the couch and he said to him, "Imagine something brown, firm, with smooth curves."

The patient thought for a moment and said, "A football."

"Good", said the psychiatrist. "What do you think of when two arms slide around your waist?"

"A tackle."

"Good", he said. "Now picture a pair of firm thighs."

"A half-back!", came the reply.

"Your reactions are quite normal", said the psychiatrist. "You'd be surprised at some of the stupid answers I get."

***

"I've got to a change jobs", the patient said to his psychiatrist. "I've worked in a pickled onion factory for ten years, and last week I started to get this uncontrollable urge to put my dick in the onion peeler."

The psychiatrist explained about workplace stress and told him he must learn to relax.

But a week later, the patient was back.

"I don't think I can control myself much longer", he said. "The urge is getting greater. I'm going to put my dick in the onion peeler any day now."

The psychiatrist prescribed Valium.

A month later, the patient was back on the psychiatrist's couch.

"I've lost my job", he said. "I finally stuck my dick into the onion peeler."

"My God!", said the psychiatrist. "What happened then?"

"I got fired. And Betty, the onion peeler, got fired too."

SINGLES BARS

Zeke was only in town for one night so he headed for the singles bar for a quick pick-up. He approached the first woman he saw.

"I'm only in town for one night", he said, "and I can't waste time. Do you fuck or don't you?"

"Well", she replied coyly, "I don't usually, but you've sweet talked me into it."

A guy meets a girl in the bar and she goes home with him. When they are relaxing after making love, he asks, "Am I the first guy you ever made love to?"

She looks at him for a few moments and says, "Of course you are!" she said. "Why do you men always ask that same stupid question?"

***

Max was desperate for some female company. He started a conversation with a blonde in the corner who accepted his invitation to an expensive hotel restaurant. She had two servings of every course, thoroughly enjoying her outing.

"Do you always eat this much?", asked Max, thinking about the cost.

"Only when I've got a heavy period", replied the blonde.

***

They had just met that night and were having a post-coital conversation.

"If I get pregnant", she said, "what will we call the baby?"

Pulling off his condom, tying it in a knot and flushing it down the toilet, he said, "Well, if he gets out of that, we'll call him Houdini."

***

After a few drinks and small talk, she invited him back to her apartment. Just before they turned out the light, he asked, "How do you like your eggs in the morning?"

"Unfertilised", she replied.

***

"How about a screw?", he asked.

"Your place or mine?", she replied.

"If you're going to argue, forget it!", he said.

***

She was sitting at the bar with a lonely look on her face. He sidled up to her and whispered in her ear, "What would you say if I stole a kiss?"

"The same thing I'd say to any dickhead who had the chance to steal a car but only took the hubcaps!" she said.

***

He was driving her home after an enjoyable night at the Singles Disco. He pulled into a shady lane and started to grope her.

"Do you know what good clean fun is?" she said, pushing his hand away.

"No", he replied, "What good is it?"

***

TOP TEN PICK UP LINES

1 How'd you like to sit on my knee and we'll talk about the first thing that pops up?

2 That dress would look great on the floor next to my bed.

3 How'd you like to see something swell?

4 Excuse me, do you want to fuck or should I apologise?

5 Hey babe, how about a pizza and a fuck? What's wrong - don't you like pizza?

6 Want to play carnival? You sit on my face and I guess how much you weigh.

7 I love every bone in your body - especially mine.

8 My face is leaving in ten minutes - be on it!

9 Sit on my face and let me get to nose you better.

10 You've got the whitest teeth I ever want to cum across.

***

When she met him in the Singles Bar, she told him she was Libra on the cusp of Scorpio. He replied that he was Taurus with penis rising.

It was her first night at the Singles Bar and the handsome young guy had asked her home to watch some videos.

"No funny business? Nothing serious?", she asked.

"Trust me. We'll just watch a few movies."

"But what if I've seen the movies?"

"Well, you can put your clothes on and go home."

SPORTING HEROES

Ossie approached the umpire after a series of bad decisions.

"If I called you a stupid bastard who didn't know the first thing about the rules of football, what would you do?", he said.

"I'd report you and you'd be fined", replied the umpire.

"What if I didn't say it and I just thought it?", said Ossie.

"Well, there's nothing I can do about that."

"O.K.", said Ossie, "we'll just leave it at that."

***

A young footballer was shipwrecked on a tropical island with Miss Universe. He couldn't believe his luck, but she was prim and proper.

"You live on one side of the island, and I'll live on the other", she said, "and we'll meet once a week to discuss any rescue prospects."

This went on for a month, and when they next met, they were both as horny as hell.

"We might as well do it", he said, "we could spent the rest of our lives here."

"I agree", she said, and tore her clothes off. They screwed for hours.

"Let's meet again tomorrow", said Miss Universe.

"Could you do me a favour?", said the football player.

"Sure", she said.

"I've got some shirts and trousers here", he said. "Could you dress up as a man?"

She reluctantly consented, thinking he was a bit kinky.

Next day as she walked up the beach dressed like a man the footballer walked up beside her.

G'day mate", he said, slapping her on the back, "you'll never guess who I fucked last night."

***

The young guy was a weight lifter and very proud of his physique.

"After I won Gold at the Olympics", he told his new girlfriend, "I got quite a few advertising contracts. Have a look at this." He rolled up his sleeves. On each of his biceps he had 'NIKE' tattooed.

"A thousand dollars for each arm", he said.

He removed his shirt. 'SLAZENGER' was tattooed over his chest.

"I got $10,000 for that one."

He removed his trousers and displayed 'PUMA' tattooed on his legs. "And I got $5,000 for this", he added.

But when she saw 'AIDS' tattooed on his penis, she was horrified and ran for the door.

"Don't go!", he said. "If you stay you'll find out why I got $20,000 from Adidas."

***

The crew from the winning boat were lined up on the dais to receive their gold medal when a blonde rushed out of the crowd and kissed their cox.

***

Tony was a typical forward in the football team - big and tough. But he was in trouble. He had put on too much weight and was told if he didn't lose some quickly, he'd be dropped from the team.

He consulted a doctor at the sports clinic. "We're testing a new method of weight reduction", said the doctor, "and we'd like you to try it out. You can eat anything you like, and as much as you like, but instead of eating it, you must consume it anally."

"What! Shove it up my arse?", asked Tony.

"That's right", the doctor replied. "But there is one possible side effect... there's a 50% chance you may become homosexual."

Tony was very concerned about this but really wanted to be on the team so he agreed.

Three weeks later, Tony returned to the doctor looking trim and fitter.

"This is great!", he said. "I can eat anything I like. All I do is shove it up me bum!"

"And you look great!", said the doctor. "Any gay feelings?"

"No doc, none." said Tony smiling.

"Keep it up, and come back and see me in three weeks."

When Tony returned for his check-up, he had clearly lost more weight. He was jubilant.

"I've been eating Big Macs, Kentucky Fried and heaps of cakes. I just shove the lot up. It's great! And no gay inclinations!"

"Good!", said the doctor. "But come back next week for a final check-up."

Two weeks later, Tony was back seeing the doctor. He appeared very nervous, twitching, wriggling, standing on one foot then the other, pacing up and down the doctor's surgery and swaying his hips from side to side.

"Oh no!", said the doctor. "You've become gay!"

"Don't worry, doc. Everything's O.K. I'm just having a Mintie."

STAR GAZERS

The Hollywood talent scout had just heard a young man give a very funny and lively performance.

"That was great!", he said. "What's your name?"

"Penis van Lesbian", said the young comedian.

"Wow! We'll have to change that. How about we call you Dick Van Dyke?"

***

What did Joan Collins say to King Kong?
Is it in yet?

***

Joan Collins went to the gyno for an examination. As the doctor moved his head down between her legs he said excitedly, "That's the biggest one I've ever seen! That's the biggest one I've ever seen!"

"You didn't have to say it twice!", she said with embarrassment.

"I didn't!" he replied.

***

Hugh Grant has just been diagnosed with cancer - they found a big black mole on the end of his penis.

During the first quarter of the next New Moon, go outside at 11 p.m. and face the South. Bend over at the waist to form a ninety degree angle. Bend the knees at a forty five degree angle. Then, get a hand mirror and hold it between your legs. With a bit of luck, if all the angles are correct, you should see Uranus.

THE DIFFERENCE IS

What do you get when you cross a disobedient dog with a rooster.
You get a cock that won't come.

***

Why is English beer like making love in a boat?
They're both fucking near water.

***

What's the difference between a woman in a singles bar and a proctologist?
The proctologist only has to deal with one arse-hole at a time.

***

What's the difference between cholesterol and fat?

You'll never wake up in the morning with half a cholesterol.

***

What's got 3 balls and flies through space?
The Extra Testicle.

***

What's the difference between Jurassic Park and I.B.M.?

One is a high tech theme park dominated by dinosaurs. The other is a Steven Spielberg film.

***

What's the difference between erotic and kinky?

Erotic is when you use a feather.
Kinky is when you use the whole chicken.

***

What's the difference between a vitamin and a hormone?

You can't hear a vitamin.

***

What's the difference between a slut and a bitch?

A slut will sleep with anyone.

A bitch will sleep with anyone but you.

TOURISTS

Two Australians in London were down on their luck saw an advertisement for two footmen at Buckingham Palace. "References essential", it said. "That's O.K.", said Col, "We can write them out for each other."

They arrived at the Palace and offered the Queen two glowing references. "Our servants dress in formal Scottish attire. This means wearing kilts, so drop your trousers while I check your knees."

The Aussies were a little surprised, but they did so. The Queen gave the knees a nod of approval and said, "Okay, now let me see those testimonials."

After they were thrown out of the Palace, Col said, "Y'know, if we'd understood the local lingo, I reckon we could've got that job."

***

The two women were side by side in their deckchairs on the Q.E.2 enjoying a round-the-world cruise. The first one said, "My husband worked hard all his life so we could have a trip like this."

The other woman looked at her and said haughtily, "Oh, your first trip, is it? I have had fifteen trips like this. My husband works for Cunard."

"Well!" said the first, "my husband works fuckin' hard too, but I don't swear about it!"

***

As the young fella boarded his flight in Cairns, the hostess noticed the newspaper parcel under his arm.

"Mud crabs", he said, "I'm taking them home to Melbourne for a gourmet meal tonight."

The hostess took the package, assuring him that storage in refrigeration would keep them fresh.

The flight landed, and as the aircraft taxied in, the passengers were welcomed over the PA system and asked to remain seated until the plane came to a halt..."And would the gentleman who gave me the crabs in Cairns please come and see me?"

***

Bill had just returned home from a sales convention in Hong Kong. He spent his days at the convention and his nights in the Red Light district, and was now suffering from a painful and inflamed penis. He hurried to the doctor, who diagnosed it as the Hong Kong Dong and told Bill he would have to have his penis amputated.

Bill was shocked and sought a second opinion, only to be given the same advice - amputation.

A friend recommended a Chinese doctor who practised traditional medicine. The Chinese doctor confirmed the Hong Kong Dong diagnosis but said there was no need for amputation.

"I'm so relieved!", said Bill.

"Yes", said the Chinese medico, "in a week's time it will drop off by itself."

***

Bob had just returned from Hong Kong and the doctor had diagnosed the Hong Kong Dong.

"I'm afraid it's got to come off", he said.

Bob was horrified.

"Don't worry", said the doctor. "You can have a transplant."

"How much would that cost?", asked Bob.

"$500 for a standard model, $1,000 for a big one and $2,000 for a big black one", replied the doctor.

"I'll have to talk this over with my wife", responded Bob.

Bob returned to the doctor the next day.

"Don't worry about the transplant doc. We've decided to get a new kitchen instead." he said.

A man in a Japanese restaurant calls to the waiter, "This chicken is rubbery!"

The waiter smiled and said, "Ah, thank you very much!"

***

The young tourist was exploring the Red Light district of Bangkok and thought he would try one of the well known Parlours.

"Sorry", said the Madam "there are no girls available tonight."

Disappointed, he turned to leave.

"Wait!", said the Madam, "we do have a beautiful young female pig available, and she's very popular with many of our clients. I can guarantee you'll enjoy it."

"Why not!", he thought.

He paid his money and had his way with the pig.

It was so enjoyable that he was back at the same Parlour the next night, asking for the pig.

"I'm sorry", said the Madam, "the pig's not available, but there's a good show on tonight - a donkey with one of our girls."

He paid his money and took his seat behind the two-way mirror.

"Gee", he said to the man sitting next to him, "this is incredible."

"It's nothing", said the stranger. "You should have been here last night. There was a man fucking a pig."

UNEMPLOYED

John was attending the employment office looking for a job.

"What sort of experience have you had?", asked the employment counsellor.

"Practically nothing", replied John.

"Come on", urged the counsellor. "You must have done something with your life."

John thought. "I've committed adultery. I defrauded the Mothers Club of some of their savings. I've been charged a few times with assaulting children. And I suppose, for most of my life I've taken advantage of people that have trusted me."

"We've got just the job for you!", said the counsellor. "A Christian Brother at the local Catholic school!"

VEGETARIAN

"I heard you married again."

"Yes, for the fourth time."

"What happened to the first three?'

"They all died."

"What happened?"

"My first wife ate poison mushrooms."

"How sad. What happened to your second wife?"

"She ate poison mushrooms too."

"What about the third wife. Did she eat poison mushrooms?"

"No, she died of a broken neck."

"Had an accident, eh?"

"No. She wouldn't eat her mushrooms."

***

Cinderella wasn't really a hard-done-by scullery maid. She was a nymphomaniac. And when the Fairy Godmother appeared to prepare her for the Prince's ball, she scolded Cinderella. "If you don't stop screwing around, I'll wave my wand over your pussy and turn it into a pumpkin at 12 o'clock."

But Cinderella could not restrain herself and had half a dozen quickies at the back of the Palace before the Prince raced off with her as the clock struck twelve. And sure enough, her pussy turned into a pumpkin.

When the Fairy Godmother next appeared, Cinderella had a big smile on her face and she said, "Fairy Godmother, meet my new boyfriend, Peter Peter."

VIVE LA FRANCE

An Australian, an Englishman and a Frenchman were discussing the meaning of *'savoir faire'*. The Australian gave an example:

"Say a man comes home and finds his best mate screwing his wife in bed. He says, 'G'day Shirley, g'day George. Never mind me, just carry on. I'll go and get a beer.' That's savoir faire!"

The Englishman said, "By jove, that's a good one, but we'd do it a little differently. A chap comes home and finds his chum in bed with his wife and says, 'Good evening, Shirley, good evening George, old chap. Never mind me, just carry on whilst I make a gin and tonic.' Now that's savoir faire!"

The Frenchman said, "Non! Non! Zee Frenchman comes home and finds 'is best friend in bed making zee passionate love to his wife, he says, 'Bonjour mon ami, bonjour Shirlee. Never mind me, just carry on while I pour a glass of champagne.' And my friend *continues* to make love to my wife, that's *savour faire!*"

***

Several young French boys were called by the Paris Authorities for a medical check-up to determine the father of a teenage girl's baby.

Pierre was first in, and after a few minutes, came out and said, "Don't worry, they'll never find out 'oo it was. They're taking samples from the finger."

***

What's the difference between a French girl and a bowling ball?

You can only get three fingers in a bowling ball.

***

The French couple asked their ten year old son what he wanted for Christmas.

"I wanna watch", he replied.

So they let him.

***

A Jew, an Indian and a Frenchman were travelling across Texas when their car broke down. They knocked on a farmers' door and asked for accommodation for the night.

"I can only put up two", said the farmer, "one will have to sleep in the barn."

"I will sleep in the barn", said the Jew.

Five minutes later there was a knock on the door. "There's a pig in the barn", said the Jew, "I cannot sleep with a pig."

"O.K., I'll go", said the Indian.

Five minutes later, there was a knock on the door. "There's a cow in the barn", said the Indian,

"I am a Hindu, I cannot sleep with a cow."

"I'll go", said the Frenchman.

Five minutes later, there was another knock on the door. It was the pig and the cow.

***

A Frenchman was on holidays in Australia and, while taking a drive in the countryside, saw a young child being chased by a raging bull. The Frenchman slammed on his brakes, jumped out of the car, vaulted a high fence and sprinted with amazing speed towards the bull.

Unknown to him, an Australian journalist was passing, and noticed his incredible feat. The Frenchman reached the bull and held it by the horns just five metres from the child. He flipped the bull over onto its back, twisted its head and broke its neck. He picked the child up and comforted him and carried him gently back to the side of the road.

The Australian journalist was astounded. He ran over to the Frenchman and said, "Shit-a-brick! That was incredible mate! I've never seen a man so athletic, with such strength and courage! It makes me proud to be an Australian. I'm going to put this story on the front page of every newspaper! Just give me some details about yourself. Born around here, were you?"

Next day the headlines appeared on the front page:

"FRENCH PAEDOPHILE KILLS CHILD'S PET".

***

Jean Paul was so exhausted after his marriage to Suzette that when he got to the honeymoon suite he went to sleep the moment his feet hit the pillow.

***

Take your glasses off, Pierre", Fifi demanded. "They are tearing my stockings."

Pierre did as he was commanded.

"You'd better put them back on again", she said a few minutes later. "You're licking the carpet."

***

Marcel was caught screwing his boss's fiancee. The boss sent a letter challenging Marcel to a duel.

Marcel replied in writing: "I have received your circular letter and will be present at the gathering."

***

VOLVOS

What's the difference between driving a Volvo and putting your hand in a black man's trouser pocket?

Driving a Volvo, you'll feel a much bigger prick.

WANKERS

He's so conceited that when he masturbates, he calls out his own name when he comes.

***

He fakes orgasm when he masturbates.

***

"Wake up Paula!" Peter yelled at 2am. You won't believe what just happened! I went to have a leak and a strange light came on from nowhere. When I finished the light went out again. It's a miracle!"
"No, it's not," said Paula. "You've pissed in the bloody fridge again!"

***

What's a Yankee?
Same as a quickie except you do it alone.

***

The football coach went beserk. His team were in the middle of the ground, their shorts and jock straps round their ankles, and wanking themselves.

"What the hell are you doing?", he demanded.

"Well", said the captain, "you told us to get out here and pull ourselves together."

***

The sex expert was being interviewed, "Our research proves that half the population sing in the shower and the other half masturbate. Do you know what the singers sing?"

"No", replied the interviewer.

"I didn't think you did."

***

What's the ultimate rejection?

When your hand falls asleep while you're masturbating.

***

What's the difference between an omelette and a wank?

You can beat an omelette, but you can't beat a wank.

***

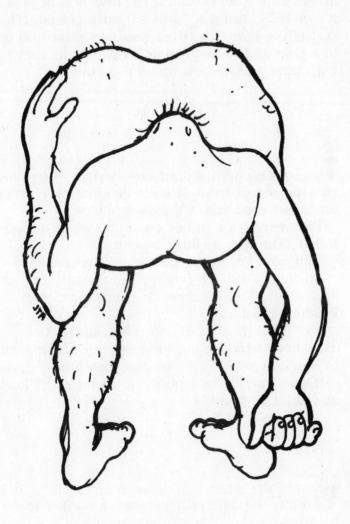

"I'm perfectly happy with my lot in life."

— from *Rude and Politically Incorrect Jokes* by Allan Pease

Fortunately the penis is one of the few things still exempt from taxation. The reason is because it's usually hanging around unemployed. The rest of the time, it's either hard up, pissed off or in a hole. It also has two dependants and they're both nuts and its best friend is a cunt.

***

The young parents used code words when discussing sex in front of their children. The term for intercourse was "washing machine".

They were lying in bed one night when he said to her, "Darling, washing machine."

"Not now, I've got a headache", she replied.

An hour later, he ran his hand down her leg and said, "Darling, washing machine, please! Washing machine."

"I've got a headache!", she complained.

An hour later, feeling sorry for him, she turned to him and said, "O.K., washing machine."

"Don't worry", he replied, "it was a small load so I did it by hand."

***

What is the difference between a wanker and a banker?

A wanker knows what he's doing.

***

"**D**octor, I feel weak and faint."

"How many times do you have sex?", asked the doctor.

"Five or six times a night."

"Obviously that's the cause of your problem", said the doctor.

"What a relief, doc. I was afraid it might be the masturbation."

UNHAPPY MARRIAGE

"**I**'m divorcing my wife" Peter told his mates at the pub. "She has disgusting habits. I went to piss in the sink this morning, and it was still full of dirty dishes!"

***

Marriage has its good side. It teaches you loyalty, forbearance, tolerance, self-restraint, and other valuable qualities you wouldn't need if you'd stayed single.

***

A man came home to find his wife in bed with his friend.

"What's going on here?" demanded the husband.

"See," said the wife to her lover, "I told you he was stupid."

***

A music lover married a woman because he was infatuated by her voice. He didn't realise how ugly she was until the first morning of the honeymoon when he sat in bed and saw her without her make-up.

He stared at her for a while, then shook her and yelled: "Sing ya bitch, sing!"

***

A man died and his wife put a death notice in the paper, saying that he died of gonorrhoea. His brother phoned and complained angrily saying, "You know very well that he died of diarrhoea, not gonorrhoea."

"I know he died of diarrhoea." she replied, "But I want people to remember him as a great lover rather than the big shit he really was."

***

Bob likes to run their wedding video backwards so he can watch himself walk out of the church, a free man.

The husband comes home early from work and finds his neighbour in bed with his wife.

"I've looked after you for all these years, you bastard!" he shouted at his neighbour, "I've lent you money, loaned you my car, after all I've done for you ... and stop doing that while I'm talking to you!"

***

Valerie had just found out that her wealthy husband Roy was having an affair with another woman.

"It's not that I don't love you", said Roy. "It's just that this other woman is so passionate. When we make love, she low moans and groans, while you just lay there and don't show any emotion."

Valerie thought about the possibility of losing Roy's fortune, and decided to work on improving their sex life. She bought new perfume and sexy underwear and seduced Roy into bed. When Roy was screwing away, she remembered Roy's mistress's speciality of low moaning while they were having sex.

"Oh Roy, what I day I've had today", moaned Valerie. "First the washing machine broke down, then I was short changed at the supermarket, the bus was late... "

***

What are the three words you don't want to hear while making love?

"Darling, I'm home."

***

Advice for the man who wants excitement in his sex life:

Try "Rodeo Screwing". Mount your wife from behind and whisper, "This is how I do it with your sister", and try to stay on for eight seconds.

***

Fred had been grinding away for thirty minutes.

"What's wrong, why are you taking so long?", his wife demanded.

"I'm trying", said Fred, "but I just can't think of anyone."

***

Their love life was getting a bit boring.

"Let's do something exciting", he said, "Let's do it back to back."

"That sounds great!", she said, "how do we do that?"

"We invite another couple", he replied.

***

Adam was lonely in the garden of Eden so he spoke to God.

"Hey God, how about some company?"

"OK," said God, "I'll send you Woman. She'll be beautiful, charming and intelligent. She'll cook and clean for you and she'll never argue".

"Sounds great!" said Adam "But how much will she cost?"

"An arm and a leg, Adam."

"Gee... what can I get for just a rib?".

***

Two friends were discussing their sex life.

"Our sex life has become boring", said one. "There doesn't seem to be any interest there any more. We don't worry about it much now. In fact, I haven't had a good screw for six months."

"Well", said the other, "it's up to you. You've got to make things interesting. I buy my wife a box of chocolates and a bunch of flowers. We sip a glass of champagne on the rug in front of the fire. Then I rip off her underclothes and screw her right there on the lounge floor. You should try that."

Next time they met, the friend asked, "Did you take my advice?"

"I sure did. Sex is fantastic now, and I just love that bear skin rug on your lounge room floor."

***

Never forget that your wife is a romantic. She still enjoys wine, flowers and chocolate. Let her know that you, too, remember these things, by speaking of them occasionally.

***

How many men does it take to change a toilet roll?

We don't know 'cos it's never happened.

***

"I want a divorce", she told her solicitor.

"On what grounds?"

"Bigamy. He can't have his Kate and Edith too."

***

Ivan looked worried. He was explaining to his friend about his experience after the party the night before.

"I was so pissed", he said, "I can hardly remember a thing. All I know is that I woke up on top of this woman. I didn't know what to do, so I gave her $20, rolled over and went to sleep. When I woke up this morning, I was at home in bed and I realised it was my wife that I'd given the $20 to."

"Well, what's the problem?" said his friend.

"She gave me $10 change", Ivan replied.

***

"Harry - have you ever thought about burying your nose in the newspaper like other men?"

— from *Rude and Politically Incorrect Jokes* by Allan Pease

Dave watched his flat chested wife try on her new bra.

"What do you want a bra for? You've got nothing to put in them", he smirked.

"I don't complain when you buy underpants", she replied.

***

Revenge is what you feel when you seduce your enemy's wife, but sweet revenge is when you find out that she's a lousy lay.

***

George wasn't feeling too good. He felt worn out.

"How's your sex life?" asked the doctor.

"Every Saturday, Sunday, Tuesday and Thursday, never fail", said George.

"Why not cut out Sunday?", suggested the doctor.

"I can't do that. It's the only day I'm home."

**

Why does the bride always smile when she walks down the aisle?

Because she knows she'll never have to give another blow job again.

**

WHAT'S IN A NAME?

The Indian brave asked his father why the people of his tribe had such unusual names like Running Bear, White Eagle, Red Fox and Flying Cloud.

"We Indians name our children after first thing we see after conception. Why do you ask these questions, Broken Rubber?"

***

What do you call a woman who can suck a golf ball up a garden hose?

"Darling."

***

The Liberal Party decided to form a youth group, so they called it the Young Libs.

The Labor Party took up the challenge and started the Young Labs.

What did the Country Party call their youth group?

A young man got onto a bus and took a seat beside a most beautiful redhead.

"Hi", he said as he sat down.

"Hello", she replied, "It's a nice day, isn't it? I saw my psychiatrist today and he said that I had a problem."

"What sort of problem?", asked the young man.

"I can't tell you", replied the beautiful young thing. "I don't even know you."

"Well, sometimes it's good to talk over your problems with a perfect stranger", he replied.

"Well", she said, "my psychiatrist said that I'm a nymphomaniac who only likes to have sex with Jewish cowboys. By the way, my name's Shirley."

"Pleased to meet you, Shirley", replied to young man. "My name's Hopalong Goldberg."

WHITE COLLAR CRIME

"Oh no, it's my husband!", she said to her boyfriend on hearing the front door slam. "Quick, hide in the wardrobe!"

He grabbed his clothes and dashed from the bed to the wardrobe. After a few minutes, another voice said quietly, "It's damn dark in here, isn't it?"

The man, shivering in the nude, said, "Who's there?"

The little voice replied, "Give me $50 and I won't yell out to Dad and tell him who you are."

In no position to argue, he handed over the

money, and at the appropriate time made a quick dash out the window.

The following week, Junior came home with a brand new set of roller blades. His mother queried, "Where did you get the money for those?"

"I had $50", he replied.

"Where did you get that kind of money?", but Junior wasn't telling.

Convinced her son was up to no good, she ordered him to go to Church. "Confession will fix you up, my boy. You'll have to tell the Priest", and she pushed him into the confessional box and shut the door.

"It's damn dark in here", he said out loud.

"Now, don't start that again!", said the Priest.

***

What do you get when you cross a nun with an apple?

A computer that will never go down on you.

***

Three young priests were going to visit a church in Pitt Street. And they were delivering a new chest of drawers. At the railway station, the ticket clerk wore a very low cut blouse and displayed a magnificent pair of tits. The young priests could not take their eyes off them.

"Three pickets to Tit Street", stammered the first, before turning away in embarrassment.

Impatiently, the second priest moved up to the window and asked, "Three tickets to Pitt Street please... and we'd like some room for our breast of drawers."

"I don't know what's wrong with you lot", said the third priest. "Leave this to me" as he took the money and walked up to the counter.

"I will have three tickets to Pitt Street, Miss. And some room for our chest of drawers!", he said firmly, "and if you don't dress more modestly, St Finger will point his Peter at you."

***

The local priest was asked to give some sex education lessons to three young nuns. He dropped his trousers and, pointing to his male appendage, asked, "Do you know what this is?"

"That's your cock", said the first nun.

"You brazen hussy! Go and rinse your mouth out with soap and water!", said the priest.

Fuming, he asked the second nun if she knew what it was.

"That's your prick", she replied.

"Get out of here, you disgusting little tramp! Scrub your mouth out with soap and water."

When he asked the third if she knew what it was, she replied, "I have no idea."

"Oh, you wonderful, innocent child", he said. "This is my penis."

She responded, "You call THAT a penis? A penis is long, thick and black!"

The old lady had purchased a pair of white cockatoos for company. She wanted to name them Joey and Polly but she was unable to identify which was male and which was female, so she enquired at the pet shop.

The pet shop proprietor told her to watch them and she would be able to identify the male when they were mating.

The old lady watched and waited. One day, she heard squawks and saw feathers flying and she was easily able to identify Joey. So that she would always be able to identify him, she put a white band around his neck.

Some time later, the old lady gave an afternoon tea party for the Church. Joey spotted the Vicar and flew onto his shoulder and squawked, "So they've caught you fuckin' round too, eh?"

***

The Parish Priest felt that the Church was not turning out young Priests in the same mould as they did in the past. His new Curate was a really sharp dresser and he'd turned up in his B.M.W. sports car.

The new Curate had only been around for a couple of days when he asked his senior to lend him $30.

"And what would you be wanting that for?", enquired the Father.

"A nookie", replied the Curate.

This puzzled the old Priest. He didn't know what a nookie was, but he handed over the money.

The next day, when the Priest was visiting the convent, he asked the Mother Superior, "What's a nookie?"

"$30", she replied.

***

An American advertising firm was doing research in Italy for an export sex product. A researcher approached an Italian gentleman in a black suit.

"Would you take part in a survey?", asked the researcher.

"Certainly", said the gentleman.

"How many times do you have sex, sir?"

"About six times a year", replied the man.

"What!", said the amazed researcher. "I thought Italians were supposed to be the greatest lovers on earth."

"Well", came the reply, "I'm not doing too badly for a sixty five year old priest without a car."

***

Bishop O'Riordan had just completed an inspection of the prison to check out the conditions. He told the Governor how delighted he was to hear that a social event had been planned that evening.

"What social event?", asked the Governor?

"Well, one of the prisoners wanted to sell me a ticket for the Warden's Ball."

"That's not a dance, Your Grace, that's a raffle."

WILD LIFE

Why does a male elephant have four feet?

Because six inches would never satisfy a female elephant.

***

Why do hippos make love in the water?

How else can you keep a two tonne fanny wet for two hours?

***

Two old ladies were looking at the giraffe in an enclosure at the Zoo. It's arse was at eye level.

"Have a look at its balls!", one said to the other. "I reckon I could squeeze them from here!"

And squeeze them she did.

The giraffe jumped clean out of its enclosure, jumped the Zoo fence and was heading for the horizon.

A zoo keeper came up and asked the startled old ladies what had happened. When they told him, he dropped his trousers and said, "You'd better squeeze mine, 'cos I've got to catch the bastard."

***

A bear and a rabbit were having a crap in the woods.

"Do you have any trouble with shit sticking to your fur?" asked the bear.

"No", replied the rabbit.

So the bear picked up the rabbit and wiped his arse with him.

WHY OH WHY?

Why do men like to have sex with the light on?

It makes it easier for them to remember your name.

***

Did you hear about the girl who went fishing with five men?

She came home with a red snapper.

***

"Why does that guy in the corner attract all the women?" asked a drinker. "He's not handsome, he's not a flashy dresser, he's not a good conversationalist, he just sits there... licking his eyebrows..."

***

Why does Mike Tyson cry after sex?
He's got mace in his eyes.

***

What do you get when you cross a rooster with a jar of peanut butter?
A cock that sticks on the top of your mouth.

XMAS

It was just a couple of weeks before Christmas and the postmaster in the small country town sorted a letter addressed to Santa Claus. He opened it and was touched by its message.

"Dear Santa", it read. "Do you think you could give me $100 to buy a bike? It's not that I want it for myself – it's for my family. My father died last month and my mother has five children and we are very poor. If I had a bike, I would be able to deliver papers so that I could earn money to buy medicine for my little brother".

The postmaster was so touched that he took the letter along to his Rotary meeting and read it aloud to the members. A quick whip-around resulted in $95. The postmaster slipped the $95 into a Rotary envelope, addressed it to the boy and posted it.

The following week the postmaster opened another letter to Santa from the same child. He slipped the envelope into his pocket on his way to Rotary and again, read it aloud at the meeting. It read:

"Dear Santa, Thank you for sending the money for the new bike. Next time you do this sort of thing, be sure not to send it through the Rotary Club as those thieving bastards took $5 commission".

***

Rudolph the Rednosed Reindeer always led the sled team. While Rudolph, the Brown-nosed Reindeer always brought up the rear.

***

More often than not, Rudolph the Brown-nosed Reindeer rides in the sleigh with Santa.

***

Why doesn't Santa have any children?

He only comes once a year - and that's down a chimney.

***

It was Christmas time and the housewife was waiting impatiently at the front gate for the garbage truck. One by one, she took the garbos to the bedroom and made passionate love to them.

Finally, it was the driver's turn, but he was bitterly disappointed when she gave him $20.

"What's this?", he cried.

"For Christmas", she replied. "My husband said, 'give the driver $20 and fuck the rest'."

***

What did Quasimodo give his wife for Christmas?

A wok. He thought it would help her iron his shirts.

***

YES, BUT......

The Captain was on the Bridge and there was a heavy fog. He saw a light in front of his ship. He sent a message. "I have right of way."

An answer came from the light. "No you don't. Please turn 30 degrees to port side."

The Captain was infuriated. "I'm the captain of a naval ship. Give way", he sent back.

The light answered "I'm a mariner. Turn 30 degrees to port."

The Captain became really angry. "I'm the Captain of an aircraft carrier. I will not turn!"

An answer came back. "You'll turn 30 degrees to port side. I'm a lighthouse!"

***

"Sir, I want your daughter for my wife."

"I'm not swapping 'til I see your wife."

***

The middle aged man was suffering from stress and depression.

"Relax!", was the doctor's advice.

"Do you drink alcohol?"

"No", said the patient, "never touch it."

"There's no harm in a few glasses of wine every night", said the doctor. "Even a cigarette. And have sex, at least once a week. From what you've told me, sex is essential."

Two months later, the patient returned to the doctor, saying he felt much better. He enjoyed a couple of glasses of wine and a couple of cigarettes every night.

"And sex. What about sex?", asked the doctor.

"That's a bit difficult. Only once a month", replied the patient. "I'm the parish priest in a small country town."

YES, OFFICER

The middle aged couple were driving along the suburban street when the traffic cop pulled them over. "You were doing 95 in a built up area", said the cop.

"Rubbish!", replied the husband, "I was only doing 60!"

The cop insisted on 95 and the driver was getting very agitated, when his wife leaned over and said, "Don't argue with him, officer. He's always pigheaded when he's had a few drinks."

***

The patrol car pulled over at the scene of the accident, to find a young couple bonking furiously on the side of the road.

"What the hell are you doing!" exclaimed the cop, pulling the girl off the accident victim.

I was giving him mouth to mouth resuscitation", she cried, "when we both got carried away!"

***

The Police Sergeant told the young Constable to clean up the drunks hanging around the local bar.

One drunk walked up to him and asked, "Exchuse me, offisser, could you tell me the time?"

"One o'clock", replied the Policeman, and hit him once on the head with his baton.

"Christ!", said the drunk, "I'm glad I didn't ask you an hour ago!"

***

The patrol car pulled over behind two motor bikes parked in the scrub at the side of the road. Upon investigation, the cop found two men in the bushes, one with his pants down and the other with his finger up his friend's arse.

"What's going on here?", demanded the cop.

"My mate's had too much to drink. I'm trying to make him sick."

"Well, don't put your finger in there... put it down his throat!" said the cop.

"I'm just about to do that."

***

A driver is pulled over by a Police car and the Officer asks him to blow in the breathalyser and is asked to show his licence. Upon examination, the Police Officer says, "You're wearing glasses in your licence photo. Are you long sighted or near sighted?"

"I'm near sighted", said the driver.

"Well, you should be wearing your glasses for driving. I'm issuing you with an on the spot ticket for $100."

"But I have contacts!", protested the driver.

"I don't care who you know", said the Policeman. "I'm still giving you the ticket."

***

Alec had taken his complaint to the Police Ombudsman.

"I have been persecuted," he complained. "This copper pulled me up in my car and walked around it for twenty minutes looking for some fault and he finally booked me because one of my hub caps was missing. I know that's not an offence."

"What did he book you for?", enquired the Ombudsman.

"Exposing my nuts", replied Alec.

YOU CAN BE STIFF

The roadside sign said, "Rest. Revive. Survive. Arrive", so the motorist pulled onto the side of the road and closed his eyes. He had just got off to sleep when a jogger tapped on his window and asked for the time. The motorist told him it was 6 a.m. He was just getting off to sleep when he was awakened by another jogger who asked the time. "It's 6.30", he growled.

This happened three or four more times, so he wrote a sign and stuck it on his window. It read, **"I do not have the time."** He had just got off to sleep and there was another tap on the window. It was another jogger. "It's 7.45." said the jogger.

***

Xavier was asked how he got his black eye.

"I was teaching my girlfriend the La Bamba when her father came in. How was I to know he was stone deaf?"

A burglar had broken into a house, and as he was feeling his way through the darkened room, he heard a voice. "Jesus is watching you!"

The burglar was startled and stood still for a few moments. Then he decided to continue his search for valuables. Once again, he heard the voice, a little louder, "Jesus is still watching you!"

"What's going on?", he thought. He waited a little longer before continuing his search. Again, he heard, "Jesus is watching you!"

The burglar couldn't stand it any longer. He switched on his flashlight, and there, sitting on the perch, was a parrot.

"Was that you talking?", asked the burglar.

"Yes", said the parrot.

"Well, you talk pretty well", said the burglar.

"I've been talking for fifty years", said the parrot.

"You gave me a fright when I came in", said the burglar. "What's your name?"

"Alfred", replied the parrot.

"That's a pretty weird name for a parrot", said the burglar.

"Yeh, but not as weird as 'Jesus' for a rottweiler."

***

Did you hear about the eighty five year old who was acquitted of a charge of rape?

Because the evidence wouldn't stand up in Court.

***

Herbie limped into the club to have a few beers with his mates.

"What's wrong, Herbie? You're looking a bit pale", said one.

"Well", said Herbie, looking a bit embarrassed, "I've been in jail for six months after being charged with rape."

"But, mate! You're eighty five!"

"That's the problem", said Herbie. "I pleaded guilty and I got six months for perjury!"

ZOOS

Little Johnnie was at the zoo with his Mum and Dad. He had never seen an elephant before.

"What's that thing hanging between it's front legs, mum?"

"That's it's trunk."

"And what's that thing hanging between his back legs?'

Embarrassed Mum said, "That's nothing."

Johnnie wasn't happy with this answer and asked his father for confirmation.

"What's that thing hanging between his back legs, Dad?"

"That's his penis", said Dad.

"Mum said it's nothing."

"Yes, but your mother's been spoiled."

***

The female gorilla at the local zoo had become irritable and moody. She was examined by a veterinarian.

"She's in season, and needs a mate." he said.

The zoo manager decided to advertise to get someone to have sex with his gorilla and placed an ad in the newspaper.

"Wanted. A male to have sex with a female gorilla – $10,000."

Next day, Paddy showed up at the zoo.

"I'll make love to the gorilla on three conditions", he said.

1 I don't have to kiss her.
2 If there's a baby, I won't have to pay support.
3 You'll have to give me a couple of weeks to raise the $10,000."

***

Jobs were hard to get but there was a vacancy at the zoo. On arrival, Pat was told that the gorilla had just died and that they wanted him to put on a gorilla suit and pretend to be a gorilla until another one could be found.

Pat began to enjoy his job a great deal. Eating bananas, swinging from branch to branch, entertaining the spectators and laying in the sunshine.

One day, while putting on a performance for a big crowd, he swung a bit too far and landed in the lion enclosure next door. He jumped to his feet when he saw two lions growling fiercely. He ran to the bars, screaming for help. He turned round and faced the lions and one said, "If you don't stop that bloody screaming and shouting, we'll all lose our jobs."

***

COMEDY

Why do Greek men wear gold neckchains?
So they know where to stop shaving.

***

How do you know when you've had a good blow job?
All the sheets are sucked up your arse.

***

If Mama Cass had shared her sandwich with Karen Carpenter they'd both be alive today.

***

What happens when a Jew walks into a wall with a fully erect penis?
He breaks his nose.

391

— from *Rude and Politically Incorrect Jokes* by Allan Pease

Why do black men always have sex on their minds?
Cos they have pubic hair on their heads.

***

What's a Lesbian?
Just another woman trying to do a man's job.

***

How can you avoid AIDS?
Sit tight and keep your mouth shut.

***

Why does a man weigh less after sex?
Because his brain is empty.

***

Two men drive into a carwash. Which one is the Irishman?
The one on the motorbike.

***

Did you hear about the dyslexic agnostic insomniac?
He'd lay awake all night wondering if there really was a dog.

BEFORE MARRIAGE

— from *Rude and Politically Incorrect Jokes* by Allan Pease

Why do women fake orgasm?
Because they think men care.

***

Why don't men fake orgasm?
Cos no man would pull those faces on purpose.

***

A recent survey shows that 36 million American men said that they would never make love to Madonna - again.

***

What does a blonde say after sex?
"So...do you all play for the same team?"

***

What's the difference between a blonde and the Titanic?
Only 880 people went down on the Titanic!

***

The blonde's boyfriend said he wanted to kiss her where it smells, so she drove him to the dump.

What's the difference between getting piles and breaking off an engagement to a blonde?

When the piles clear up you get your ring back.

***

How does a blonde get rid of unwanted pubic hair?

She spits it out.

***

Why do blondes wear blouses with thick shoulder pads?

So that men have somewhere comfortable to rest their knees.

***

What's the difference between a blonde and a fridge?

A fridge doesn't fart when you take your meat out.

***

What does the blonde use for protection during sex?

A bus shelter.

Why is it called Rap music?
Because the "C" fell off at the printer.

***

What's the difference between a used car tyre and one thousand used condoms?
One's a Goodyear and the other's a fucking good year.

***

What does the Starship *Enterprise* have in common with a piece of toilet paper?
Both circle Uranus looking for Klingons.

***

Did you read Salman Rushdie's new book?
It's called, "Hey Buddha, you big fat prick!"

***

If the answer is "Infatuation, prick!' what's the question?
The question is, "How do you want your Dim Sims cooked?"

***

Why don't Government employees look out the window in the morning?
Because they'd have nothing to do after lunch.

— from *Rude and Politically Incorrect Jokes* by Allan Pease

LYN: "If you could sleep with any man, who would it be?"

CHERYL: "I'd sleep with Santa Claus."

LYN: "Santa Claus? He only comes once a year!"

CHERYL: "Yes, but he fills your stocking."

***

Here's a telephone joke: call someone and say "What's got a huge dick (or boobs) and hangs up telephones?" When they say they don't know, hang up the phone.

***

How do we know that Jesus was Jewish?

Because he lived at home until he was 30, he went into his father's business, his mother thought he was divine and he thought she was a virgin.

***

"— from *Rude and Politically Incorrect Jokes* by Allan Pease

Bill went to the doctor complaining of stomach cramps. After diagnosis the doctor told him that he had Terminal Diarrhoea.

"What can you do to help me, doctor?" pleaded Bill.

"Nothing" said the doctor, "it runs in your genes."

***

Jesus stood before the Disciples at the Last Supper and held up a glass of water. "I will take this water and turn it to wine!" he declared.

"No bloody way Mate!" yelled St. John from the other end of the table. "You'll put $20 in the centre like the rest of us!"

***

A man called the King Brothers Chinese Restaurant for some food:

"Hello...King Brothers Restaurant." a man answered.

"Are you Wang-King, the Manager?"

"No...I'm Foo-King, the Chef."

"Sorry...I'll call back when your not busy."

***

MICHAEL: "Hey Carol, if you woke up in the morning with a grass stains on your hands and knees, your knickers around your ankles and a used condom on the bed beside you, would you tell anyone?"

CAROL: " Hell, no!"

MICHAEL: "Then how about a picnic tomorrow?"

Ben applied for a job as bartender at the local hotel. The owner had heard that Ben had been fired from his last hotel job because he was always late, money was often missing from the till and it was rumoured that he was gay.

"I'll give you a chance" said the new employer "but if there's any money missing or you're late you will be fired immediately. Now give me a kiss and get to work."

***

Justin and Melissa were walking across a bridge over a small country stream.

"I'm dying to have a pee" she said, "but there's no toilets."

"Don't worry" said Justin "just stick your arse over the bridge and I'll hold onto your hands."

She pulled up her skirt and sat with her arse over the edge.

"My God" she screamed "there's a man in a canoe down there!"

Justin peered over the edge. "No, that's just a reflection."

***

In a child custody case the judge took the unprecedented step of allowing the child to decide his own future. "Do you want to live with your father?" he asked.

"No" replied the child "he beats me all the time".

"Well do you want to live with your mother?"

"No" said the child "she beats me too."

"Well, who do you want to live with?" asked the judge.

"I want to live with the Australian Cricket Team" replied the child, "they never beat anyone."

***

It was Bill's first day in the prison lunchroom. A guy at the next table stood up and shouted "Number 39!" Everyone burst into laughter. A guy at the table behind him stood up and shouted "Number 324!" Again they cheered clapped. A guy on Bill's table stood up and called out "Number 91!" and everyone giggled and clapped again.

"What's going on here?" Bill enquired of one of the other inmates.

"It's joke-telling time on Tuesdays," he said, "but we've only got one joke book in the prison library and we've all read it, so rather than making us hear the jokes over and over we just call out the numbers. If everyone likes the number they clap or laugh."

Another prisoner stood up and called "Number 184!" but no-one laughed. "Number 628!" he yelled, but still no-one laughed. "Number 474!" he mumbled. The prisoners began to shout at him and told him to sit down.

"What happened to him?" asked Bill.

"Well" said the fellow inmate "some people can tell 'em and some people can't."

***

"just when you thought you were in front."

— from *Rude and Politically Incorrect Jokes* by Allan Pease

Luigi was given the job of painting the ceiling of the local Catholic church. He had been laying on his back on the scaffolding for two weeks and it was becoming boring. One morning he saw a big fat Italian woman enter the church dressed in black. She knelt at the statue of Virgin Mary and began to pray. Luigi decided he'd have a bit of fun. "Hey you down there," he yelled, "this is Jesus Christ talking to you in person!"

The Italian woman stopped praying and looked up to the ceiling where the voice came from. "Hey you upa there!" she screamed, "shuddupa you face - I'ma speaka to your Mudda!"

***

Luigi heard that if you speak to the Virgin Mary you can get anything you want in life. He decided he wanted a new bike, so he wrote a letter to Virgin Mary promising to say his prayers everyday. But no bike arrived. So he wrote a second letter and asked Virgin Mary again for the bike. He promised not only to say his prayers but to take the garbage out twice a week. But still no bike appeared. He wrote a third letter asking again. This time promised he would take the garbage out, do his homework and help little old ladies across the road. But still no bike appeared. He decided to write a final letter. He sat at his fathers desk, took the cross of Jesus off the wall put it in a drawer, locked it with the key and wrote the following letter -"Dear Virgin Mary, if you every want to see your son again..."

What's the difference between cheating on your wife and cheating on the taxman?

If you get caught, the taxman will still want to screw you.

***

Bill was seventy five years old when he decided to take up walking. He began by walking five kilometres every day and soon he was in such great health that he had the body of a fifty year old. He met an old friend who said "Bill I didn't even recognise - you look fantastic". This encouraged Bill to join a health club, so he started walking five kilometres a day and working out at the gym 4 days a week. Soon he had the body of a 40 year old. One day at the gym he met an old girlfriend who said "Bill you look fantastic! I didn't even recognise you!" He was so inspired by this he joined a singles club and began disco dancing 3 nights a week plus working out at the gym plus walking five kilometres a day. Six months later he has the body of a thirty year old. He fell in love with a twenty one year old woman and proposed marriage. She accepted. In their honeymoon suite on the eleventh floor of the Hilton Hotel he said "Darling this is the happiest day of my life, I'm going to jog across to the bottle shop and buy us a bottle of Moet champagne." He jogged eleven floors down the hotel staircase, straight across the road and was hit by a Mac truck. He was killed instantly and went straight to Heaven. On arrival at the Pearly gates he approached God

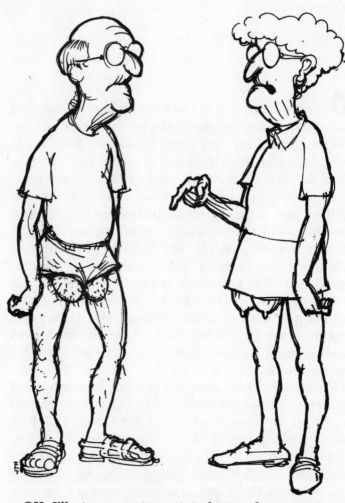

OK. I'll stop wearing mini skirts when you stop wearing those stupid shorts!!!.

— from *Rude and Politically Incorrect Jokes* by Allan Pease

and said "Why did you do it God? Why did you take me now? It was the happiest day of my life!" God looked at him at said "Bill, is that you? I didn't even recognise you! You look fantastic!"

***

Terry joined the army and was terrified about having to make his first parachute jump. On the day of the jump he told his wife that he couldn't do it but she reassured him and sent him off for the jump. On his return she asked him how it went.

"Dreadful!" he said. "When the plane got to 10,000 feet, we lined up for the jump and when it got to my turn I just froze in the doorway!"

"So what happened?" she pressed.

"The Sergeant came up behind me pulled out his huge dick and said that if I didn't jump he'd stick it right up my arse!" said the embarrassed husband.

"Well did you jump?" she asked

"Yes, - a little bit at first..."

Stress Diet

This diet is designed to help you cope with daily stress

Breakfast
Half grapefruit

1 slice wholemeal
  toast
300ml skim milk
Decaffeinated coffee

Lunch
80gm grilled chicken
  breasts
1 serve steamed
  carrots
1 herb tea
1 Tim-Tam

Afternoon Tea
Rest of Tim-Tams
2 pints of ice-cream
1 jar fudge sauce
nuts, cherries,
whipped cream

Dinner
2 loaves garlic bread
1 large supreme
  pizza
6 glasses of wine
3 Milky Ways

Evening Snack While Watching TV
Entire frozen cheesecake direct from freezer

Rules For This Diet

1. If you eat something and no-one sees you eat it, it has no calories

2. If you drink a diet soft drink when eating chocolate, the diet soft drink cancels out any calories in the chocolate

3. When eating with someone else, your calories don't count if you eat less than they do

4. Calories in food used for medicinal purposes **NEVER** count e.g., hot chocolate, brandy, etc.

5. Movie-related foods do not add calories because they are part of the entire entertainment package. e.g. Jaffas. buttered popcorn, Minties etc.

6. Biscuit pieces contain no calories because the process of breakage causes calorie leakage.

7. Things licked off knives and spoons have no calories if you are in the process of preparing something because calories only become part of the complete meal when it is cooked, e.g. ice cream off a spoon, icing off a knife etc.

8. Foods that have the same colour have the same number of calories. Examples are spinach and pistachio ice cream, mushrooms and white chocolate.

NOTE: The harmful effects of caffeine, fat and sugar in hot chocolate drinks or cappuccinos will be neutralised when you drink them with skim milk.

A mean-looking guy takes a seat at the bar. He's 6' 6", has tattoos all over, earrings in his nose and a scarred face. He turns to the guys sitting on his left and says "All the guys on this side of the bar are motherfuckers! Anyone got a problem with that?"

He turns to his right and yells "All the guys on this side of the bar are cocksuckers! Anyone got a problem with that?"

No-one wants to mess with this guy so they ignore him. A man on the left side of the bar walks towards the tough guy.

"What's your problem?" demands the tough guy.

"I'm on the wrong side of the bar."

***

How do you confuse an Archeologist?

Give him a tampon and ask which period its from.

***

What do men say when they play hide-and-seek or have sex?
Coming, ready or not.

***

How many animals can you fit into a pair of pantyhose?

Ten little piggies, two calves, one ass, one pussy, an unknown number of hares, and one dead fish no one can find.

God spoke to Adam. "Adam I have good news and bad news. The good news is that I will give you two organs to give you great power and pleasure. I will give you a brain to enable you to think and to control the world. And I will give you a penis to give great pleasure in lovemaking."

"Sounds great God!" said Adam. "But what's the bad news?"

"You only have enough blood to work one at a time."

***

A little girl was telling Santa what she wanted for Christmas and as she listed one thing after another she said, "...and I want a G.I. Joe and Barbie, and..."

"But Honey," Santa interrupted, "you mean you want a Ken and Barbie?"

"No, Santa!" she said. "I want a G.I. Joe and Barbie!"

"But Barbie comes with Ken!" Santa insisted.

"No!" the little girl exclaimed. "Barbie comes with G.I. Joe! She only fakes it with Ken."

***

An eskimo was riding his snowmobile when it broke down. He got off, and noticed a gas station nearby. He went over, got the mechanic and brought him over to the machine. The mechanic bent down, fiddled with the motor, looked back up and said to the eskimo, " I think you just blew a seal."

"No," said the eskimo, "that's just frost on my moustache."

Not all bosses are arseholes!

— from *Rude and Politically Incorrect Jokes* by Allan Pease

WHO'S THE BOSS?

When God made man, all the parts of the body argued over who would be boss. The brain explained that since he controlled all the parts of the body, he should be boss. The legs argued that since they took the man wherever he wanted to go, they should be boss.

The stomach countered with the explanation that since he digested all the food, he should be boss. The eyes said that without them, man would be helpless, so they should be boss. Then the asshole applied for the job. The other parts of the body laughed so hard that the asshole became mad and closed up. After a few days the brain went foggy, the legs got wobbly, the stomach got ill, the eyes got crossed and unable to see. They all conceded and made the asshole boss. This proves that you don't have to be a brain to be boss..... just an asshole.

***

TASTELESS JOKES

How does a Tasmanian know that his sister has her period?

His brother's dick tastes funny.

413

What's the similarity with a mobile telephone and a clitoris?

Both turn on with the touch of a finger and every cunt's got one.

***

Why is it called a 'papsmear'?

Because no woman would have one if it was called a cuntscrape.

***

If the bird of peace is the dove then then the bird of true love is the swallow.

***

A woman went to the Doctor with an unusual problem.

"Doctor, I've got three breasts." she declared.

"Please undress." said the doctor.

"Doctor, I'm worried that when you see my problem you'll laugh." she said nervously.

"Don't be concerned Miss," said the Doctor, "I'm a medical man and I'm fully trained to handle such problems."

She took off her blouse revealing her three breasts and the Doctor burst into uncontrollable laughter. So she lifted her arm and pissed in his face.

— from *Rude and Politically Incorrect Jokes* by Allan Pease

What's the definition of Eternity?

It's the time between when you come and she goes.

***

What's the difference between an Irishman and a trampoline?

You take your boots off before you jump on a trampoline.

***

What's the difference between BSE and PMT?

One is Mad Cow's Disease and the other is an agricultural infection.

***

Ray, the local Stationmaster, was having a beer at the pub with his mates. "I had an incredible experience last night," he said. "I saw something lying on the tracks so I went to investigate. I found a woman who had tied herself to the tracks!"

"So what did you do?" asked his mates.

"I untied her and took her back to my place and made a strong cup of coffee. Then I poured a couple of drinks, put on some soft music, one thing led to another, and I finished up having the wildest night of sex I've ever had!" he bragged.

"Was she good looking?" asked a drinker.

"Dunno" said Ray, "I couldn't find her head.

Turn this page upside down and cover her face with your hand.

— from *Rude and Politically Incorrect Jokes* by Allan Pease

MALE CHAUVINIST JOKES

Why did God give men penises?
So they'd have at least one way to stop a woman talking.

***

What's the difference between a paycheque and your dick?
You don't have to beg a woman to blow your pay cheque.

***

What's it called when a woman is paralysed from the waist down?
Marriage.

***

What are the small bumps around a woman's nipples?
It's Brail for "suck here".

***

What's the difference between a woman with PMS and a Rottweiler?
Lipstick.

***

How do you fuck a fat chick?
  Have a wank in your hand then throw it at her.

***

If your wife keeps coming out of the kitchen to nag you, what have you done wrong?
  Made her chain too long.

***

Why are hurricanes normally named after women?
  When they come they're wild and wet, but when the go they take your house and car.

***

Why did the army send so many women with PMS to the Gulf war?
  They fought like animals and retained water for four days.

***

Why is a fat woman like a skateboard?
  They're both fun to ride, but you wouldn't want your friends to see you on either.

***

What's the best thing about a blow job?
  Seven minutes silence.

"It's not the constant sex I object to...it's the bloody accent!"

— from *Rude and Politically Incorrect Jokes* by Allan Pease

ANIMALS

A man takes his Rottweiler to the vet and says, "My dog's cross-eyed, is there anything you can do for him?

"Well," says the vet, "let's have a look at him." He picks the dog up and examines his eyes, then checks his teeth. Finally, he says,

"I'm going to have to put him down."

"What? Because he's cross-eyed?"

"No, because he's really heavy."

***

A man is browsing in a pet shop and sees a parrot sitting on a little perch. It doesn't have any feet or legs. The guy says aloud, "I wonder what happened to this parrot?" The parrot says, "I was born this way. I'm a phyically disadvantaged parrot."

"Holy cow," the guy replies, "You actually understood me and answered me!"

"I got every word," says the parrot. "I happen to be a highly intelligent, thoroughly educated bird."

The guy asks, "Then answer this – how do you hang onto your perch without any feet?"

"Well," the parrot says, "this is very embarrassing but since you asked, I wrap my weenie around this wooden bar like a little hook. You can't see it because of my feathers."

"Wow," says the guy. "You really can understand and speak English, can't you?"

"Actually, I speak both Spanish and English, and I can converse with reasonable competence on almost any topic: politics, religion, sports, physics, philosophy. I'm especially good at ornithology. You really ought to buy me. I'd be a great companion."

The guy looks at the $500 price tag. "Sorry, but I just can't afford that."

"Pssssssst," says the parrot, "I'm defective, so the truth is, nobody wants me 'cause I don't have any feet. You can probably get me for $50, just make the guy an offer!" The guy offers $50 and walks out with the parrot. Weeks go by. The parrot is sensational. He has a great sense of humour, he's interesting, he's a great pal, he understands everything, he sympathizes, and he's insightful. The guy is delighted.

One day the guy comes home from work and the parrot motions him over with one wing. "I don't know if I should tell you this or not, but it's about your wife and the postman."

"What are you talking about?" asks the guy.

"When the postman delivered the mail today, your wife greeted him at the door in a sheer black nightie and kissed him passionately."

"What?" the guy asks incredulously. "Then what happened?"

"Well, then the postman came into the house and lifted up her nightie and began carressing her all over," reported the parrot.

"Oh no! Then what?"

"Then he got down on his knees and began to kiss her all over, starting with her breasts and slowly going down…"

"Well," demands the frantic guy, "Then what happened?"

"Damned if I know. I got a hard-on and fell off my perch!"

What is a Cat?

1. Cats do what they want.
2. They rarely listen to you.
3. They're totally unpredictable.
4. When you want to play, they want to be alone.
5. When you want to be alone, they want to play.
6. They expect you to cater to their every whim.
7. They're moody.
8. They leave hair everywhere.

Conclusion: Cats are tiny women in little fur coats.

***

What is a Dog?

1. Dogs spend all day sprawled on the most comfortable piece of furniture in the house.
2. They can hear a package of food opening half a block away, but don't hear you when you're in the same room.
3. They can look dumb and loveable all at the same time.
4. They growl when they are not happy.
5. When you want to play, they want to be alone.
6. When you want to be alone, they want to play.
7. They leave their toys everywhere.
8. They do disgusting things with their mouths and then try to give you a kiss.
9. They go right for your crotch as soon as they meet you.

Conclusion: Dogs are tiny men in little fur coats.

A farmer went to the market to buy a rooster to service his 300 hens. He found a likely looking bird and asked the price.

"$200", said the vendor.

"That's a mighty high price for a rooster" replied the farmer.

"This rooster's name is Shagger. He's the greatest stud you'll ever find. He'll fix up all your hens in one day".

The farmer took Shagger home and, sure enough, it screwed all 300 hens before lunch. Then he screwed 4 ducks, 6 geese and 10 turkeys.

Later that day, the farmer saw a dozen vultures circling overhead and saw Shagger lying dead on the ground.

"Why did you have to kill yourself on the first day, Shagger?" cried the farmer.

"Quiet!" whispered Shagger, "they're about to land!"

***

One day a farmer's donkey fell into a well. The animal cried piteously for hours as the farmer tried to figure out what to do.

Finally he decided the animal was old and the well needed to be covered up anyway. It just wasn't worth it to retrieve the donkey.

He invited all his neighbors to come over and help him. They all grabbed a shovel and began to shovel dirt into the well. At first, the donkey realised what was happening and cried horribly. Then, to everyone's amazement, he quietened down.

A few shovel loads later, the farmer finally looked into the well and was astonished at what he saw. With every shovel of dirt that hit his back, the donkey was doing something amazing. He would shake it off and take a step up. As the farmer's neighbors continued to shovel dirt on top of the animal, he would shake it off and take a step up. Pretty soon, everyone was amazed as the donkey stepped up over the edge of the well and kicked the crap out of the farmer who tried burying him.

The Lesson
Life is going to heap all kinds of crap on you. The trick is to shake it off and take a step up. Each of our troubles is a stepping stone.

We can get out of the deepest holes by never giving up! Shake off the crap and take a step up!

The Moral
When you try to cover your ass, it always comes back to get you.

**

A shepherd was looking after his sheep on the side of a deserted road.

Suddenly a new Porsche screeched to a halt. The driver, a young man dressed in an Armani suit, Ray Bans, Tag Heuer watch, white Cerutti shoes and tailor-made mauve shirt with a Boss tie got out and said to the shepherd, "If I can guess how many sheep you have, can I keep one?"

The shepherd looked at the large flock of sheep and said, "Okay'.

The young man connected his laptop to his mobile phone, entered the NASA website, scanned the field using his GPS, opened a database linked to 60 Excel tables filled with logarithms and pivot tables, then printed out a 150 page report on his high tech mini printer. He studied the reports and said, "You have 1586 sheep". Shocked, the shepherd replied, "You're right! You can have the pick of my flock."

The young man packed away his equipment, looked at the flock and put one into the boot of the Porsche. As he was about to leave, the shepherd said, "If I can guess what your profession is, will you return the animal to me?"

The young man thought for a minute and said, "Okay'".

The shepherd said, "You are a Management Consultant".

Amazed, the young man said, "Correct, but how did you know?"

The shepherd answered, "Simple. First, you came here without being invited. Second, you charge me a fee for something I already knew. Third, you don't understand anything about my business. Now, can I have my dog back?"

***

Once upon a time, in a nice little forest glen, there lived an orphaned bunny and an orphaned snake. By a surprising coincidence, both were blind from birth.

One day, the bunny was hopping through the forest, and the snake was slithering through the forest, when the bunny tripped over the snake and fell down. This knocked the snake about quite a bit.

'Oh, my,' said the bunny, 'I'm terribly sorry. I didn't mean to hurt you. I've been blind since birth, so I can't see where I'm going. In fact, since I'm also an orphan, I don't even know what I am.'

'It's quite OK,' replied the snake. 'Actually, my story is much the same as yours. I, too, have been blind since birth, and also never knew my mother. Tell you what, maybe I could slither all over you, and work out what you are, so at least you'll know.'

'Oh, that would be wonderful' replied the bunny.

So the snake slithered all over the bunny, and said, 'Well, you're covered with soft fur; you have really long ears; your nose twitches; and you have a soft cotton tail. I'd say that you must be a bunny rabbit.'

'Oh, thank you! Thank you,' cried the bunny, in obvious excitement. 'Maybe I could feel you all over with my paw, and help you the same way that you've helped me', the bunny suggested to the snake.

So the bunny felt the snake all over, and re-marked, 'Well, you're smooth and slippery, and you have a forked tongue, no backbone and no balls. You must be a lawyer'.

***

Management Lesson Number One

A crow was sitting atop a ladder, doing nothing all day. A small rabbit saw the crow, and asked him, "Can I also sit like you and do nothing all day long?"

The crow answered: "Sure, why not." So the rabbit sat on the ground below the crow, and rested. All of a sudden, a fox appeared, jumped on the rabbit and ate it.

Moral

If you want to sit around all day doing nothing, you must be sitting high up the ladder.

***

Management Lesson Number Two

A turkey was chatting with a bull. "I would love to be able to get to the top of that tree" sighed the turkey, "but I haven't got the energy."

"Well, why don't you nibble on some of my droppings?" replied the bull. "They're packed with nutrients."

The turkey pecked at a lump of dung and found that it actually gave him enough strength to reach the lowest branch of the tree. The next day, after eating some more dung, he reached the second branch. Finally after a fourth night, there he was proudly perched at the top of the tree. Soon he was promptly spotted by a farmer, who shot the turkey out of the tree.

Moral

Bullshit might get you to the top, but it won't keep you there.

***

Management Lesson Number Three

A little bird was flying North for the winter. It was so cold the bird froze and fell to the ground in a large field. While it was lying there, a cow came by and dropped some dung on it. As the frozen bird lay there in the pile of cow dung, it began to realise how warm it was. The dung was actually thawing him out! He lay there all warm and happy, and soon began to sing for joy. A passing cat heard the bird singing and came to investigate. Following the sound, the cat discovered the bird under the pile of cow dung, and promptly dug him out and ate him.

Moral
1. Not everyone who shits on you is your enemy.
2. Not everyone who gets you out of shit is your friend.
3. And when you're in deep shit, and happy, keep your mouth shut!

***

A man goes on a safari in Africa and takes his faithful pet dog along for company. One day the dog starts chasing butterflies and before long discovers that he is lost. Wandering about he notices a leopard heading rapidly in his direction with the obvious intention of having lunch. The dog thinks, "Ok Fuck, I'm in deep shit now." (He's an Irish setter)... Then he notices some bones on the ground close by, and immediately settles down to chew on the bones with his back to the approaching cat. Just as the leopard is about to leap, the dog exclaims loudly, "That was one delicious leopard. I wonder if there are any more around here..." Hearing this, the leopard halts his attack in mid stride, as a look of terror comes over him, and slinks away into the trees. "Whew", says the leopard. "That was close. That dog nearly had me."

Meanwhile, a monkey who has been watching the whole scene from a nearby tree, figures he can put this knowledge to good use and trade it for protection from the leopard.

But the dog sees the monkey heading after the leopard with great speed, and figures that something must be up. The monkey soon catches up with the leopard, spills the beans and strikes a deal for himself with the leopard. The leopard is furious at being made a fool of and says, "Here monkey, hop on my back and see what's going to happen to that conniving canine bitch." The dog sees the leopard coming with the monkey on his back, and thinks, "What the hell am I going to do now?" But instead of running, the dog sits down with his back to his attackers pretending he hasn't seen them yet. And just when they get close enough to hear, the dog says, "Where's that fucking monkey. I just can never trust him. I sent him off half an hour ago to bring me another leopard, and he's still not back!!"

***

A little rabbit is happily running through the forest when he stumbles upon a giraffe rolling a joint. The rabbit looks at her and says, "Giraffe my friend, why do you do this? Come with me running through the forest, you'll see, you'll feel so much better!"

The giraffe looks at him, looks at the joint, tosses it and goes off running with the rabbit. Then they come across an elephant doing coke, so the rabbit again says, "Elephant my friend, why do you do this? Think about your health. Come running with us through the pretty forest, and you'll see, you'll feel so good!"

The elephant looks at them, looks at his razor, mirror and all, then tosses them away and starts running with the rabbit and giraffe. The three animals then come across a lion about to shoot up and the rabbit again says, "Lion my friend, why do you do this? Think about your health! Come running with us through the sunny forest, you will feel so good!"

The lion looks at him, puts down his needle, and starts to beat the shit out of the rabbit. As the giraffe and elephant watch in horror, they look at him and ask, "Lion, why did you do this?... He was merely trying to help us all!"

The lion answers, "That little prick! He makes me run around the forest like an idiot every time he's on ecstasy!"

***

A gorilla is walking through the jungle. He parts the bushes by the watering hole and sees a lion taking a drink of water with his butt sticking up in the air. So the gorilla thinks to himself: "Wouldn't it be fun if I snuck up behind the 'King of the jungle' and slipped him the old sausage?"

So the gorilla sneaks up behind the lion, grabs him by the hips, and starts pumping him in the butt as hard as he can. Then he pulls out and runs away, laughing his ass off.

The lion, however, doesn't think it's so funny. He lets out a mighty roar and takes off after the gorilla. But gorilla can't run very fast and the lion is catching up with him, so he ducks into a camp-site, pulls some safari duds off the clothesline, puts them on, picks up a newspaper and sits down by the fire, holding the paper up to hide his face.

Just then, the lion comes busting through the jungle. Hey you!" he says, "Did you just see a big gorilla come running through here?"

The gorilla starts shaking behind the paper. "Um...d-do you mean the one that just s-screwed you in the a-a-ass?" The lion sits up with a start and says: "Jeez! It's in the fucking newspapers already?"

BLONDES

A blonde is involved in a serious car crash; there's blood everywhere. The paramedics arrive and drag her out of the car till she's lying flat out on the floor.

Medic: 'OK, I'm going to check if you're concussed.'

Blonde: 'OK...'

Medic: 'How many fingers am I putting up?'

Blonde: 'Oh my god... I'm paralysed from the waist down!'

A blonde nurse walks into a bank. Preparing to endorse a cheque, she pulls a rectal thermometer out of her pocket and tries to write with it. She looks up at the teller, pauses for a moment realising her mistake, and says, "Well, that's great... just great...some asshole's got my pen."

***

A blind man enters a ladies bar by mistake. He finds his way to a barstool and orders a drink. After sitting there for a while, he yells to the bartender, "Hey, you wanna hear a blonde joke?" The bar immediately falls quiet. In a very deep, husky voice, the woman next to him says, "Before you tell that joke, sir, I think it is just fair – given that you are blind – you should know five things; The bartender is a blonde girl, the bouncer is a blonde girl, I'm a 6 foot tall, 220lb. blonde woman with a black belt in karate. The woman sitting next to me is blonde and a professional weight lifter. The lady to your right is a blonde and is a professional wrestler. Now think about it seriously, Mister. Do you still wanna tell that joke?" The blind man thinks for a second, shakes his head, and declares, "Nah, not if I'm gonna have to explain it five times..."

***

Two guys are moving about in K-Mart when their shopping trolleys collide. One says to the other, "Excuse me, but I'm looking for my wife."

The other answers... "What a coincidence, so am I and I'm getting a little desperate."

"Well, maybe I can help you. What does your wife look like?"

"She's tall, with long blonde hair, long legs, firm boobs, and a tight arse. What's your wife look like?"

"Never mind, let's just look for yours."

***

A blonde calls her boyfriend and says "Please come over here and help me, I have a killer jigsaw puzzle, and I can't figure out how to get it started."

Her boyfriend asks, "What is it supposed to be when it's finished?"

"According to the picture on the box, it's a tiger..."

Her boyfriend decides to go over and help with the puzzle. She lets him in and shows him where she has the puzzle spread all over the table. He studies the pieces for a moment, then looks at the box, then turns to her and says, "First of all, no matter what we do, we're not going to be able to assemble these pieces into anything resembling a tiger. Second, I'd advise you to relax. Let's have a cup of coffee, then put all these Frosties back in the box."

***

It was Postman Pat's last day on the job after 35 years of carrying the mail through all kinds of weather to the same neighborhood. When he arrived at the first house on his route, he was greeted by the whole family there, who all hugged and congratulated him and sent him on his way with a gift cheque for $500. At the second house they presented him fine Cuban cigars in an 18-carat gold box. The folks at the third house handed him a case of 30-year old Scotch whisky. At the fourth house he was met at the door by a dumb blonde in her see-through lingerie. She took him by the arm and led him upstairs to the bedroom where she blew his mind with the most passionate, dirtiest shag he had ever experienced.

When he had had enough they went downstairs, where the dumb blonde fixed him a giant breakfast: eggs, tomatoes, bacon, sausage, mushrooms, toast and freshly-squeezed orange juice. When he was truly satisfied she poured him a cup of steaming coffee. As she was pouring, he noticed a $50 note sticking out from under the cup's bottom edge. "All this was just too wonderful for words," he said, "but what's the $50 for?" "Well," said the dumb blonde, "last night, I told my husband that today would be your last day, and that we should do something special for you. I asked him what to give you. He said, 'Fuck him! Give him fifty dollars.'"

She smiled prettily. "The breakfast was my idea..."

***

The blonde asked her doctor how latex gloves were made.

"Well" said the doctor, "there is a big tank of latex in China and workers put their hands in it. When the latex is dry, they peel the latex glove off."

"Really!" replied the blonde, "Do they make condoms the same way?"

***

A blonde read in a magazine that 1 in 5 people in the world are Chinese. "There are five people in my family" she said to herself. "I wonder which one of them it is? It could be my mum or my dad... or maybe my older brother Colin, or my younger brother Ho-Chi-Lim...but I'm pretty sure it's Colin."

***

A police officer stops a blonde for speeding and asks her very nicely if he could see her licence. She replies in a huff, "I wish you guys would get your act together. Just yesterday you take away my licence and then today you expect me to show it to you!"

***

A blonde pushes her BMW into a gas station. She tells the mechanic it died. After he works on it for a few minutes, it is idling smoothly. She says, "What's the story?"

He replies, "Just crap in the carburettor."

She asks, "How often do I have to do that?"

A blonde was driving down the M1 when her car phone rang. It was her boyfriend, urgently warning her, "Treacle, I just heard on the news that there's a car going the wrong way on the M1. Please be careful!"

"It's not just one car!" said the blonde, "There are hundreds of them!"

***

What do you call a smart blonde?
A golden retriever.

***

A blonde was having financial troubles so she decided to kidnap a child and demand ransom. She went to a local park, grabbed a little boy, took him behind a tree and wrote this note: "I have kidnapped your child. Leave $10,000 in a plain brown paper bag behind the big oak tree in the park tomorrow at 7am, signed, "The Blonde". She pinned the note inside the little boy's jacket and told him to go straight home.

The next morning, she returned to the park to find the $10,000 in a brown bag behind the big oak tree, just as she had instructed. Inside the bag was the following note... "Here is your money. I cannot believe that one blonde would do this to another!"

***

What did the blonde say when she found out she was pregnant? "Are you sure it's mine?"

A brunette, redhead and blonde were at a special magic Amusement Park. One of the rides was a long slide at the end of which was a magic pool. On the way down the slide, all the rider had to do was shout out his or her favourite drink, and hey-presto they would land in a pool full of this drink. So off they went. The brunette went first. On her way down she shouted out "Vodka" at the top of her voice, and sure enough she landed in a pool of the finest vodka. After filling several bottles and glasses she went home, happy but a little unsteady.

Next the redhead – who loved 10 year old malt – went flying down shouting "Whisky", and into a pool of whisky she fell. She had to be dragged away practically unconscious.

Now it was the blonde's turn. She was very excited, and on her way down she was enjoying the ride so much she shouted – "Weeeeeee..."

***

A policeman pulls over a swerving car on a lonely back road and approaches the blonde driver. "Ma'am," he says, "is there a reason why you're weaving all over the road?"

The woman replies: "Oh officer, thank goodness you're here! I almost had an accident. I looked up and there was a tree right in front of me. I swerved to the left and there was another tree in front of me. I swerved to the right and there was another tree in front of me!"

"Ma'am," the officer replies, tapping the blonde's windshield, "that's your air freshener."

A man walks into a bar and sees a beautiful blonde sitting alone at a table. After a few drinks, he decides to approach her. Soon they are chatting like old friends. Finally, the man asks why someone as stunning as her is sitting alone.

"Well…" she says, "every man I go out with thinks I'm too kinky."

The man sees an opportunity and mentions that he, too, likes to get kinky. So she invites him to her place. When they arrive, she excuses herself 'to slip into something more comfortable.' Ten minutes later, she walks back into the room wearing crotchless rubber panties, carrying a riding crop and a tube of KY jelly. To her dismay, the man is pulling up his pants and getting ready to leave.

"Where do you think you're going?" she asks in dismay. "I thought that we were going to get kinky!"

"Hey lady," the man replies "I screwed your dog, I crapped in your purse… I'm outta here!"

***

A blonde walks into a pharmacy and asks the assistant for some rectum deodorant. The pharmacist, a little bemused, explains to the woman that they don't sell rectum deodorant, and never have.

Unfazed, the blonde assures the pharmacist that she has been buying the stuff from this store on a regular basis and would like some more.

"I'm sorry," says the pharmacist, "we don't have any."

"But, I always buy it here," says the blonde.

"Do you have the container that it came in?" asks the pharmacist.

"Yes," said the blonde, "I'll go home and get it."

She returns with the container and hands it to the pharmacist who looks at it and says to her, "This is just a normal stick of underarm deodorant."

Annoyed, the blonde snatches the container back and reads out loud from the container... "TO APPLY, PUSH UP BOTTOM."

***

A blonde is overweight, so her doctor puts her on a diet. "I want you to eat regularly for two days, then skip a day, and repeat this procedure for two weeks. The next time I see you, you'll have lost at least five pounds."

When the blonde returns, she's lost nearly 20 pounds. "That's amazing!" the doctor says. "Did you follow my instructions?" The blonde nods. "I'll tell you, though, I thought I was going to drop dead that third day. "From hunger, you mean?" asks the doctor. "No, from all that skipping."

***

A Russian, an American, and a Blonde were talking one day.

The Russian said, "We were the first in space!"

The American said, "We were the first on the moon!"

The Blonde said, "So what, we're going to be the first on the sun!"

The Russian and the American looked at each other and shook their heads. "You can't land on the sun, you idiot! You'll burn up!" said the Russian.

The Blonde replied, "We're not stupid, you know. We're going at night!"

***

A blonde was playing Trivial Pursuit one night. It was her turn. She rolled the dice and she landed on 'Science & Nature.' Her question was, "If you are in a vacuum and someone calls your name, can you hear it?" She thought for a time and then asked, "Is it on or off?"

***

A blonde is walking down the street with her blouse open and her right breast hanging out. A policeman approaches her and says, "Ma'am, are you aware that I could cite you for indecent exposure?"

"Why, officer?"

"Because your breast is hanging out."

She looks down and says, "Oh God!... I left the baby on the bus again!"

***

A bartender is sitting behind the bar on a typical day, when the door bursts open and in come four exuberant blondes. They come up to the bar, order five bottles of champagne and ten glasses, take their order over and sit down at a large table. The corks are popped, the glasses are filled and they begin toasting and chanting, "51 days, 51 days, 51 days!"

Soon, three more blondes arrive, take up their drinks and the chanting grows. "51 days, 51 days, 51 days!"

Two more blondes show up and soon their voices are joined in raising the roof. "51 days, 51 days, 51 days!" Finally, the tenth blonde comes in with a picture under her arm.

She walks over to the table, sets the picture in the middle and the table erupts. Up jump the others, they begin dancing around the table, exchanging high-fives, still chanting, "51 days, 51 days, 51 days!" The bartender can't contain his curiosity any longer, so he walks over to the table. There in the center is a beautifully framed child's puzzle of the Cookie Monster.

When the frenzy dies down a little bit, the bartender asks one of the blondes, "What's all the chanting and celebration about?"

The blonde who brought in the picture says, "Everyone thinks that blondes are dumb and they make fun of us. So, we decided to set the record straight. Ten of us got together, bought that puzzle and put it together. The side of the box said 2–4 years, but we put it together in 51 days!"

BLOW JOBS

One afternoon a little girl returned from school, and announced that her friend had told her where babies come from. Amused, her mother replied:

"Really, sweetie, why don't you tell me all about it?"

The little girl explained, "Well... OK... the Mummy and Daddy take off all of their clothes, and the Daddy's thingee sort of stands up, and then Mummy puts it in her mouth, and then it sort of explodes, and that's how you get babies."

Her mum shook her head, leaned over to meet her eye to eye and said, "Oh, Darling, that's sweet, but that's not how you get babies. That's how you get jewellery!"

***

Colin told his wife she had three choices. She could go hunting with him or he could bum screw her or she could give him a blow job. The first two didn't appeal to her at all, so she settled on a blow job.

While she was doing her best, she said, "Hey, your dick tastes like shit".

"Yeah", said Colin, "the dog didn't want to go hunting either".

***

A young man walks up and sits down at the bar.

"What can I get you?" the bartender inquires.

"I want six shots of ouzo," responds the young man.

"Six shots? Are you celebrating something?"

"Yeah, my first blowjob."

"Well, in that case, let me give you a seventh on the house" says the bartender.

"No offense, sir. But if six shots won't get rid of the taste, nothing will."

COUNCIL COMPLAINTS

These are genuine clips from Housing Commission complaint letters.

My bush is really overgrown round the front and my back passage has fungus growing in it.

The man living below has this huge tool that vibrates the whole house and I just can't take it anymore.

It's their dog's mess that I find hard to swallow.

I want some repairs done to my cooker as it has backfired and burnt my knob off.

I wish to report that tiles are missing from the outside toilet roof. I think it was bad wind the other night that blew them off.

I request permission to remove my drawers in the kitchen.

The toilet is blocked and we cannot bath the children until it is cleared.

Will you please send a man to look at my water; it is a funny colour and not fit to drink.

I want to complain about the farmer across the road; every morning at 6am his cock wakes me up and it's now getting too much for me.

I have had the clerk of works down on the floor six times but I still have no satisfaction.

The man next door has a large erection in the back garden, which is unsightly and dangerous.

I am a single woman living in a downstairs flat and would you please do something about the noise made by the man on top of me every night.

Please send a man with the right tool to finish the job and satisfy my wife.

CROSS CULTURAL

An Englishman, an Irishman and a Scotsman go into a pub. They all suffer from a severe stutter.

"What's it to be?" asks the stunningly beautiful landlady.

"Th th th th th th three pi pi pi pi pi..." says the Englishman.

Up steps the Irishman. "Threeee p pints of of of of gui gui gui gui..."

445

Then the Scotsman tries."Th th th thth th th th th th th th th th..."

"Oh bugger this!" says the beautiful landlady and walks away to serve someone else.

She returns ten minutes later and asks if they are ready to order yet.

"Th th th th th th three pi pi pi pi pi", stutters the Englishman.

"Three pints of gui gui gui gui..." tries Paddy.

And then Scotty starts "Th th th th th th th th th th th th th th th thth...".

"Look" says the beautiful landlady, who loves a bet, "If any one of you can answer a question without stuttering I'll let you shag me!"

Quite confident that no one will win, she turns to the Englishman.

"Where do you live?" "M M M M Man Man Manch Manch Manch..."

"No. You lose." says the beautiful landlady. Turning to the Scotsman, she asks, "Where do you live Scotty?" trying not to laugh.

"E E E E EEd Ed Ed Edin Edin Edin Edin Edin Edin Edinb..."

"Sorry, you lose." says the gorgeous woman. "And Paddy, where do you live?" she purrs at the Irishman.

"London" blurts out the Irishman

"Oh. Bugger!" says the landlady. A great cheer goes up in the pub and the landlady reluctantly takes Paddy by the hand and leads him upstairs.

Once in the bedroom she strips to her underwear, next she takes off her bra exposing a voluptuous bosom. Finally she slides off her panties then climbs into bed. Paddy climbs aboard and goes for glory, and then right at the climaxing stroke, he suddenly screams out, "B B B B B B B B... Belfast!!!"

DATING BEHAVIOUR

WHITE WOMEN:
First date: You get to kiss her goodnight.
Second date: You get to grope her all over and make out.
Third date: You get to have sex, but only in the missionary position.

*****

IRISH WOMEN:
First Date: You both get blind drunk and have sex.
Second Date: You both get blind drunk and have sex.
20th Anniversary: You both get blind drunk and have sex.

*****

ITALIAN WOMEN:
First Date: You take her to a play and an expensive restaurant.
Second Date: You meet her parents and her Mom makes spaghetti & meatballs.
Third Date: You have sex, she wants to marry you and insists on a 3 carat ring.

5th Anniversary: You already have 5 kids together and hate the thought of having sex.

6th Anniversary: You find yourself a girlfriend.

***

JEWISH WOMEN:

First Date: You get dynamite head.

Second Date: You get more great head.

Third Date: You tell her you'll marry her and you never get head again.

***

POLISH WOMEN:

First Date: You go to pick her up but she isn't home. She gave you the wrong address.

Second Date: You decide to meet at a restaurant. She gets lost getting to the restaurant and then again going home.

Third Date: She's pregnant. She's not sure if it's hers.

***

CHINESE WOMEN:

First Date: You get to buy her an expensive dinner, but nothing happens.

Second Date: You buy her an even more expensive dinner. Nothing happens again.

Third Date: You don't turn up. You realise nothing is going to happen.

INDIAN WOMEN:
   First Date: Meet her parents.
   Second Date: Set the date of the wedding.
   Third date: Wedding night.

***

BLACK WOMEN:
   First Date: You buy her a real expensive dinner.
   Second Date: You buy her and her girlfriends a real expensive dinner.
   Third Date: You get to pay her rent.
   Tenth Date: She's pregnant by someone other than you.

***

LATIN WOMEN:
   First Date: You buy her an expensive dinner, get drunk on Malibu, have sex in the back of her car.
   Second Date: She's pregnant.
   Third Date: You move in with her, her two cousins, her sister's boyfriend and live happily ever after, eating rice and beans in the Bronx.

***

A Lebanese guy walks into the local Centrelink office, marches up to the counter and says, "Walla man... I hate being on the dole. I'd really rather have a job bro." The Centrelink clerk says, "Your timing is excellent. We just got a job opening from a very wealthy old man who wants a chauffeur/bodyguard for his beautiful nymphomaniac daughter. You'll drive around in his 500 SLK Mercedes and he'll supply all of your clothes. Because of the long hours, meals will be provided and you'll be expected to escort her on her overseas holiday trips. You'll have a rent-free two-bedroom apartment above the garage at Brighton Beach. The starting salary is $200,000 a year".

"You're bullshitting me!" says the Lebanese guy.

"Yeah...well, you started it..."

***

An American, a Dutchman and a Frenchman are all in Saudi Arabia, sharing a smuggled crate of booze when, all of a sudden, Saudi police rush in and arrest them. The mere possession of alcohol is a severe offence in Saudi Arabia, so for the terrible crime of being caught consuming the booze, they are all sentenced to life imprisonment.

By a stroke of luck, it was a Saudi national holiday the day their trial finished and the benevolent Sheikh decided they could be released after receiving just 20 lashes each of the whip.

As they were preparing for their punishment, the Sheikh announced: "It's my first wife's birthday today, and she has asked me to allow each of you one wish before your whipping."

The Dutchman was first in line, he thought for a while and then said:

"Please tie a pillow to my back."

This was done, but the pillow only lasted 10 lashes before the whip went through. When the punishment was done he was carried away bleeding and crying with pain. The Frenchman was next up.

After watching the Dutchman in horror he said smugly: "Please fix two pillows to my back." But even two pillows could only take 15 lashes before the whip went through again and the Frenchman was soon led away whimpering loudly (as they do).

The American was the last one up, but before he could say anything, the Sheikh turned to him and said: "You are from a most beautiful part of the world and your culture is one of the finest in the world. For this, you may have two wishes!"

"Thank you, your Most Royal and Merciful Highness", the American replied. "In recognition of your kindness, my first wish is that you give me not 20, but 100 lashes."

"Not only are you an honorable, handsome and powerful man" said the Sheikh, "you are also very brave".

"If 100 lashes is what you desire, then so be it. And what is your second wish?" the Sheikh asked.

The American replied: "Tie the Frenchman to my back."

***

Three Western men found themselves in an Arabian harem. They could not resist the temptation and started fooling around with the women.

The sheik burst in. "No-one touches the women in my harem but me!" he roared. "You will all be punished according to your profession!"

The first guy said he was a policeman, so the sheik got one of his women to shoot his penis off. The second said he was a fireman so the sheik got a woman to burn his penis off. The third said he was a lolly pop manufacturer...

***

George W. Bush and Tony Blair are sitting in a bar. A guy walks in and asks the barman, "Isn't that Bush and Blair?"

"Yep, that's them." says the barman.

So the guy walks over and says, "Hello, what are you guys doing?"

"We're planning World War III" says Bush.

"Really? What's going to happen?"

"Well, we're going to kill 10 million Iraqis and one bicycle repairman." replies Bush.

"Why would you want to kill a bicycle repairman?"

Bush turns to Blair and says, "See, I told you no one would care about another 10 million Iraqis!"

DICKS

A man one day noticed that his penis was growing larger and staying erect longer. Needless to say, he was delighted, as was his wife. But after several weeks, and nearly nine inches of additional length, the man became concerned and the couple went to see a urologist.

After an initial examination, the physician explained to the couple that, though rare, the man's condition could be cured through corrective surgery.

How long will he be on crutches?" the man's wife asked anxiously.

"Crutches?" responded the surprised doctor.

"Well, yes," the wife replied, "You're planning to lengthen his legs, aren't you?"

***

The doctor told Kevin that masturbating before sex often helped men last longer during the act. Kevin decided, "What the hell, I'll try it."

He spent the rest of the day thinking about where to do it.

He couldn't do it in his office. He thought about the restroom, but that was too open. He considered an alley, but figured that was too unsafe.

Finally, he came up with a solution. On his way home, he pulled his truck over on the side of the highway. He got out and crawled underneath as if he was examining the truck. Satisfied with the privacy, he undid his pants and started to masturbate. He closed his eyes and thought of his lover. As he grew closer to orgasm, he felt a quick tug at the bottom of his pants. Not wanting to lose his mental fantasy or the orgasm, he kept his eyes shut and replied, "What?" "This is the police.

What's going on down there?" "I'm checking out the rear axle…it's busted." the man replied. "Well, you'd better check your brakes too while you're down there because your truck rolled down the hill five minutes ago."

***

A man can't obtain an erection so he goes to the doctor. The doctor tells him the muscles at the base of his penis are broken down and there's nothing he can do unless he's willing to try an experimental surgery.

The guy asks what the surgery is. The doctor tells him they take the muscles from the base of a baby elephant's trunk, insert them in the base of his penis, and hope for the best. The guy says it sounds pretty scary but the thought of never having sex again is even scarier, so he goes ahead. The doctor performs the surgery and about six weeks later gives him the go ahead to try out his new equipment. The guy takes his girlfriend out to dinner. While at dinner he starts feeling an incredible pressure in his pants. It becomes unbearable and he figures no one can see him so he undoes his pants. Suddenly, his penis pops out, crawls across the table, grabs a dinner roll, and disappears back into his pants. It repeats this process another three times. His girlfriend sits in shock for a few moments, then gets a sly look on her face. "That was pretty cool!" she says, "Can you do it again?"

With his eyes watering and a painful look on his face, he says "Probably, but I don't know if I can fit another dinner roll up my ass!"

A man walks into a sperm bank and declares, "I'm of Royal blood and have an I.Q. of 165. I'd like to make a donation."

The nurse gives him a sealed cup and directs him to a private room.

Twenty minutes later the man still hasn't come out, so the nurse knocks on the door. "Is there a problem?" she asks.

"I'm so embarrassed," the man explains. "I used my right hand. I used my left hand. I poured cold water on it and hot water on it. Could you help me?"

The nurse replies, "I don't usually do this, but you are kinda cute…"

She gets on her knees and begins to give him a blow job.

After a few minutes, the man speaks. "I really appreciate this, but I actually just need help getting the cap off the jar!"

***

A man was having problems with premature ejaculation so he decided to go to the doctor. He asked the doctor what he could do to cure his problem.

The doctor said, "When you feel like you are getting ready to ejaculate try startling yourself."

So the man went to the store and bought himself a starter's pistol and runs home to his wife. Much to his delight, he discovers his wife is in bed, naked and waiting for him. Within minutes, they find themselves in the 69 position. Moments later, he feels the building urge to cum so in order to startle himself, he fires the starter pistol.

The next day, the man went back to the doctor and told him what happened. "How did it go?" the doctor asked.

"Not so good, doc. The wife shit on my face, bit 3 inches off my cock and the mailman jumped out of the closet with his hands in the air!"

***

During a hard day's work on the farm, one of the day laborers needs to take a leak. He goes to the edge of the field and pulls out his dick. Just then, a bee lands on his knob, and before he can react, the bee stings him!

The pain is unbearable, but the laborer remembers what his mother once told him: 'Milk is the best tonic for a beesting!' So he runs to the dairy house and sticks his dick in a bucket of fresh milk. At that moment, the farmer's daughter comes into the dairy house and is frozen by the sight of the laborer.

"What's the matter? Haven't you ever seen one of these before?" the laborer asks.

"Oh, I've seen one before," replies the farmer's daughter, "but this is the first time I've ever seen one being re-loaded!"

***

I, the Willy, hereby request a raise in salary for the following reasons:

- I do physical labour.
- I work at great depths.

- I plunge headfirst into everything I do.
- I do not get weekends or public holidays off.
- I work in a damp environment.
- I work in a dark workplace that has poor ventilation.
- I work in high temperatures.
- My work exposes me to contagious diseases.

Dear Willy,

After assessing your request, and considering the arguments you have raised, the administration rejects your request for the following reasons:

- You do not work 8 hours straight.
- You fall asleep after brief work periods.
- You do not always follow the orders of the management team.
- You do not stay in your designated area and are often seen visiting other locations.
- You do not take initiative – you need to be pressured and stimulated to start working. You leave the workplace untidy at the end of your shift.
- You don't always observe necessary safety regulations, such as wearing protective clothing.
- You will retire well before you are 65.
- You are unable to work double shifts.
- You sometimes leave your designated work area before you have completed the assigned task.
- And you have been seen constantly entering and exiting the work place carrying two suspicious-looking bags.

Sincerely,
The Management

A young wife bought a mirror at an antique shop. One morning while dressing, she looked in the mirror and said, "Mirror, mirror, on the door, make my bustline 44." There was a flash of light and her breasts swelled to size 44.

She told her husband that night, and he had a go. "Mirror, mirror, on the door, make my penis touch the floor". There was a flash of light and his legs dropped off.

***

The government announced today that it is changing it's emblem to a condom because it more clearly reflects the government's political stance. A condom stands up to inflation, halts production, destroys the next generation, protects a bunch of pricks, and gives you a sense of security while it's actually screwing you.

***

Roger said to the doctor, "Doctor, I've got a problem, and if you're going to treat it, you've have to promise not to laugh."

"Of course I won't laugh," the doctor said. "I'm a professional. In over twenty years I've never laughed at a patient."

"Okay" Roger said, and proceeded to drop his trousers, revealing the tiniest penis the doctor has ever seen.

Unable to control himself, the doctor fell laughing to the floor.

Ten minutes later he was able to struggle to his feet and regain his composure.

"I'm so sorry," he said. "I don't know what came over me. On my honor as a doctor and a gentleman, I promise it won't happen again. Now what seems to be the problem?"

"It's swollen..."

DOCTORS

A young lady in the maternity ward just prior to labor is asked by the midwife if she would like her husband to be present at the birth.

"I'm afraid I don't have a husband" she replies.

"O.K., do you have a boyfriend?" asks the midwife.

"No, no boyfriend either."

"Do you have a partner then?"

"No, I'm unattached. I'll be having my baby on my own."

After the birth the midwife again speaks to the young woman. "You have a healthy girl, but I must warn you before you see her that the baby is black."

"Well," replies the girl. "I was very down on my luck, with no money and nowhere to live, so I accepted a job in a porno movie. The lead man was black."

"Oh, I'm very sorry," says the midwife, "that's really none of my business and I'm sorry I have to ask you these awkward questions but I must also tell you that the baby has blonde hair."

"Well yes," the girl again replies, "you see I desperately needed the money and there was this Swedish guy also involved in the movie...what else could I do?"

"Oh, I'm sorry," the midwife repeats, "I really shouldn't pry further but your baby has slanted eyes."

"Well yes," continues the girl, "I was incredibly hard up and there was a little Chinese man also in the movie... I really had no choice."

The midwife again apologises, collects the baby and presents her to the girl, who immediately proceeds to give baby a slap on the bum. The baby starts crying and the mother exclaims, "Well thank God for that!"

"What do you mean?" says the midwife, shocked.

"Well... I had this horrible feeling that it was going to bark."

***

After a long night of making love, the young guy rolled over, pulled out a cigarette from his jeans and searched for his lighter. Unable to find it, he asked the girl if she had one.

"There might be some matches in the top drawer," she replied. He opened the bedside table drawer and found a box of matches sitting neatly on top of a framed picture of another man.

The guy began to worry. "Is this your husband?" he inquired nervously. "No, silly," she replied, snuggling up to him.

"Your boyfriend then?" he asked.

"No, not at all," she said, nibbling away at his ear.

"Well, who is he then?" demanded the bewildered guy.

"That's me before the operation."

***

George went to see his urologist. The receptionist was a loud-mouthed bully. "You're here to see about your impotence?" she said loudly. The waiting room was full and George felt very embarrassed as everyone stared at him and smiled.

"No", said George, "I'm here to have a sex change operation and I want the same doctor that did yours!"

***

A lovely but naïve young lady went to see a gynaecologist. He asked her to disrobe and lie on the examination table. He started to stroke the inside of her thigh and asked her if she knew what he was doing.

"Yes. You are checking for dermatological abnormalities".

"That's right", said the doctor.

Then he stroked her breasts. "Do you know what I am doing now?" he asked.

"Yes. You are examining my breasts for lumps or cancer".

The doctor then mounted his patient and started screwing her. "Do you know what I'm doing now?" he asked.

"Yes. You're catching herpes, which is why I came to see you in the first place".

***

A man staggers into an emergency room with two black eyes and a five iron wrapped tightly around his throat. Naturally the doctor asks him what happened. "Well, it was like this", said the man. "I was having a quiet round of golf with my wife when she sliced her ball into a pasture of cows. We went to look for it, and while I was searching around, I noticed one of the cows had something white at its rear end. I walked over and lifted up the tail and sure enough, there was my wife's golf ball...stuck right in the middle of the cow's butt. That's when I made my mistake."

"What did you do?" asks the doctor.

"Well, I lifted the tail and yelled to my wife, 'Hey, this looks like yours!"

***

After her sixth child, Jane decided that she should have some cosmetic surgery 'down below' to restore herself to her former youthful glory because her bomb doors were dangling a bit too low and looked like a ripped-out fireplace.

Time and childbirth had taken their toll and she reckoned that, with six children now being the limit, she'd tidy things with a nip here and a tuck there so it looked more like a piggy bank slot rather than a badly packed kebab. Following the operation she awoke from her anesthetic to find three roses at the end of the bed. "Who are these from?" she asked the nurse, "they're very nice, but I'm a bit confused about why I've received them."

"Well" said the nurse, "the first is from the surgeon – the operation went so well and you were such a model patient that he wanted to say thanks."

"Ah, that's really nice" said Jane.

"The second is from your husband; he's delighted that the operation was such a success that he can't wait to get you home. Apparently it'll be the first time he's touched the sides for years and he's very excited!"

"Brilliant!" said Jane.

"And the third?"

"That's from Eric, a patient in the burns unit" said the nurse. "He just wanted to say thanks for his new ears..."

***

Five surgeons are discussing who has the best patients to operate on. The first surgeon says, "I like to see accountants on my operating table because when you open them up, everything inside is numbered." The second responds, "Yes, but you should try electricians! Everything inside them is colour coded." The third surgeon says, "No, I really think librarians are the best; everything inside them is in alphabetical order." The fourth surgeon chimes in: "You know, I like construction workers. Those guys always understand when you have a few parts left over at the end or when the job takes longer than you said it would." But the fifth surgeon shut them all up when he observed: "You're all wrong. Politicians are the easiest to operate on. There's no guts, no heart, no balls, no brains and no spine, and the mouth and the arse are interchangeable."

***

A couple went to the hospital for the delivery of their first baby. The doctor said, "I have invented a new machine, which allows the baby's father to bear some of the excruciating pain of delivery. Do you want to use it?"

The couple agreed and the machine was put in place. As the delivery of the baby began, the doctor set the machine for the father to receive 15% of the pain.

"How's that?" he asked the husband.

"It's nothing at all – give me more!" the husband replied. The doctor increased the figure to 50%.

The laboring wife indicated that the reduction of her intense pain was dramatic, but the husband still insisted that he easily could take much more.

The doctor set the equipment to give the father 95% of the pain of the baby's delivery, and the procedure was completed with the new mother relieved of pain almost completely.

The doctor congratulated the husband on his remarkable strength and courage. The husband choked and said in a low voice, "Believe me, Doctor, I hardly felt anything out of the ordinary." Everyone stood in admiration of him. Two days later the couple left the hospital with the new baby and returned to their home.

There they discovered their mailman lying dead on the front porch.

***

A man was visiting his wife in hospital where she has been in a coma for several years. On this visit he decides to rub her left breast instead of just talking to her. On doing this, she lets out a sigh. The man runs out and tells the doctor who says this is a good sign and suggests he should try rubbing her right breast to see if there is any reaction. The man goes in and rubs her right breast and this also brings a moan. From this, the doctor suggests that the man should go in and try oral sex, saying he will wait outside as it is a very personal act and he doesn't want the man to be embarrassed. The man goes in then comes out about five minutes later, white as a sheet and tells the doctor his wife is dead. The doctor asks what happened to which the man replies: "She choked."

***

Two lawyers boarded a flight out of Seattle. One sat in the window seat, the other sat in the middle seat. Just before takeoff a physician got on and took the aisle seat next to the two attorneys. The physician kicked off his shoes, wiggled his toes and was settling in when the lawyer in the window seat said, "I think I'll get up and get a coke."

"No problem," said the doctor, "I'll get it for you."

While he was gone, one of the lawyers picked up the doctor's shoe and spat in it. When he returned with the coke, the other lawyer said, "That looks good, I think I'll have one too."

Again, the physician obligingly went to fetch it and while he was gone, the other lawyer picked up the other shoe and spat in. The doctor returned and they all sat back and enjoyed the flight. As the plane was landing, the doctor slipped his feet into his shoes and knew immediately what had happened. "How long must this go on?" he asked. "This fighting between our professions? This hatred? This animosity? This spitting in shoes and pissing in cokes..."

***

A woman in her forties went to a plastic surgeon for a face-lift.

The surgeon told her about a new procedure called 'The Knob' where a small knob is placed on the back of a woman's head and can be turned to tighten up her skin to produce the effect of a brand new face lift.

The woman said she definitely wanted 'The Knob.'

Over the course of the years, the woman tightened the knob, and the effects were wonderful – she remained young looking and vibrant. After fifteen years, the woman returned to the surgeon with two problems. "All these years, everything has been working just fine. I've had to turn the knob many times and I've always loved the results. But now I've developed two annoying problems; First, I have these terrible bags under my eyes and the knob won't get rid of them." The doctor looked at her closely and said, "Those aren't bags, those are your breasts."

"Well, I guess there's no point in asking about the goatee beard."

***

A woman was very distraught at the fact that she had not had a date or sex in quite some time. She was afraid she might have something wrong with her, so she decided to employ the medical expertise of a sex therapist. Her doctor recommended that she go see Dr Chang, the well-known Chinese sex therapist. Upon entering the examination room, Dr Chang said, " OK, preeze take off all your crose."

The woman did as she was told.

"Now, get down and craw reery reery fass to udder side of loom."

Again, the woman did as she was instructed. Dr Chang then said, "OK, now craw reery reery fass back to me."

So she did. Dr Chang slowly shook his head and said, "Your probrem vewy bad. You haf 'Ed Zachary Disease.' Worse case I ever see. Dat why you not haf sex or dates."

Confused, the woman asked, "Oh my God, Dr Chang, what is 'Ed Zachary Disease'?"

"Disease is when your face rook Ed Zachary rike your arse."

DRINKING

A loud pounding on the door wakes a man and his wife at 3 o'clock in the morning. The man gets up and goes to the door where a drunken stranger, standing in the pouring rain, is asking for a push.

"Not a chance," says the husband, "it's three o'clock in the morning!"

He slams the door and returns to bed.

"Who was that?" asked his wife.

"Just some drunk guy asking for a push," he answers.

"Did you help him?"

"No, I did not...it's three in the morning and it's pouring rain!"

"Well, you have a short memory," says his wife.

"Can't you remember about three months ago when our car broke down and those two guys helped us? I think you should help him, and should be ashamed of yourself!"

The man gets dressed, and goes out into the pounding rain. He calls out into the dark, "Hello, are you still there?"

"Yes," comes back the answer.

"Do you still need a push?" calls out the husband.

"Yes, please!" came the reply from the dark.

"Where are you?"

"Over here on the swing!"

***

A guy sitting at an airport bar noticed a beautiful woman sitting next to him. He thought to himself, "Wow, she's so gorgeous she must be a flight attendant; but which airline does she work for?"

Hoping to pick her up, he leaned towards her and whispered the Delta Airlines slogan: "Love to fly and it shows?"

She gave him a blank, confused stare and he immediately thought to himself that she didn't work for Delta.

A few seconds later, the American Airlines slogan popped into his head. He leaned towards her again, "Something special in the air?"

She gave him the same confused look. He mentally kicked himself, and scratched off the list.

Next he tried United: "I would really love to fly your friendly skies…" This time the woman turned and barked back at him "What the fuck do you want, you dickhead?"

The man smiled and slumped back in his chair, "Aahhhh, British Airways".

***

One night, a police officer was staking out a particular rowdy bar for possible violations of the Drink Driving laws. At closing time, he saw a fellow stumble out of the bar, trip on the curb, and try his keys on five different cars before he found his. Then he sat in the front seat fumbling around with his keys for several minutes. Meanwhile, everyone left the bar and drove off. Finally, he was able to start his engine and began to pull away. The police officer was waiting for him. He stopped the driver, read him his rights and administered the

Breathalyzer test. The results showed a reading of zero. The puzzled officer demanded: "How can this be?"

"Because tonight, officer, I'm the designated decoy!"

***

A guy walks into a bar with a pet alligator by his side. He puts the alligator up on the bar. He turns to the astonished patrons and says, "I'll make you a deal. I'll open this alligator's mouth and place my genitals inside. Then the gator will close his mouth for one minute. He'll then open his mouth and I'll remove my wedding tackle, unscathed. In return for witnessing this spectacle, each of you will buy me a drink." The crowd murmured their approval. The man stood up on the bar, dropped his trousers, and placed his privates in the alligator's open mouth. The gator closed his mouth as the crowd gasped. After a minute, the man grabbed a beer bottle and whacked the alligator hard on the top of its head. The gator opened his mouth and the man removed his genitals unscathed as promised. The crowd cheered and the first of his free drinks were delivered.

The man stood up again and made another offer. "I'll pay anyone $100 who's willing to give it a try." A hush fell over the crowd.

After a while, a hand went up in the back of the bar and a woman timidly spoke up. "I'll try it, but you have to promise not to hit me on the head with the beer bottle".

A businessman entered a tavern, sat down at the bar, and ordered a double scotch on the rocks. After he finished the drink, he peeked inside his shirt pocket, then ordered another double scotch. After he finished it, he peeked inside his shirt pocket again and ordered another. "Look, buddy, I'll bring you drinks all night long, but you have tell me why you look inside your shirt pocket before you order another" demanded the bartender.

"I'm looking at a photo of my wife" he said. "When she starts to look good, then I know it's time to go home."

***

Two women went out for a drinking weekend without their husbands. As they came back, right before dawn, both of them drunk, they felt the urge to pee but the only place to stop was a cemetery. Scared and drunk, they stopped and decided to go there anyway.

The first one did not have anything to wipe herself with, so she took off her panties, used them to clean herself and discarded them. The second, not finding anything either, didn't want to throw away her panties so she used the ribbon off a flower wreath to clean herself.

The next morning, the two husbands were talking on the phone, and one said "We have to be on the lookout...it seems our wives were up to no good last night, my wife came home without her panties..." "You're lucky", the other one responded, "Mine came home with a card stuck to her ass that read, 'We will never forget you."

A guy walks into a bar and sees a gorgeous babe nursing a drink.

Walking up behind her he said, "Hi, there, good looking! How's it going?"

Having already downed a few power drinks she turned around, faced him, looked him straight in the eye and said, "Listen! I'll screw anybody, any time, anywhere, your place, my place, front door, back door, it doesn't matter to me. I've been doing it for years and I just love it!"

"No kidding!" he responded, "I'm a lawyer too! What firm are you with?"

***

George, an Englishman, was working on a construction site with two Frenchmen. Every night after work they went to the pub for a drink. One day, George fell 200 feet from the top of the building. His face was unrecognizable. When the Police arrived, they asked the Frenchmen if George had any distinguishing marks so he could be identified. The two Frenchmen thought for a while and said, "George had two rectums".

"You're kidding me", said the cop. "How do you know?"

"Well, every night when we went to the pub for a drink, the barman used to say, "Here comes George with the two arseholes".

***

A very shy man goes into a bar and sees a beautiful woman sitting at the bar. After an hour of gathering up his courage, he finally goes over and says: "Um...excuse me, but would you mind if I sat here beside you?"

She responds by yelling, at the top of her lungs, "No! I don't want to sleep with you!"

Everyone in the bar turns to stare at them. The guy is hopelessly and completely embarrassed and he slinks back to his table. After a few minutes, the woman walks over to him and apologizes. She smiles at him and says: "I'm sorry if I embarrassed you. You see, I'm a graduate student in psychology and I'm studying how people respond to embarrassing situations."

At the top of his lungs the man yells, "What do you mean, $200?"

FAIRY TALES

CINDERELLA wants to go to the ball, but her wicked stepmother won't let her. As Cinderella sits crying in the garden, her Fairy Godmother appears, and promises to provide Cinderella with everything she needs to go to the ball, but only on two conditions. "First, you must wear a diaphragm." Cinderella agrees. "What's the second condition?" "You must be home by 2:00 a.m. Any later, and your diaphragm will turn into a pumpkin." Cinderella agrees to be home by 2:00 a.m. The appointed hour comes and goes, and Cinderella doesn't show up. Finally, at 5:00 a.m. Cinderella shows up, looking love struck and very satisfied.

"Where have you been?" demands the Fairy Godmother. "Your diaphragm was supposed to turn into a pumpkin three hours ago!" "I met a prince, Fairy Godmother. He took care of everything." "I know of no prince with that kind of power! Tell me his name!" the Fairy Godmother demanded. "I can't remember, exactly,... Peter, Peter, something or other..."

***

PINOCCHIO had a human girlfriend who would sometimes complain about splinters when they were having sex. Pinocchio went to visit Gepetto to see if he could help. Gepetto suggested he try a little sandpaper and Pinocchio skipped away enlightened. A couple weeks later, Gepetto saw Pinocchio bouncing happily through town and asked "How's your girlfriend?" "Who needs a girlfriend?"

***

LITTLE RED RIDING HOOD was walking through the woods when suddenly the Big Bad Wolf jumped out from behind a tree and, holding a sword to her throat, said, "Red, I'm going to screw your brains out!" To that, Little Red Riding Hood calmly reached into her picnic basket and pulled out a .44 magnum and pointed it at him and said, "No, you're not. You're going to eat me, just like it says in the book."

MICKEY MOUSE and MINNIE MOUSE were in divorce court and the judge said to Mickey, "You say here that your wife is crazy." Mickey replied, "I didn't say she was crazy, I said she's fucking Goofy."

***

SNOW WHITE saw Pinocchio walking through the woods so she ran up behind him, knocked him flat on his back, and then sat on his face crying, "Lie to me! Lie to me!"

***

JANE met TARZAN in the jungle one day. She was very attracted to him and during her questions about his life she asked him how he managed to have sex. "What's that?" he asked. She explained to him what sex was and he said, "Oh, I use a hole in the trunk of a tree." Horrified, she said, "Tarzan, you have it all wrong but I will show you how to do it properly." She took off her clothes, laid down on the ground and spread her legs. "Here," she said, "you must put it in here." Tarzan removed his loincloth, stepped closer and then gave her an almighty kick in the crotch. Jane rolled around in agony. Eventually she managed to gasp, "What the hell did you do that for?" "Just checking for bees," said Tarzan.

***

THE SEVEN DWARFS are on holiday, traveling the World. On their journey, they stop off in Rome, where Dopey wants to see the Pope. They go to Vatican City, and stand outside the Papal home.

The other six Dwarfs stand back a way whilst Dopey walks up to the Pope's residence, and knocks on the Pope's door. The Pope answers his door, and Dopey falls to his knees, and clutches the Popes robe.

"Father, please, tell me for I must know. Are there any Dwarf Nuns in Rome?"

"No, my son," replies the Pope, "there are no Dwarf Nuns in Rome." Happy smiled.

"Father, Father – in that case, are there any Dwarf Nuns in Italy?"

"No, my son," replies the Pope, "there are no Dwarf Nuns in Italy." Happy grinned, but the other Dwarfs smirked.

"Well, then!" exclaimed Dopey, "are there any Dwarf Nuns in Europe at all?"

"No, my son – there are no European Dwarf Nuns." replied the Pope. By this stage, Happy has tears running from his eyes, and is almost laughing out loud. The other Dwarfs seem barely able to control themselves.

"Please Father – tell me this!" implores Dopey, "are there **any** Dwarf Nuns **anywhere** in the World?"

"I am truly sorry, my son, but there is no such thing as a Dwarf Nun."

Happy rolls around on the floor, holding his sides and chortling at the top of his voice. Even grumpy is smiling.

"Dopey screwed a penguin! Dopey screwed a penguin!" they sang.

Mary had a little skirt, with splits right up the sides

And every time that Mary walked the boys could see her thighs.

Mary had another skirt, 'twas split right up the front…but she didn't wear that one very often!

***

Mary had a little lamb
Her father shot it dead.
Now it goes to school with her,
Between two chunks of bread.

***

Mary had a little lamb
It ran into a pylon.
10,000 volts went up it's ass
And turned its wool to nylon!

***

Little Miss Muffet sat on a tuffet,
Her clothes all tattered and torn.
It wasn't the spider that crept up beside her,
But Little Boy Blue with his horn.

***

Simple Simon met a pieman, going to the fair.
Said Simple Simon to the pieman,
What have you got there?
Said the pieman unto Simple Simon,
"Pies, you dickhead!"

Humpty Dumpty sat on a wall
Humpty Dumpty had a great fall.
All the kings' horses and all the kings' men,
Said "Fuck him, He's only an egg!"

***

Georgie Porgy pudding and pie,
Kissed the girls and made them cry.
When the boys came out to play,
He kissed them too, 'cause he was gay.

***

Jack and Jill
Went up the hill
To have some hanky panky.
Jill the dill forgot her pill
And now there's little Frankie!

***

Old Mother Hubbard
Went to the cupboard
To fetch her poor dog a bone.
When she bent over
Rover took over,
And gave her a bone of his own!

***

Little Boy Blew.
Hey, he needed the money!

It's a sunny morning in the Big Forest and the Bear family is just waking up. Baby Bear goes downstairs and sits in his small chair at the table. He looks into his small bowl. It is empty. "Who's been eating my porridge?" he squeaks. Daddy Bear arrives at the table and sits in his big chair. He looks into his big bowl. It is also empty! "Who's been eating my porridge?" he roars.

Mummy Bear puts her head through the serving hatch from the kitchen and yells, "For heaven's sake, how many times do we have to go through this? It was Mummy Bear who got up first. It was Mummy Bear who woke up everybody else in the house. It was Mummy Bear who unloaded the dishwasher from last night and put everything away. It was Mummy Bear who went out into the cold early morning air to fetch the newspaper and the wood for the fire. It was Mummy Bear who set the table. It was Mummy Bear who put the cat out, cleaned the litter box and filled the cat's water and food dish. And now that you've decided to come down stairs and grace me with your presence, listen good because I'm only going to say this one more time... I haven't made the fucking porridge yet!"

FARTS

A woman goes into a Sports store to buy a rod and reel for her grandson's 21st birthday. She doesn't know which one to get, so she just grabs one and goes over to the counter. A check-out clerk is standing there wearing dark glasses. "Excuse me, sir" she says, "Can you tell me anything about this rod and reel?"

"Ma'am, I'm completely blind, but if you'll drop it on the counter, I can tell you everything you need to know about it from the sound it makes."

She doesn't believe him, but drops it on the counter anyway. He says, "That's an eight-foot surf caster Shakespeare graphite 667 Model rod fitted with a Shimano Calcutta 400 reel, spooled with 20lb Berkley Fireline. It's a good all around combination, and it's on sale this week for only $199.00." "It's amazing that you can tell all that just by the sound of it dropping on the counter. I'll take it!" she says.

As she opens her purse, her credit card drops on the floor. She bends down to pick it up and accidentally farts. At first she's really embarrassed, but then realises it's not likely that the blind clerk could tell it was she who farted. He may not even know that she was the only person around. The man rings up the sale and says, "That'll be $254.50 please."

The woman is totally confused by this and asks, "Didn't you tell me it was on sale for $199.00? How did you get $254.50?"

He replies, "Yes, Ma'am, the rod and reel is $199.00, but the duck caller is $36.00 and the fishing bait is $19.50."

***

There was a married couple who had been happily married for 40 years. The only friction in their marriage was the husband's habit of loudly farting every morning as he awoke. The noise would wake his wife and the smell would make her eyes water and make her gasp for air. Every morning she would plead with him to stop farting as it was making her sick. He told her he couldn't stop it and that it was perfectly natural for a man to do it. She told him to see a doctor, as she was concerned that one day he was going to fart his guts out. The years went by and he continued to rip them out. Then, one Christmas morning as she was downstairs preparing the turkey for dinner and he was upstairs sound asleep, she looked at the bowl where she had just put the turkey innards, neck, gizzards, liver and all the spare parts and a malicious thought came to her. She took the bowl upstairs where her hubby was sound asleep and gently pulling back the bed covers, she slid down his underwear at the back and emptied the bowl of turkey guts into them.

Several hours later she heard her husband waken with his usual ripping and trumpeting farts, followed by a bloodcurdling scream and the sound of frantic footsteps as he ran to the bathroom. The wife could hardly control herself as she rolled on the floor laughing with tears in her eyes. After years of torture she reckoned she had now got her own back. About twenty minutes later, her husband came downstairs in his bloodstained underwear with a look of horror on his face. She bit her lip as she asked "What's the matter?"

"Honey, you were right!" he said. "All those years you warned me and I didn't listen to you."

"What do you mean?" she asked.

"Well, you always told me that one day I would

end up farting my guts out and today it finally happened. But...by the grace of God, some Vaseline and these two fingers, I think I got most of them back in."

***

Cameron got a job working in a pharmacy. He wasn't really into retail sales and wasn't taking much money so the boss put him on notice. "If you don't sell product to the next customer, you're fired!" he said.

A man came in with a really bad cough and wanted some cough lozenges. Cameron couldn't find them, so gave him a packet of laxatives and told him to eat the whole packet. After the man left, the boss told Cameron that laxatives would not cure a cough.

"Yes they will" said Cameron, "after he's taken those, he'll be too scared to cough".

***

Lyn went to Chris' house to meet his mother and have lunch. She was served a large plate of baked beans. Lyn soon felt a fart coming on but held back until her eyes started to water. She finally let go. It was silent but very smelly. At Lyn's feet lay the family dog. Chris' mum shouted, "Rover, come here!"

Soon, Lyn felt another fart coming on. She didn't hesitate. She felt confident that the dog would again be blamed and dropped a prize winning fart.

"Rover, come here!" Chris' mum said sternly.

When Lyn felt a third fart come on, she first lifted her leg and let fly with a real gold medal fart. Chris' mum again spoke sternly to the dog. "Rover, come here at once before she shits on you!"

***

A lady walks into a Mercedes dealership. She browses around, then spots the perfect car and walks over to inspect it. As she bends to feel the fine leather upholstery, she drops a loud fart. Very embarrassed, she looks around nervously to see if anyone has noticed her little accident and hopes a sales person doesn't pop up right now. As she turns back, standing next to her is a salesman.

"Good morning, Madam. How may we help you today?"

"Sir, what is the price of this lovely vehicle?" she asks uncomfortably.

"Madame, if you farted just touching it, you are going to shit when you hear the price."

FINANCIAL

"Mr. Clark, I have reviewed this case very carefully," the divorce court judge said, "and I've decided to give your wife $775 a week."

"That's very fair, your honor," the husband said. "And every now and then I'll try to send her a few bucks myself."

***

A Scotsman went to the dentist and asked how much it was for an extraction. "£85 for an extraction, sir" was the dentists reply.

"Och, huv ye nay got unythin cheaper", replied the Scotsman, getting agitated. "But that's the normal charge for an extraction sir", said the dentist. "What aboot if ye didnae use uny anaesthetic?", asked the Scotsman hopefully.

"Well it's highly unusual sir, but if that's what you want, I suppose I can do it for £70", said the dentist.

"Hmmmm, what aboot if ye used one of ye dentist trainees and still wi' oot anaesthetic", said the Scotsman, "Well it's possible but they are only training and I can't guarantee their level of professionalism and it'll be a lot more painful, but I suppose in that case we can bring the price down to say £40", said the dentist.

"Och that's still a bit much, how aboot if ye make it a training session and have yon student do the extraction and the other students watchin and learnin", said the Scotsman hopefully.

"Hmmmmm, well OK...it'll be good for the students I suppose, I'll charge you only £5 in that case" said the dentist...

"Wonderful...it's a deal" said the Scotsman. "Can ye book the wife in for next Tuesday?"

A little old lady went into the Westpac Bank one day, carrying a bag of money. She insisted that she must speak with the president of the bank to open a savings account because she had a lot of money. After much hemming and hawing, the bank staff finally ushered her into the president's office. The bank president asked her how much she would like to deposit. She replied, "$165,000!" and dumped the cash out of her bag onto his desk. The president was curious as to how she came by all this cash, so he asked her, "Ma'am, I'm surprised you're carrying so much cash around. Where did you get this money?"

"I make bets," the old lady replied.

"Bets? What kind of bets?"

"Well, for example, I'll bet you $25,000 that your balls are square."

"Ha!" laughed the president, "That's a stupid bet. You can never win that kind of bet!"

"So, would you like to take my bet?" the old lady challenged.

"Sure," said the president, "I'll bet $25,000 that my balls are not square!"

"Okay, but since there is a lot of money involved, may I bring my lawyer with me tomorrow at 10:00 am as a witness?"

"Sure!" replied the confident president.

That night, the president became very nervous about the bet and spent a long time in front of a mirror checking his balls, turning from side to side, again and again. He thoroughly checked them out until he was sure that there was absolutely no way his balls were square and that he would win the bet. The next morning, at precisely 10:00 am, the little old lady appeared with her lawyer at the president's office. She repeated the bet: "$25,000 says the president's balls are square!"

The president agreed with the bet again and the old lady asked him to drop his pants so they could all see. The president complied. The little old lady peered closely at his balls and then asked if she could feel them.

"Well, Okay," said the president, "$25,000 is a lot of money, so I guess you should be absolutely sure." Just then, he noticed that the lawyer was quietly banging his head against the wall. The president asked the old lady, "What the hell's the matter with your lawyer?"

"Nothing," she replied, "except I bet him $100,000 that at 10:00 am today, I'd have the Westpac Bank's president's balls in my hand."

***

The Madam opened the brothel door and saw a frail, elderly gentleman.

"Can I help you?" the madam asked.

"I want Natalie," the old man replied.

"Sir, Natalie is one of our most expensive ladies, perhaps someone else would be suitable?"

"I must see Natalie!"

Natalie appeared and announced to the old man that she charges $1,000 per visit. Without blinking, the man reached into his pocket and handed her ten $100 bills. The two went up to a room for an hour, where upon the man calmly left.

The next night he appeared again demanding to see Natalie. Natalie explained that no one had ever come back two nights in a row and that there were no discounts. It was still $1,000 a visit. Again the old man took out the money; the two went up to the room and an hour later, he left. When he showed up the third consecutive night, no one could believe it. Again he handed Natalie the money and up to the room they went. At the end of the hour Natalie questioned the old man:

"No one has services three nights in a row. Where are you from?"

The old man replied, "I'm from Wagga Wagga."

"Really?" replied Natalie. "I have family who live there."

"Yes, I know," said the old man. "Your father died, and I'm your sister's attorney. She asked me to give you $3,000."

***

Two couples were playing cards one evening. Dave accidentally dropped some cards on the floor. When he bent down under the table to pick them up, he noticed that Mike's wife's legs were spread and she wasn't wearing any underwear! Shocked by this, and on trying to sit back up again, he hit his head on the table and emerged red-faced. Later, Dave went to the kitchen to get some refreshments. Mike's wife followed and asked, "Did you see anything that you liked under there?"

Surprised by her boldness, Dave courageously admitted that, well, indeed he did.

"Well, you can have it but it will cost you $500." she said.

After taking a minute or two to assess the financial situation as well as the moral costs of this offer, Dave indicated that he was indeed interested.

She told him that since her husband, Mike, worked Friday afternoons and Dave didn't, that Dave should be at her house around 2pm Friday afternoon. When Friday rolled around, Dave showed up at Mike's house for the planned time at 2pm sharp and after paying her the agreed $500, they went to the bedroom and, as Mike's wife had promised, she bonked him senseless.

Afterwards, Dave quickly dressed and left. As usual, Mike came home from work at 6pm and upon entering the house, asked his wife abruptly,

"Did Dave drop by the house this afternoon?"

With a lump in her throat, she answered,

"Why yes, he did stop by for a few minutes this afternoon."

Her heart nearly skipped a beat when her husband curtly asked, "And did he give you $500?"

In terror, she assumed that somehow he had found out, and after mustering up her best poker face, replied, "Well, yes, in fact he did give me $500".

"Good. I was hoping he did. Dave came by the office this morning and borrowed $500 from me. He promised me he'd stop by our house this afternoon on his way home and pay me back."

***

When NASA first started sending up astronauts, they quickly discovered that ballpoint pens would not work in zero gravity. To combat the problem, NASA scientists spent a decade and 12 billion dollars to develop a pen that writes in zero gravity, upside down, underwater, on almost any surface including glass and at temperatures ranging from below freezing to 300C. The Russians used a pencil.

***

A bloke was having a few drinks by himself at a Sydney casino when he met up with a striking but quite short and slim young woman. They got on famously and ended up in bed. The next morning she told him she was a jockey and that if he came to the races that day, she'd tip him the winner of each race she was riding in by giving him a sign as she rode out of the saddling paddock.

In Race 2, she rode out rubbing both her boobs. The bloke looked through the race book and found "Two Abreast" on which he placed $100 at 5-1. It won by two lengths.

In Race 4 she rode out rubbing her fingers around her eyes. He put the lot on "Eyeliner" at 10-1 and was then $5000 in front.

In the last race she came out standing up in the stirrups and rubbing her fanny. He backed nothing. After the races, he met up with her and thanked her for the winners in Races 2 and 4.

"What about 'Itchy Mickey' in the sixth?" she asked. "It paid a fortune!"

"Shit", he said, "I thought you were telling me that the cunt was scratched!"

***

A man and woman are getting all snugly in bed. The passion is heating up. But then the lady stops and says, "I don't feel like it, I just want you to hold me."

The guy says "What?"

The lady explains that he must be in tune with her emotional needs as a woman. He realises that nothing is going to happen tonight and he might as well deal with it. So the next day the man takes her shopping at a big department store. He walks around and has her try on three very expensive outfits. She can't decide what to get. He tells her to take all three of them. They get matching shoes worth $300 a pair, then they go to the Jewellery Department where she gets a set of diamond earrings.

The lady is so excited and thinks her guy has flipped out, but she doesn't care. She goes for the tennis bracelet.

"You don't even play tennis, but OK, if you like it then let's get it!" he says.

The woman is jumping up and down so excited she cannot even believe what is going on.

"I'm ready to go... let's go to the cash register." she says.

"No, I don't feel like buying all this stuff now." the man says.

The woman's face goes blank.

He continues – "I just wanted you to hold this stuff for a while."

The look on her face is indescribable and she is about to explode.

The guy says, "You need to be in tune with my financial needs as a Man."

***

A little kid was talking to his friends about the fancy house on his street. They said it was the place to get some nookie. The little kid said, "Well, I'm going to get some!" He went up to the door of the place and knocked. A beautiful woman answered and said "What do you want?"

"I want some nookie!"

"It's fifty dollars." she said.

"I've only got fifty cents." the kid said.

"Then... get lost kid!" she said.

He banged on the door again and said, "Give me some nookie!"

"OK" she said. She took his fifty cents, raised up her dress and rubbed his face right in it.

Then she pushed him out the door.

"I'm glad I only had fifty cents" the kid said, "I don't think I could have taken fifty dollars worth."

***

A young kid moves to Sydney and goes to a big department store looking for a job. The manager asks, "Do you have any sales experience?"

"Yeah, I was a salesman back home" the kid answers.

The manager liked the kid, so he gave him the job. His first day on the job was rough but he got through it. After the store was locked up, the manager came over and asked, "How many sales did you make today?"

"One..." says the kid.

The manager groans, "Just one? Our sales people average 20 or 30 sales a day. How much was the sale for?"

The kid replies "$101,237.64".

"$101,237.64? What did you sell him?" the manager exclaims.

"Well, first I sold him a small fish hook. Then I sold him a medium fish hook. Then I sold him a new fishing rod. Then I asked him where he was going fishing, and he said down at the coast, so I told him he was gonna need a boat, so we went down to the boat department and I sold him a twin engine Chris Craft. Then he said he didn't think his Honda Civic would pull it, so I took him down to the automotive department, and I sold him a Toyota Four Wheel Drive."

"You mean a guy came in here to buy a fish hook and you sold him a boat and truck?" exclaimed the manager.

"No…" replied the kid, "He came in here to buy a box of tampons for his wife and I said, "Well, since your weekend's stuffed you might as well go fishing".

***

A guy is walking along the tourist strip in a big city when a knockout looking hooker catches his eye. He strikes up a conversation and eventually he asks the hooker, "How much do you charge?"

The hooker replies, "It starts at $500 for a hand-job."

"$500 dollars! For a hand-job! No hand-job is worth that kind of money!"

"Do you see that restaurant on the corner?" the hooker asks.

"Yes."

"Do you see the restaurant about a block further down?"

"Yes."

"And beyond that, do you see that third restaurant?"

"Yes."

"Well," says the hooker, smiling invitingly, "I own those. And, I own them because I give a hand-job that's worth $500."

The guy says, "What the hell? You only live once. I'll give it a try." They go to a nearby motel.

A short time later, the guy is sitting on the bed realizing that he just experienced the hand-job of a lifetime, worth every bit of $500. He is so amazed, he says, "I suppose a blow-job is $1,000?"

The hooker replies, "$1,500."

I wouldn't pay that for a blow-job!"

The hooker replies, "Step over here to the window, big boy. Do you see that casino just across the street? I own that casino outright. And I own it because I give a blow-job that's worth every cent of $1,500."

The guy, basking in the afterglow of that terrific hand-job, decides to put off the new car for another year or so, and says, "Sign me up."

Ten minutes later, he is sitting on the bed more amazed than before. He can hardly believe it but he feels he truly got his money's worth.

He decides to dip into the retirement savings for one glorious and unforgettable experience. He asks the hooker, "How much for some pussy?"

The hooker says, "Come over here to the window, I want to show you something. Do you see how the whole city of is laid out before us, all those beautiful lights, hotels, and theatres?"

"Damn!" the guy says, in awe, "You own the whole city?"

"No," the hooker replies, "but I would if I had a pussy."

***

A beautiful brunette moved in next door to Danny. She loved sunbathing in the nude. Danny would go out in the garden, looking through a crack in the fence, every sunny day. She had the most perfect breasts he had ever seen. He couldn't stand it any longer. He knocked on her front door and offered her $10,000 if he could kiss her breasts. She agreed to the deal. She stripped off her blouse and sat on the bed.

Danny bent down and snuggled his nose between her breasts, he cupped each breast in his hands and sighed with delight.

"Come on – kiss them" she said.

"I can't" said Danny.

"Why not?" she asked angrily.

"I haven't got $10,000".

***

A company, feeling it was time for a shake-up, hires a new CEO. The new boss is determined to rid the company of all slackers. On a tour of the facilities, the CEO notices a guy leaning on a wall. The room is full of workers and he thinks this is his chance to show everyone he means business! The CEO walks up the guy and asks, "And how much money do you make a week?"

Undaunted, the young fellow replies, "I make $300.00 a week. Why?"

The CEO then hands the guy $300 in cash and screams, "Here's a week's pay, now get out and don't come back!"

Feeling pretty good about his first firing, the CEO looks around the room and asks, "Does anyone want to tell me what that slacker did here?"

With a sheepish grin, one of the other workers muttered, "He's the pizza delivery guy."

GOLF

Tiger Woods drives his BMW into a petrol station in a remote part of the Irish countryside. The attendant at the pump greets him in a typically relaxed Irish manner, completely unaware of who the golfing legend is.

"Top of the mornin' to yer, sor" says the attendant. Tiger nods a quick 'hello' and bends forward to pick up the nozzle. As he does so, two tees fall out of his shirt pocket onto the ground. "What are dey den, son?" asks the attendant. "They're called tees" replies Tiger. "Well, what on de good earth are dey for?" inquires the Irishman. "They're for resting my balls on when I'm driving" says Tiger. "Jaysus" says the Irishman, "Dem boys at BMW tink of everything!"

Two women are playing golf on a sunny afternoon when one of them slices her shot into a foursome of men. To her horror, one of the men collapses in agony with both hands in his crotch. She runs to him apologising profusely, explaining that she is a physical therapist and can help ease his pain.

"No thanks...just give me a few minutes... I'll be fine..." he replies quietly with his hands still between his legs. Taking it upon herself to help the poor man, she gently undoes the front of his pants and starts massaging his genitals.

"Doesn't that feel better?" she asks.

"Well...yes...that feels pretty good," he admits. "But my thumb still hurts like hell."

***

A couple were on their honeymoon, laying in bed, about ready to consummate their marriage, when the new bride says to the husband, "I have a confession to make...I'm not a virgin."

"That's no big thing in this day and age" the husband replies.

"Yeah, I've been with one other guy."

"Oh yeah? Who was the guy?" he asks.

"Tiger Woods."

"Tiger Woods the golfer?"

"Yeah."

"Well he's rich, famous and handsome" he says. "I can see why you went to bed with him."

The husband and wife then make passionate love. When they are finished, the husband gets up and walks to the telephone.

"What are you doing?" says the wife.

The husband says, "I'm hungry. I was going to call room service and get some food."

"Tiger wouldn't do that," she says calmly.

"Oh yeah? What would Tiger do?"

"He'd come back to bed and do it a second time."

The husband puts down the phone and goes back to bed to make love with his wife a second time. When they finish, he gets up and goes over to the phone.

"What are you doing?" she says.

"I'm still hungry so I was going to call room service to get some food." he says.

"Tiger wouldn't do that."

"Oh yeah? What would Tiger do?"

"He'd come back to bed and do it one more time."

The guy slams down the phone and goes back to bed and makes love to his wife one more time. When they finish he's tired and exhausted. He drags himself over to the phone and starts to dial. "Are you calling room service?" she asks.

"No! I'm calling Tiger Woods to find out what's par for this hole!"

***

Two old friends were just about to tee off at the first hole of their local golf course when a chap carrying a golf bag called out to them, "Do you mind if join you? My partner didn't turn up."

"Sure," they said, "You're welcome."

So they started playing and enjoyed the game and the company of the newcomer. Part way around the course, one of the friends asked the newcomer, "What do you do for a living?"

"I'm a hitman," was the reply.

"You're joking!" was the response.

"No, I'm not," he said, reaching into his golf bag, and pulling out a beautiful Martini sniper's rifle with a large telescopic sight. "Here are my tools."

"That's a beautiful telescopic sight," said the other friend, "Can I take a look? I think I might be able to see my house from here."

So he picked up the rifle and looked through the sight in the direction of his house.

"Yeah, I can see my house all right. This sight is fantastic. I can see right in the window."

"Wow, I can see my wife in the bedroom. Ha Ha... I can see she's naked! Wait a minute...that's my neighbour in there with her...he's naked as well! The bitch!"

He turned to the hitman, "How much do you charge for a hit?"

"I do a mate's rate, for you, one thousand dollars every time I pull the trigger."

"Can you do two for me now?"

"Sure, what do you want?"

"First, shoot my wife; she's always been mouthy, so shoot her in the mouth. Then the neighbor, he's a mate of mine, a bit of a lad, so just shoot his dick off to teach him a lesson."

The hit man took the rifle and took aim, standing perfectly still for a few moments.

"Are you going to do it or not?" said the friend impatiently.

"Just wait a moment...be patient," said the hitman calmly, "I think I can save you a grand here..."

One fine day in Ireland, Pat is out golfing and gets up to the 16th hole.

He tees up and cranks one. Unfortunately, it goes into the woods on the side of the fairway. He goes looking for his ball and comes across this little chap with this huge lump on his head, and the golf ball lying right beside him.

"Goodness," says Pat, and proceeds to revive the poor little fellow. Upon awaking, the little guy says, "Well, you caught me fair and square. I am a leprechaun. I will grant you three wishes." The man says, "I can't take anything from you, I'm just glad I didn't hurt you too badly" and walks away.

Watching the golfer depart, the leprechaun says "Well, he was nice enough, and he did catch me, so I have to do something for him. I'll give him the three things that I would want. I'll give him unlimited money, a great golf game, and a great sex life."

Well, a year goes past and Pat is again out golfing on the same course at the 16th hole. He gets up and hits one into the same woods and goes off looking for his ball. When he finds the ball, he sees the same little guy and asks how he is going.

The leprechaun says, "I'm fine, and might I ask how your golf game is?"

The golfer says, "It's great! I hit under par every time." The leprechaun says, "I did that for you. Might I ask how your money is holding out?"

The golfer says, "Well, now that you mention it, every time I put my hand in my pocket, I pull out a hundred dollar bill." The leprechaun smiles and says, "I did that for you, too. And might I ask how your sex life is?"

The golfer looks at him a little shyly and says,

"Well, maybe once or twice a week." The leprechaun is floored and stammers, "Once or twice a week? Is that all?!" The golfer looks at him and says, "Well, that's not too bad for a priest in a small parish!"

JEWISH

Six retired Jewish men were playing poker in the condo clubhouse when Meyerwitz loses $500 on a single hand, clutches his chest and drops dead at the table.

Showing respect for their fallen comrade, the other five continue playing, standing up. Finkelstein looks around and asks, "So, who's gonna tell his wife?"

They draw straws, and Goldberg picks the short one. They tell him to be discreet, be gentle, don't make a bad situation any worse.

"Discreet? I'm the most discreet guy you'll ever meet. Discretion is my middle name. Leave it to me!"

Goldberg goes over to the Meyerwitz apartment and knocks on the door. The wife answers and asks what he wants.

"Your husband just lost $500 and is afraid to come home." says Goldberg.

"Tell him to drop dead!" the wife says.

"I'll go tell him."

A reporter goes to Israel to cover the fighting. She is looking for something emotional, positive and of human interest. In Jerusalem, she hears about an old Jew who has been going to the Wailing Wall to pray, twice a day, every day, for a long, long time. So she goes to check it out. She goes to the Wailing Wall and there he is! She watches him pray and after about 45 minutes, when he turns to leave, she approaches him for an interview.

"Rebecca Smith, CNN News. Sir, how long have you been coming to the Wailing Wall and praying?"

"For about 50 years."

"What do you pray for?"

"For peace between the Jews and the Arabs. For all the hatred to stop. For our children to grow up in safety and friendship."

"How do you feel after doing this for 50 years?"

"Like I'm talking to a fucking brick wall!"

***

A man arrives at Tel Aviv International Airport with two large bags. The customs agent opens the first bag and finds it full with money in different currencies. The agent asks the passenger, "How did you get this money?"

"You will not believe it" the man says, "but I traveled all over Europe, I went into public restrooms and each time I saw a man pee, I grabbed his penis and said, 'donate money to Israel or I will cut your balls off...'"

The customs agent said, "well...it's a very interesting story...what do you have in the other bag?"

"You would not believe how many people in Europe do not support Israel"...

Father O'Brien was called away for an emergency. Not wanting to leave the confessional unattended, he called his rabbi friend from across the street and asked him to cover for him. The rabbi told him he wouldn't know what to say, but the priest told him to come on over and he'd stay with him for a while and show him what to do. The rabbi comes and he and the priest are in the confessional. A few minutes later, a woman comes in and says, "Father forgive me for I have sinned." The priest asks "What did you do?"

Woman: "I committed adultery."

Priest: "How many times?"

Woman: "Three times."

Priest: "Say two Hail Marys, put $5 in the box and go and sin no more." A few minutes later a man enters the confessional. He says, "Father forgive me for I have sinned."

Priest: "What did you do?"

Man: "I committed adultery."

Priest: "How many times?"

Man: "Three times."

Priest: "Say two Hail Mary's, put $5 in the box and go and sin no more." The rabbi tells the priest that he thinks he's got it so the priest leaves. A few minutes later another woman enters and says, "Father, forgive me for I have sinned."

Rabbi:"What did you do?"

Woman: "I committed adultery."

Rabbi: "How many times?"

Woman: "Once."

Rabbi: "Go do it two more times. We have a special this week, three for $5."

***

A man was called in for an audit by the Tax Office. He asked his accountant for advice on what to wear. "Wear your worst clothing and an old pair of shoes. Let them think you are a pauper," the accountant said.

Then he asked his lawyer the same question, but got the opposite advice: "Don't let them intimidate you. Wear your best suit and an expensive tie."

Confused, the man went to his Rabbi who would surely know the correct answer. He told him of the conflicting advice he had received, and asked what he should do.

"Let me tell you a story," replied the Rabbi. "A woman, about to be married, asked her mother what to wear on her wedding night. Her mother advised, 'Wear a heavy, long, flannel nightgown that goes right up to your neck and wool socks.' But when the woman asked her best friend, she got conflicting advice: 'Wear your sexiest negligee, with a V-neck right down to your navel.'"

The man did not understand: "But Rabbi, what does all this have to do with my problem with the Tax Office?"

"I'll give you the same advice I gave her when she asked me", replied the Rabbi, "It doesn't matter what you wear – you're going to get screwed."

***

A man goes to see the Rabbi. "Rabbi, something terrible is happening and I have to talk to you about it."

"What's wrong?" the Rabbi asked.

"My wife is poisoning me."

The Rabbi, very surprised by this, asks, "How can that be?"

"I'm telling you, I'm certain she's poisoning me. What should I do?"

The Rabbi then offers, "Tell you what...let me talk to her, I'll see what I can find out and I'll let you know."

A week later the Rabbi calls the man and says, "I spoke with your wife. I was on the phone with her for three hours. Do you want to hear my advice?"

"Yes, yes!" the man says anxiously.

"Take the poison..."

***

A rabbi, a priest and a minister were discussing how they divided up the collection plate. The priest said he left it up to God. He drew a circle and threw the contents of the plate into the air. Everything landing inside the circle was for the poor and needy and all on the outside was for his expenses.

The minister had a similar method. He also left it up to God. He drew a straight line then threw the contents into the air. One side was for the parish and the other was his.

The rabbi also said he left it up to God. He threw the contents into the air and God could keep all he caught.

The Tax Office sends their auditor to a synagogue. The auditor is doing all the checks and then turns to the Rabbi, and says, "I noticed that you buy a lot of candles."

"Yes," answered the Rabbi.

"Well, Rabbi, what do you do with the candle wax drippings?" he asked.

"A good question," noted the Rabbi. "We actually save them up and when we have enough, we send them back to the candle maker and every now and then, they send us a free box of candles."

"Oh," replied the auditor. "Rabbi, what about all these matzo purchases? What do you do with the crumbs from the matzo?"

"Ah, yes," replied the Rabbi calmly, "we actually collect up all the crumbs from the matzo and when we have enough, we send them in a box back to the manufacturer and every now and then, they send a box of matzo balls."

"Oh," replied the auditor, thinking hard how to fluster the Rabbi. "Well, Rabbi," he went on, "what do you do with all the foreskins from the circumcisions?"

"Yes, here too, we do not waste," answered the Rabbi. "What we do is save up all the foreskins, and when we have enough we actually send them to The Tax Office."

"The Tax Office?" questioned the auditor in disbelief.

"Ah, yes," replied the Rabbi, "The Tax Office... and about once a year, they send us a little prick like you."

KIDS

A young family moved into a house next door to an empty plot. One day a construction crew turned up to start building a house there.

The young family's 5-year-old daughter naturally took an interest in all the activity going on next door and started talking with the workers. She hung around and eventually the construction crew, all of them rough diamond types, more or less adopted her as their project mascot. They chatted with her, let her sit with them while they had coffee and lunch breaks, and gave her little jobs to do here and there to make her feel important.

At the end of the first week they even presented her with a pay envelope containing $5. The little girl took this home to her mother who praised the girl with words of admiration and suggested that they take the money she had received to the bank the next day to start a savings account. When they got to the bank the clerk was equally impressed with the story and asked the little girl how she had come by her very own wage packet at such a young age. The little girl proudly replied, "I worked all last week with a crew building a house."

"My goodness," said the clerk, "and will you be working on the house again this week, too?"

"I will if those useless pricks at the hardware store ever bring us the fucking plasterboard..."

***

An adorable little girl, all blonde curls and blue eyes walks into a pet shop and asks in the sweetest little lisp: "Excuthe me mithter, do you keep widdle wabbits?" The shopkeeper's heart melts and he gets down on his knees so that he's on her level, and asks, "Do you want a widdle white wabbit, or a thoft and fuwwy bwack wabbit or maybe one like that cute widdle bwown wabbit over there?"

She, blushing, rocks on her heels, puts her hands on her knees, leans forward and says in a quiet voice, "I don't fink my python weally givth a phuck...

***

The boss of a big company needed to call one of his employees about an urgent problem with one of the main computers. He dialed the employee's home phone number and was greeted with a child's whisper,

"Hello."

"Is your daddy home?" he asked.

"Yes," whispered the small voice.

"May I talk with him?"

The child whispered, "No."

Surprised, and wanting to talk with an adult, the boss asked, "Is your mommy there?"

"Yes."

"May I talk with her?"

Again the small voice whispered, "No."

Hoping there was somebody with whom he could leave a message, the boss asked, "Is anybody else there?"

"Yes," whispered the child, "a policeman."

Wondering what a cop would be doing at his employee's home, the Boss asked, "May I speak with the policeman?"

"No, he's busy" whispered the child.

"Busy doing what?"

"Talking to Daddy and Mommy and the Fireman," came the whispered answer.

Growing concerned and even worried as he heard what sounded like a helicopter through the earpiece on the phone the boss asked, "What is that noise?"

"A hello-copper," answered the whispering voice.

"What is going on there?" asked the boss, now alarmed.

In a whispering voice the child answered, "The search team just landed the hello-copper."

Alarmed, concerned, and even more than just a little frustrated the boss asked, "What are they searching for?"

Still whispering, the young voice replied along with a muffled giggle:

"Me..."

***

A mother was working in the kitchen, listening to her five-year-old son playing with his new electric train in the living room.

She heard the train stop and her son saying, "All of you bastards who want to get off, get the hell off now, 'cause this is the last stop! And all of you bastards who are getting on, get your arse in the train, cause we're going down the tracks."

The horrified mother went in and said, "We don't use that kind of language in this house. Now I want you to go to your room and stay there for two hours. When you come out, you may play with your train, but I want you to use nice language."

Two hours later, the son came out of the bedroom and resumed playing with his train. Soon the train stopped and the mother heard her son say, "All passengers who are disembarking the train please remember to take all of your belongings with you. We thank you for travelling with us today and hope your trip was a pleasant one."

She hears the little boy continue, "For those of you just boarding, we ask you to stow all of your hand luggage under your seat. Remember, there is no smoking on the train. We hope you will have a pleasant and relaxing journey with us today."

As the mother began to smile, the child added, "For those of you who are pissed off about the two hours delay, please see the fat arse bitch in the kitchen."

***

One day a 12-year-old boy was walking down the street when a car pulled up beside him and its window was wound down.

"I'll give you a bag of sweets if you get in the car," said the driver.

"No way...get stuffed!" replied the boy.

"How about a bag of sweets and $10?" the driver asked.

"I said, no way!" replied the irritated youngster.

" What about a bag of juicy sweets and $50, eh?" quizzed the driver, still rolling slowly to keep up with the walking boy.

"No! I'm not getting in the damn car!" answered the boy.

"Okay, okay. I know what you want. I'll give you $100 and a bag of sweets," the driver offered.

"No!" screamed the boy.

"What will it take to get you into the car?" asked the driver in a long sigh. The boy replied: "Listen Dad, you bought the bloody Volvo, you live with it!"

***

A little boy went to his father and asked: "Dad, where did all of my intelligence come from?"

"Well, son, you must have gotten it from your mother, 'cause I still have mine" the father replied.

***

A group of 3rd, 4th and 5th graders, accompanied by two female teachers, went on a field trip to the local racetrack to learn about thoroughbred horses and the industry. When it was time to take the children to the bathroom it was decided that the girls would go with one teacher and the boys would go with the other. The teacher assigned to the boys was waiting outside the men's room when one of the boys came out and told her that none of them could reach the urinal.

Having no choice, she went inside, helped the boys with their pants, and began hoisting the little boys up one by one, assisting each one to direct the flow away from their clothes. As she lifted one, she couldn't help but notice that he was unusually well endowed. Trying not to show that she was staring the teacher said, "You must be in the 5th grade."

"No, ma'am!" he replied. "I'm the jockey riding Silver Arrow in the seventh!"

LAST MINUTE STUFF

Two women are new arrivals at the Pearly Gates, and are comparing stories on how they had died.

First woman: "I froze to death."

Second woman: "You froze to death? How horrible!"

First woman: "Well, it wasn't so bad. After I quit shaking from the cold, I began to get warm and sleepy, and finally died a peaceful death. And you?"

Second woman: "I died of a massive heart attack. I suspected that my husband was cheating, so I came home early to catch him in the act. But instead, I found him all by himself in the den, watching TV. I was so sure there was another woman somewhere that I started running all over the house, looking. I ran up into the attic and searched and down to the basement. Then I went through every closet and checked under every bed. I kept this up until I had looked everywhere, and I finally became so exhausted that I just keeled over with a heart attack and died."

First woman: "Too bad you didn't look in the freezer – we'd both still be alive."

***

Paul McCartney is doing his Xmas shopping and decides to buy Heather a new artificial leg. He wraps it up, takes it home and hides it in the wardrobe. A couple of days later, Heather is doing her housework and finds it. She 'phones Paul and says, "That's a really nice present Paul but I hope it's not my main Xmas present!"

"No...it's just a stocking filler!"

***

Two guys are walking through the woods and come across a big deep hole.

"Wow...that looks deep!"

"Sure does...toss a few pebbles in there and see how deep it is."

They pick up a few pebbles and throw them in and wait...but no noise.

"Gee...that is **really** deep. Throw some of these great big rocks down there. They should make a noise."

They pick up a couple of football-sized rocks and toss them into the hole and wait, and wait. But nothing. They look at each other in amazement.

One gets a determined look on his face and says, "There's a railway sleeper over there. Help me carry it over. When we toss **that** in, it's gotta make some noise!"

512

They drag the heavy sleeper over to the hole and heave it in. But not a sound comes from the hole. Suddenly, out of the nearby woods, a goat appears, running like the wind. It rushes toward the two men, then runs right past them, running as fast as its legs will carry it. Suddenly, it leaps in the air and disappears into the hole. The two men are astonished at what they've just seen. Then, out of the woods comes a farmer who spots the men and ambles over.

"Hey...have you guys seen my goat?"

"You bet we did! Craziest thing we've ever seen! It came running like the wind and jumped into this hole!"

"Nah," says the farmer, "that couldn't have been my goat. My goat was chained to a railway sleeper"!

***

I was on the Highway recently when I decided to stop at a rest stop to use the men's room. The first stall was occupied so went in the second. I was barely sitting down when a voice from the other stall said, "Hi, how are you?"

I'm not the type to start a conversation or fraternize in men's rooms at a rest stop and I don't know what got into me, but I answered, somewhat embarrassed, "Not bad!"

"So what's up with you?" he asked.

"Ah... I'm like you, just traveling east!" I stammered.

The guy nervously said... "I'll have to call you back; there's an idiot in the next stall who keeps answering all my questions!"

A stock broker, on his way home from work, came to a dead halt in traffic. "This traffic seems worse than usual. Nothing's even moving." he thought.

He noticed a police officer walking back and forth between the lines of cars, so he rolled down his window and asked, "Officer what's the hold up?"

"Hillary Clinton is so depressed about Americans making her the butt of so many jokes, she stopped her motorcade in the middle of the freeway and she's threatening to douse herself in petrol and set herself on fire. She says her husband is running around on her more than ever and the Democrats told her to forget about ever going for the presidency. So we're taking up a collection for her."

"Oh really? How much have you got so far?" the broker asks.

"About 15 litres, but a lot of folks are still siphoning."

***

A salesman drives into this small town where a circus was in progress. A sign read:

"Don't miss the amazing Scotsman".

He buys a ticket and sits down. There, on centre stage, was a table with three walnuts on it. Standing next to it is an old Scotsman. Suddenly the old man lifts his kilt, whips out a huge willy and smashes all three walnuts with three mighty swings! The crowd erupts in applause as the elderly Scot is carried off on their shoulders.

Ten years later the salesman visits the same

little town and he sees a faded sign for the same circus saying, "Don't Miss the Amazing Scotsman."

He can't believe the old guy is still alive much less still doing his act! He buys a ticket. Again, the centre ring is illuminated. This time, instead of walnuts, three coconuts are placed on the table. The Scotsman stands before them, then suddenly lifts his kilt and smashes the coconuts with three swings of his amazing dick. The crowd goes wild! Flabbergasted, the salesman requests a meeting with him after the show.

"You're incredible," he tells the Scotsman. "But I have to know something. You're older now, why switch from walnuts to coconuts?"

"Well...me eyes are not what they used to be..."

***

WANTED
A tall well-built woman with good
reputation, who can cook frog's
legs, who appreciates a good fuc
hsia garden, classical musical music and tal
king without getting too serious.

But please only read lines 1, 3 and 5.

***

The European Commission has just announced an agreement whereby English will be the official language of the European nation rather than German, which was the other possibility.

As part of the negotiations, Her Majesty's Government conceded that English spelling had some room for improvement and has accepted a 5-year phase-in plan that would become known as "Euro-English".

In the first year, "c" will replace the soft "s". Sertainly, this will make the sivil servants jump with joy. The hard "c" will be dropped in favour of the "k". This should klear up konfusion, and keyboards kan have one less letter. There will be growing publik enthusiasm in the sekond year when the troublesome "ph" will be replaced with the "f". This will make words like fotograf, 20% shorter.

In the third year, publik akseptanse of the new spelling kan be expekted to reach the stage where more komplikated changes are possible. Governments will encourage removal of double letters which have always ben a deterent to akurate speling. Also, al wil agre that the horibl mes of the silent "e" in the languag is disgrasful and it should go away.

By the fourth yer peopl wil be reseptiv to steps such as replasing "th" with "z" and "w" with "v".

During ze fifz yer, ze unesesary "o" kan be dropd from vords kontaining "ou" and after ziz fifz yer, ve vil hav a reil sensibl riten styl.

Zer vil be no mor trubl or difikultis and evrivun vil find it ezi tu understand ech oza. Ze drem of a united urop vil finali kum tru.

***

This woman walks into a chemist's shop and tells the pharmacist she wants to buy some arsenic.

"What do you want with arsenic?" he asks.

"I want to kill my husband because he cheats on me by having sex with another woman."

"I can't sell you arsenic so you can kill your husband, lady, even if he is having sex with another woman" says the pharmacist.

She reaches into her pocket and pulls out a picture of her husband having sex with the pharmacist's wife.

"Oh, I didn't realize you had a prescription."

***

A guy and his wife fancied a pet ferret they saw in a pet shop. They couldn't afford to buy it, so when no-one was looking, they stole it. On their way home, the guy was exceeding the speed limit and was pulled over by the Police. The guy thought they were after him for stealing the ferret, so he said to his wife, "Put the ferret up your dress and hold it between your thighs."

"But it'll smell like hell!" said his wife.

"I know" said the guy, "just hold his nose and he'll be ok".

***

A blind man walked into a restaurant. He explained to the waiter that he couldn't read the menu and asked for three dirty forks from previous meals. "Ah!" he said after smelling the forks, "I'll have the chicken parmagiana".

A few days later, the blind man returned. Again he asked for three forks, smelt them and this time ordered spaghetti marinara.

A few days later, the blind man returned again. The waiter thought he'd play a joke on him. "Would you like to try today's special?" he asked.

"Let me smell the fork", requested the blind man.

The waiter went to the kitchen and asked the cook to wipe the fork on her panties and then took it to the blind man.

"Ah!" said the blind man, "how long has Susie been working here?"

***

While waiting for my first appointment in the reception room of a new dentist, I noticed his certificate, which bore his full name. Suddenly, I remembered that a tall, handsome boy with the same name had been in my high school class some 30 years ago. After seeing him however, I quickly discarded any such thought. This balding, grey-haired man with the deeply lined face was far too old to have been my classmate. After he had examined my teeth, I asked him if he had attended the local high school.

"Yes," he replied.

"When did you graduate?" I asked.

"In 1971. Why?"

"You were in my class!" I exclaimed.

He looked at my face closely and asked, "What did you teach?"

***

Three men were sitting together bragging about how they had given their new wives duties. The first man had married a woman from Albania, and bragged that he had told his wife she was going to do all the dishes and house cleaning that needed done. He said that it took a couple days till he saw any action but on the third day he came home to a clean house and the dishes were all washed and put away. The second man had married a woman from Korea. He bragged that he had given his wife orders that she was to do all the cleaning, dishes, and the cooking. He told them that the first day he didn't see any results, but the next day it was better. By the third day, his house was clean, the dishes were done, and he had a huge dinner on the table. The third man had married an Australian girl. He boasted that he told her that her duties were to keep the house cleaned, dishes washed, the lawn mowed, laundry done and hot meals on the table for every meal. He said the first day he didn't see anything, the second day he didn't see anything, but by the third day most of the swelling had gone down and he could see a little out of his left eye.

MARRIAGE

For all those men who say about marriage... "why buy the cow when you can get the milk for free?", here's an update for you. Today, 80% of women are against getting married because women realise it's not worth buying an entire pig just to get a little sausage.

If you're a man, don't get married. Find a woman you hate with two kids, buy her a house and car and give her a cheque every week, then go and live with your parents. It's a lot easier and saves time.

*****

A married man and his secretary were having a wild affair. One afternoon they couldn't contain their passion, so they rushed over to her place where they spent the afternoon making passionate love. When they were finished, they fell asleep, not waking until 8 o'clock. They got dressed quickly. Then the man told his secretary to take his shoes outside and rub them on the lawn. Bewildered, she did as he asked, thinking him pretty weird. The man finally got home and his wife met him at the door. Upset, she asked where he'd been. The man replied, "I cannot tell a lie. My secretary and I are having an affair. Today we left work early, went to her place, spent the afternoon making love, and then fell asleep. That's why I'm late."

The wife looked at him, took notice of his shoes and yelled, "I can see those are grass stains on your shoes. You liar! You've been playing golf again, haven't you?"

*****

John O'Riley was a member of an Irish Toast Masters Club. One evening at their meeting, a contest was held to see who could deliver the best toast. John won the contest for the best toast of the evening:

"Here's to the best years o' me life, spent between the legs o' me wife."

When John arrived home his wife asked him how the Toast Masters meeting went and he said, "I won the contest for the best toast of the evening." She asked him what his toast was, and he said, "Here's to the best years o' me life, spent in Church wi' me wife."

"John, that's so nice of you to include me in your toast."

The next morning, Mrs. O'Riley was shopping and ran into the local policeman on the beat who had been at the Toast Masters meeting with her husband. "Hello Mrs. O'Riley...that was some great toast that your husband John gave at the Toast Masters meeting last evening. He won first prize".

"Yes, that's right," she said "but he wasn't quite honest with the facts: he's only been there twice, the first time he fell asleep and the second time I had to pull him by the ears to make him come."

***

Fresh from her shower, a woman stands in front of the mirror, complaining to her husband that her breasts are too small. Instead of his standard response of reassuring her that that wasn't the case, comes up with a suggestion. "If you want your breasts to grow, then every day take a piece of toilet paper and rub it between your breasts for a few seconds." Willing to try anything, the wife gets a piece of toilet paper and stands in front of the mirror, rubbing it between her breasts. "How long will this take?" she asks.

"They'll grow larger over a period of years," he replies.

"Why do you think rubbing a piece of toilet paper between my breasts every day will make my breasts grow over the years?"

"Worked for your arse, didn't it?"

***

A man goes to a shrink and says, "Doctor, my beautiful, sexy, young wife is unfaithful to me. Every evening, she goes to the Arrow Bar and picks up men. In fact, she goes to bed with anybody who asks her! I'm going crazy. What do you think I should do?"

"Relax," says the Doctor, "take a deep breath and calm down. Now, tell me, where exactly is the Arrow Bar?"

***

A man came home from work, sat down in his favorite chair, turned on the TV, and said to his wife, "Quick, bring me a beer before it starts." She looked a little puzzled, but brought him a beer. When he finished it, he said, "Quick, bring me another beer. It's gonna start." This time she looked a little angry, but brought him a beer. When it was gone, he said, "Quick, another beer before it starts." "That's it!" she says, blowing her top.

"You bastard! You waltz in here, flop your fat ass down, don't even say hello to me and then expect me to run around like your slave. Don't you realize that I cook and clean and wash and iron all day long?" The husband sighed, "Oh Shit…it's started."

***

A couple was celebrating their golden wedding anniversary. Their domestic tranquility had long been the talk of the town.

'What a peaceful and loving couple' everyone said. A local newspaper reporter was inquiring as to the secret of their long and happy marriage.

"Well, it dates back to our honeymoon," explained the man. "We visited the Grand Canyon and took a trip down to the bottom of the canyon by horse. We hadn't gone too far when my wife's horse stumbled. My wife quietly said, 'That's once.'

'We proceeded a little further and the horse stumbled again. Once more my wife quietly said, 'That's twice.'

'We hadn't gone a half-mile when the horse stumbled the third time. My wife quietly removed a revolver from her purse and shot the horse dead.'

'I started an angry protest over her treatment of the horse, when she looked me straight in the eye and quietly said, 'That's once'.

'And we lived happily ever after.'

***

A mild-mannered man was tired of being bossed around by his wife, so he went to a psychiatrist.

The psychiatrist said he needed to build his self-esteem, and so gave him a book on assertiveness, which he read on the way home. He had finished the book by the time he reached his house. The man stormed into the house and walked up to his wife.

Pointing his finger in her face, he said, "From now on, I want you to know that I am the man of this house, and my word is law! I want you to prepare me a gourmet meal tonight, and when I'm finished eating my meal, I expect a sumptuous dessert afterward. Then, after dinner, you're going to draw me my bath so I can relax. And, when I'm finished with my bath, guess who's going to dress me and comb my hair?"

"No need to guess – I know" said his wife, "The fucking funeral director."

***

An elderly couple was on a cruise and it was very stormy. They were standing on the back of the boat watching the moon, a wave came up and washed the old woman overboard. They searched for days and couldn't find her, so the captain sent the old man back to shore with the promise that he would notify him as soon as they found something. Three weeks went by and finally the old man got an email from the captain. It read:

"Sir, sorry to inform you, we found your wife dead at the bottom of the ocean. We hauled her up to the deck and attached to her bum was an oyster and it had a pearl worth $50,000...please advise".

The old man emailed back : "Send me the pearl and re-bait the trap"

***

A funeral service is being held for a woman who has just passed away. At the end of the service, the pall bearers are carrying the casket out when they accidentally bump into a wall, jarring the casket. They hear a faint moan! They open the casket and find that the woman is actually alive! She lives for ten more years, and then dies. Once again, a ceremony is held, and at the end of it, the pall bearers are again carrying out the casket.

As they carry the casket towards the door, the husband cries out, "Watch that wall!"

***

A man goes to visit his doctor. "Doc, you've gotta help me! My wife just isn't interested in sleeping with me anymore! No passion, nothing! Haven't you got a pill or something I can give her?"

"Look, I can't prescribe..."

"Doc, we've been friends for years. Have you ever seen me this upset? I'm desperate! I can't think; I can't concentrate; my life is falling apart! You've got to help me man!"

The doctor opens his desk drawer and removes a small bottle of pills.

"Okay. Ordinarily, I wouldn't do this. These are experimental; the tests so far indicate that they're very powerful. Don't give her more than one, understand? Just one – in her coffee."

The man goes home, where his wife has dinner waiting. When dinner is finished, she goes to the kitchen to bring dessert. The man quickly takes out the pills, then slips one into her coffee. And then he begins to wonder...'The doc said they were powerful...' Out of the blue, he drops a pill into his own coffee, just to see what it's like.

His wife returns and they enjoy their dessert and coffee. Sure enough, a few minutes after they finish, she shudders, sighs deeply, and a strange look comes over her face. In a guttural tone, she moans: "I...need...a man..."

When the husband hears this, his eyes well up with tears and his hands begin to tremble. In a passion-choked voice, he exclaims: "So do I!"

***

A young boy asks his father, "Dad, is it OK for us guys to notice all the different kind of boobs?"

Surprised, the father answers, "Well, sure son, we wouldn't be normal if we didn't...there are all kinds of breasts...depending on a woman's age.

In her twenties, a woman's breasts are like melons, round and firm. In her thirties to forties, they are like pears, still nice but hanging a bit. After fifty, they are like onions."

"Onions, Dad?"

"Yeah, you see them and they make you cry..."

Not to be outdone, his sister asks her mother, "Mom, how many kind of weenies are there?"

"Well, a man goes through three phases. In a man's twenties, a man's weenie is like an oak, mighty and hard. In his thirties and forties, it is like a birch, flexible but reliable. After his fifties, it is like a Christmas tree."

"A Christmas tree?"

"Yep, dried up and the balls are only there for decoration..."

***

A woman went into a store to buy her husband a pet for his birthday. After looking around, she found that all the pets were very expensive.

She told the clerk she wanted to buy a pet, but she didn't want to spend a fortune.

"Well," said the clerk, "I have a very large bullfrog. They say it's been trained to give blowjobs!"

"Blowjobs!" the woman exclaimed.

"We've sold 30 of them this month," he said.

The woman thought it would be a great gag gift, and what if it's true...no more blowjobs for her! She bought the frog. When she explained froggy's ability to her husband, he was extremely skeptical and laughed it off. The woman went to bed happy, thinking she may never need to perform this less than riveting act again. In the middle of the night, she was awakened by the noise of pots and pans flying everywhere, making loud banging and crashing sounds. She ran downstairs to the kitchen to find her husband and the frog reading cookbooks.

"What are you two doing at this hour?" she asked.

The husband replied, "If I can teach this frog to cook, you're outta here.

A man walks into a drug store with his 13-year old son. They walk by the condom display and the boy asks, "What are these, Dad?"

"Those are called condoms, son. Men use them to have safe sex." the man replies, matter-of-factly.

"Oh," replied the boy. "I've heard of that in health class at school."

He picks up a package of 3 and asks, "Why are there 3 in this package?"

"Those are for high-school boys. One for Friday, one for Saturday, and one for Sunday," the dad replies.

"Cool!" says the boy.

He notices a 6-pack and asks, "Then who are these for?"

"Those are for college men," the dad answers. "Two for Friday, two for Saturday, and two for Sunday."

"Wow!" exclaimed the boy.

"Then who uses these?" he asks, picking up a 12-pack. With a sigh, the dad replies, "Those are for married men. One for January, one for February, one for March..."

***

Recently a "Husband Shopping Centre" opened in Sydney where women could go to choose a husband from a range of many men.

It was laid out in five floors, with the men increasing in positive attributes as you ascended. The only rule was, once you opened the door to any floor, you **had** to choose a man from that floor; If you went up a floor, you couldn't go back down except to leave the place, never to return. A couple of girlfriends went to the shopping centre to find some husbands and went up in the elevator...

***

First floor:
The door had a sign saying, "These men have jobs and love kids."

The women read the sign and said, "Well, that's better than not having a job, or not loving kids, but I wonder what's further up?"

So up they went.

Second floor:
The sign read, "These men have high paying jobs, love kids, and are extremely good looking."

"Hmmm" said the ladies. "But, I wonder what's further up?"

Third floor:
This sign read, "These men have high paying jobs, are extremely good looking, love kids and help with the housework."

"Wow!" said the women. "Very tempting, but, there's even more further up!" And so up they went.

Fourth floor:
This door had a sign saying "These men have high paying jobs, love kids, are extremely good looking, help with the housework, and have a strong romantic streak."

"Oh, my God. But just think! What must be waiting for us further up?" So up to the fifth floor they went.

Fifth floor:
The sign on that door said, "This floor is empty and exists only to prove that women are impossible to please."

***

A woman stopped by unannounced at her recently married son's house.

She rang the doorbell and walked in. She was shocked to see her daughter-in-law lying on the couch, totally naked. Soft music was playing, and the aroma of perfume filled the room.

"What are you doing?" she asked.

"I'm waiting for my husband to come home from work," the daughter-in-law answered.

"But you're naked!" the mother-in-law exclaimed.

"This is my LOVE dress," the daughter-in-law explained.

"LOVE dress? But you're naked!"

"My husband *loves* me to wear this dress," she explained. "It excites him no end. Every time he sees me in it, he instantly becomes romantic and ravages me for hours on end. He can't get enough of me."

The mother-in-law left. When she got home, she undressed, showered, put on her best perfume, dimmed the lights, put on romantic music and laid on the couch waiting for her husband to arrive. Finally, her husband came home. He walked in and saw her laying there, provocatively.

"What are you doing?" he asked.

"This is my LOVE dress," she whispered sensually.

"Needs ironing" he said, "What's for dinner?"

Police are warning all men who frequent clubs, partygoers and unsuspecting pub regulars to be alert and stay cautious when offered a drink from any woman. A date rape drug is on the market and is used by many females to target unsuspecting men. The drug is found in a brown liquid form and is now available almost anywhere. It comes in bottles, and is used by female sexual predators at parties and bars to persuade their male victims to go home and have sex with them.

Typically, a woman needs only to persuade a guy to consume a few litres of it and then simply ask him home for no strings attached sex.

Men are rendered helpless against this approach and will often succumb to desires to perform sexual acts on horrific looking women to whom they would never normally be attracted. Men often awake with only hazy memories of exactly what happened to them the night before, often with just a vague feeling that something bad occurred. At other times these unfortunate men are swindled out of their life's savings in a familiar scam known as 'a relationship.' It has been reported that in extreme cases, the female may even be shrewd enough to entrap the unsuspecting male into a longer term form of servitude and punishment referred to as 'marriage.' Apparently, men are much more susceptible to this scam after sex is offered by the predatory female.

Please forward this warning to every male you know.

However, if you fall victim to this and the predatory women administering it, there are male support groups with venues in every town where you can discuss the details of your shocking encounter in an open and frank manner with similarly affected, like-minded men.

For the support group nearest you, just look up "Golf Courses" in the yellow pages.

***

When the husband finally died his wife put the usual death notice in the paper, but added that he died of gonorrhea. No sooner were the papers delivered when a good friend of the family phoned and complained bitterly, "You know very well that he died of diarrhea, not gonorrhea!" Replied the widow, "I nursed him night and day so of course I know he died of diarrhea, but I thought it would be better for posterity to remember him as a great lover rather than the big shit he always was."

NEW ZEALANDERS

How do you know when you're staying in a New Zealand country hotel? When you call the front desk and say "I gotta leak in my sink" and the person at the front desk says "Well...go ahead."

***

An Australian, a Kiwi and South African are in a bar one night having a beer. Suddenly, the

South African drinks his beer, pulls out a gun shoots the glass to pieces. He says "In Sooth Efrika our glasses are so cheap that we don't need to drink from the same one twice".

The Kiwi – obviously impressed by this – drinks his beer, throws his glass into the air, pulls out his gun and shoots the glass to pieces.

He says "Will mate, in Noo Zulland we hev so much sand to make the glasses that we don't need to drunk out of the same glass twice either."

The Australian, cool as a Koala, picks up his beer and drinks it, throws his glass into the air, pulls out his gun and shoots the Kiwi. He says "In Australia we have so many Kiwi's that we don't need to drink with the same one twice".

***

A seven year old boy was at the centre of a courtroom drama last week when he challenged a court ruling over who should have custody of him. The boy had a history of being beaten by his parents and the judge awarded custody to his aunt. The boy confirmed that his aunt beat him more than his parents and refused to live there. When the judge suggested that he live with his grandparents the boy cried out that they beat him more than anyone. The judge dramatically allowed the boy to choose who should have custody of him. Custody was finally granted to the All Blacks as the boy firmly believes that they are not capable of beating anyone.

***

Have you spent years trying and failing to understand what New Zealanders are saying? By following these easy steps, you too can hold a conversation with a New Zealander. (Tip – you'll need to sound these out, either in your mind or aloud.) What you hear and what it really means:

BETTING: 'Betting Gloves' are worn by betsmen playing crucket.

BRIST: Part of the human anatomy between the 'nick' and the 'billy.'

BUGGER: As in "mine is bugger than yours".

DIMMER KRETZ: Those who believe in democracy.

ERROR BUCK: Language spoken in countries like "Surria", "E-Jupp" and "Libinon".

EKKA DYMOCKS: University staff

GUESS: Flammable vapour used in stoves.

SENDELS: Thongs, open shoes

COLOUR: Terminator, murderer.

CUSS: A greeting given on the lips

DUCK HID: Term of abuse directed mainly at males.

PHAR LAP: A famous Kiwi horse, which was christened 'Philip.'

ERROR ROUTE: As in "Arnott's mulk error route buskets".

FITTER CHENEY: A type of long flat pasta not to be confused with "rugger tony"

BEARD: As in "I'm tired, so I'm going to beard now"

SEX: After 5 but before 7

***

A New Zealander, a sheep and a dog were survivors of a terrible shipwreck and found themselves stranded on a desert island. After being there for a while, they got into the habit of going to the beach every evening to watch the sun go down.

One particular evening the sky was red with beautiful clouds, the breeze was warm and gentle; a perfect night for romance. As they sat there, the sheep started looking better and better to the Kiwi.

Soon, he leaned over to the sheep and put his arm around it. But the dog got jealous, and growled so fiercely the New Zealander took his arm away from the sheep. After that, the three of them continued to enjoy the sunsets together, but there was no more cuddling.

A few weeks passed, and there was another shipwreck. The only survivor was a beautiful young woman, the most beautiful the New Zealander had ever seen. She was in a pretty bad way when they rescued her, and they slowly nursed her back to health.

When the young woman was well enough, they introduced her to their evening ritual. It was another beautiful evening, red sky, soft clouds, a warm and gentle breeze; perfect for a night of romance. Pretty soon, the New Zealander started to get those randy feelings again. He fought them as long as he could, but he finally gave in and leaned over to the young woman and whispered in her ear, "Would you mind taking the dog for a walk?"

***

Wally, a New Zealander, landed at Heathrow to watch the All Blacks play and was not feeling well, so he decided to see a doctor.

"Hey doc, I don't feel so good, ey" said Wally.

The doctor gave him a thorough examination and informed him that he had prostate problems, and that the only cure was testicular removal.

"No way doc" replied Wally, "I'm gitting a sicond opinion ey!"

The second doctor gave Wally the same diagnosis and also advised him that testicular removal was the only cure.

Not surprisingly, Wally refused the treatment. He was devastated but, with only hours to go before the All Blacks opening game he found an expat Kiwi doctor and decided to get one last opinion from someone he could trust.

The Kiwi doctor examined him and said " Wally, you huv prostate suckness, ey."

"What's the cure thin doc, ey?" asked Wally, hoping for a different answer.

"Wull, Wally" said the Kiwi doctor "Wi're gonna huv to cut off your balls."

"Phew, thunk gord for thut! "said Wally, "those Pommy bastards wanted to take my test tickets off me…"

***

Emily passed away and Wayne the Kiwi called the emergency line. The operator told Wayne that she would send someone out right away.

"Where do you live?" asked the operator.

"Et the ind of Eucalyptus Drive." Wayne replied.

"Can you spell that for me?" The operator asked.

There was a long pause and finally Wayne said "How 'bout if I drag her over to Oak Street and you pick her up there?"

***

Did you hear that they have raised the minimum drinking age in New Zealand to 32?

They want to keep alcohol out of the high schools.

***

Two New Zealanders are walking down different ends of a street toward each other, and one is carrying a sack.

When they meet, one says, "Hey Josh, what'cha got in th' bairg?"

"Jess some chuckens."

"If I giss how minny there are, kin I hev one?"

"Ya giss right and I'll guv you both of thim."

"OK. Umm...five?"

***

A New Zealander came home and found his house on fire. He rushed next door, telephoned the fire department and shouted, "Hurry over here. Me house is on fire, ey!"

OK," replied the fireman, "how do we get there?"

"Ah...don't you still have those bug rid trucks?"

A couple of New Zealand hunters are out in the woods when one of them falls to the ground. He doesn't seem to be breathing and his eyes are rolled back in his head. The other guy whips out his cell phone and calls the emergency line. He gasps to the operator, "My friend is dead, ey! What should I do?"

The operator, in a calm soothing voice says, "Just take it easy. I can help. First, let's make sure he's dead."

There is a silence, then the operator hears a shot. The Kiwi's voice comes back on the line, "OK, now what?"

OLD FOLKS

A senior citizen's group charters a bus for a Sunday's outing.

An hour into the trip, an elderly woman comes up to the driver and says, "I've just been molested!"

The driver felt that she must have fallen asleep and had a dream. So he tells her to go back to her seat, and sit down. A short time later, another old woman comes forward and claims that she was just molested too. The driver knew he had a few senile old blokes on the bus, but who would be molesting those old ladies? Ten minutes later, a third old lady comes up and says that she'd been molested too.

The bus driver decides that he's had enough, and pulls into the first rest area. When he turns the lights on and stands up, he sees an old man on his hands and knees crawling in the aisle.

"Hey gramps, what are you doing down there?" he demands.

"I lost my toupee. I thought I found it three times, but every time I grab it, it keeps jumping away..."

***

An old man marries a young woman and they are deeply in love. However, no matter what the husband does sexually, the woman never achieves orgasm so they decide to ask a sex therapist for advice. The therapist listens to their story and makes the following suggestion:

"Hire a good-looking young man and while the two of you are making love have the young man wave a towel over you, as though he is fanning you both. Make sure he is totally naked and she can see his manhood as he fans you both with the towel. That will help your wife fantasize, and should bring on a full-blown orgasm."

They go home and follow the therapist's advice. They hire a handsome young man and he strips off and enthusiastically waves a towel over them both as they make love. But it doesn't help and still the wife is unsatisfied and frustrated. Perplexed, they go back to the therapist.

"Okay", he says, "let's try it reversed. Have the young man make love to your wife and you wave the towel over them."

Once again, they follow the advice. The young man gets into bed with the wife and the husband waves the towel. The hired hand really works with great enthusiasm and the wife soon has an enormous, room-shaking, screaming, orgasm. Smiling, the husband drops the towel, taps the young man on the shoulder and says to him, triumphantly: "**That's** how you wave a towel, sonny!"

***

An elderly couple is enjoying an anniversary dinner together in a small tavern. The husband leans over and asks his wife, "Do you remember the first time we had sex together over fifty years ago? We went behind this tavern where you leaned against the fence and I made love to you."

"Yes" she says, "I remember it well."

"OK" he says, "How about taking a stroll 'round there again and we can do it for old time's sake."

"Ooh, you devil, that sounds like a good idea," she answers. There's a police officer sitting in the next booth listening to all this, and having a chuckle to himself. He thinks, "I've got to see this...two old-timers having sex against a fence." So he follows them. They walk slowly along, leaning on each other for support, aided by walking sticks. Finally they get to the back of the tavern and make their way to the fence. The old lady lifts her skirt, takes her knickers down and the old man drops his trousers. She turns around and as she hangs on to the fence, the old man moves in. Suddenly they erupt into the most furious sex that the watching policeman has ever seen. They are bucking and jumping like eighteen-year-olds. This goes on for about forty minutes! She's yelling, "Ohhh, God!" He's hanging on to her hips for dear life. This is the most athletic sex imaginable. Finally they both collapse panting on the ground. The policeman is amazed. He thinks he has learned something about life that he didn't know. After about half an hour of lying on the ground recovering, the old couple struggle to their feet and put their clothes back on. The policeman, still watching, thinks, "That was truly amazing, he was going like a train. I've got to ask him what his secret is." As the couple pass, he says to them, "That was something else; you must have been having sex for about forty minutes. How did you manage it? You must have had a fantastic life together. Is there some sort of secret?"

"No, there's no secret," the old man says, "Fifty years ago that damn fence wasn't electric."

***

An old man goes to the Wizard to ask him if he can remove a curse he has been living with for the last 40 years.

The Wizard says "Maybe, but you will have to tell me the exact words that were used to put the curse on you."

The old man says without hesitation, "I now pronounce you man and wife."

***

Little Johnny was walking down the road one day and an old man was sitting on his front porch rocking back and forth in his chair.

'Whatcha got there, son?' the old man asked.

Johnny said, 'Got me some chicken wire.'

'Whatcha gonna do with that chicken wire, son?' asked the old man.

'Gonna catch me some chickens' said Johnny.

'You can't catch chickens with chicken wire,' said the oldster.

Johnny just shrugged his shoulders and walked on down the street.

About half an hour later, Johnny came back past the old man's front porch with three chickens entangled in the chicken wire. The old man was shocked and couldn't believe his eyes.

A little later Johnny passed the old man's porch again. 'Whatcha got now, son?'

'Got me some duct tape.'

'And whatcha gonna do with that duct tape?' the old man asked.

'Gonna catch me some ducks.'

'You can't catch ducks with duct tape!' said the old man. Johnny just shrugged his shoulders and kept on walking.

About half an hour later, back comes Johnny with three ducks tangled in the duct tape. Again, the old man rubbed his eyes in disbelief.

Half an hour later, Johnny was again passing the old man's porch.

'Whatcha got now, son?' asked the old codger.

'Got me some pussy willow.'

'Wait right there while I get my shoes!'

***

The 80 year old and his wife didn't have much fun in bed any more, so they invented 'The Farting

Game.' He let go a beauty, "A five pointer", he claimed. She followed with a triple thunderclap. "Seven!" she squealed. He dropped a squeaker for four; she could only manage a fudgy fart for two points. They were level pegging. He knew he'd have to come up with something good, so he strained really hard and let one go – but crapped in the bed. "What was that?" she asked. "Half time" he said, "change sides".

***

Bob was sunbathing on the beach at the nudist colony. He had an enormous erection. Two elderly female members were walking towards him, so to avoid embarrassment, he covered himself with sand, but his erection still stood out of the sand. When the old girls got closer, one said to the other, "There's no justice...

When I was 15, I was curious about it.

When I was 20, I enjoyed it.

When I was 30, I asked for it.

When I was 40, I begged for it.

When I was 50, I paid for it.

When I was 60, I prayed for it.

When I was 70, I forgot it.

Now I'm 80, it's growing wild and I'm too old to squat!"

***

There had been a lot of bad news lately about elderly pensioners eating pet food. Ray, aged 70, walked into a convenience store and bought three tins of dog food.

"Do you have a dog?" asked the cashier.

"Yes, I do", said Ray.

"Is the dog with you?" asked the cashier.

"No, he's at home."

"I can't sell you dog food unless I see your dog", said the cashier.

The next day, Ray returned to the store and bought three tins of cat food.

"Do you have a cat?"

"Yes, I do".

"Do you have it with you?"

"No, it's at home".

"I can't sell you cat food unless I see your cat".

Next day, Ray returned to the store with a paper bag.

"Put your hand in this" Ray said to the cashier.

She put her hand in the bag, then quickly pulled it out.

"What is it?" asked Ray.

"Shit!" said the cashier.

"Right!" said Ray. "I want three rolls of toilet paper".

***

A retired gentleman went into the social security office to apply for the Age pension. After waiting in line a long time he got to the counter.

The woman behind the counter asked him for his driver's license to verify his age. He looked in his pockets and realized he had left his wallet at home. "Will I have to go home and come back later?" he asks.

The woman says, "Unbutton your shirt." So he opens his shirt revealing lots of curly silver hair. She says, "That silver hair on your chest is proof enough for me" and she processed his application.

When he gets home, the man excitedly tells his wife about his experience at the Social Security office. She said, "You should have dropped your pants, you might have qualified for the Disability pension, too."

***

There was a couple who had been married for 50 years.

They were sitting at the breakfast table one morning when the old guy said to his wife, "Just think, honey, we've been married for 50 years."

"Yeah," she replied, "Just think, fifty years ago we were sitting here at this breakfast table together."

"I know," the old man said, "We were probably sitting here naked as jaybirds fifty years ago."

"Well," Granny snickered, "What do you say... should we get naked?"

The two stripped naked and sat down at the table. "You know, honey" the little old lady whispered breathlessly, "My nipples are as hot for you today as they were fifty years ago."

"I wouldn't be surprised," replied Gramps. "One's in your coffee and the other is in your oatmeal..."

Two elderly women were eating breakfast in a restaurant one morning. Ethel noticed something funny about Mabel's ear and she said, "Mabel, did you know you've got a suppository in your left ear?"

"I have? A suppository?" She pulled it out and stared at it.

"Ethel, I'm glad you saw this thing. Now I think I know where my hearing aid is."

***

Two old ladies were outside their nursing home, having a smoke, when it started to rain. One of the ladies pulled out a condom, cut off the end, put it over her cigarette, and continued smoking.

Lady 1: What's that?

Lady 2: A condom. This way my cigarette doesn't get wet.

Lady 1: Where did you get it?

Lady 2: You can get them at any pharmacy.

The next day, Lady 1 hobbles into the local pharmacy and announces to the pharmacist that she wants a box of condoms. The pharmacist looks at the old girl kind of strangely and very delicately asks what brand she prefers. "Doesn't matter son" she said, "as long as it fits a Camel."

***

Two elderly ladies had been friends for many decades. Over the years they had shared all kinds of activities and adventures. Lately, their activities had been limited to meeting a few times a week to play cards. One day they were playing cards when one looked at the other and said, "Now don't get upset with me... I know we've been friends for a long time...but I just can't think of your name! I've thought and thought, but I can't remember it. Please tell me what your name is." Her friend glared at her. For at least three minutes she just stared and glared at her. Finally she said, "How soon do you need to know?

***

Ethel is a bit of a demon in her wheelchair and loves to charge around the nursing home taking corners on one wheel and getting up to maximum speed on the long corridors. Because the poor woman is one sandwich short of a picnic, the other residents tolerate her and some of the men actually join in.

One day, Ethel was speeding up one corridor when a door opened and Kooky Clarence stepped out with his arms outstretched.

"Stop!" he said in a firm voice. "Have you got a license for that thing?"

Ethel fished around in her handbag and pulled out a Kit Kat wrapper and held it up to him.

"OK" he said, and away Ethel sped down the hall. As she took the corner near the TV lounge on one wheel, Weird Harold popped out in front of her and shouted, "Stop! Have you got proof of insurance?"

Ethel dug into her handbag, pulled out a beer coaster and held it up to him. Harold nodded and said, "Carry on ma'am."

As Ethel neared the final corridor before the front door, Crazy Craig stepped out in front of her, stark naked, holding a very sizeable erection in his hand. "Oh, no" said Ethel, "Not the breathalyser again!"

ONE LINERS

Why do men become smarter during sex?
Because they're plugged into a genius.

***

Why don't women blink during foreplay?
They don't have enough time.

***

Why do men snore when they lie on their backs?
Because their balls fall over their bums and form an air lock.

***

Why were men given larger brains than dogs?
So they won't hump women's legs at cocktail parties.

Why did God put men on earth?
Because a vibrator can't mow the lawn.

***

Why did the man cross the road?
He heard the chicken was a slut.

***

What's the difference between men and government bonds?
The bonds eventually will mature.

***

What do you call a woman who knows where her husband is every night?
A widow.

***

Why are married women usually heavier than single women?
Single women come home, see what's in the fridge and go to bed. Married women come home, see what's in the bed and go to the fridge.

***

What did God say after creating man?
"I must be able to do better than **that**!"

What is the one thing that all men at singles bars have in common?

They're all married.

***

Adam says to God, "God, why did you make woman so beautiful?"

God says, "So you would love her."

"But God," Adam asks, "why did you make her so dumb?"

"So she would love you!"

***

Why do they call camels 'Ships of the Desert?'

Because they're full of Arab semen.

***

Two fish swim into a concrete wall.

One turns to the other and says "dam".

***

Two peanuts walk into a bar.

One was a salted.

***

A sandwich walks into a bar.

The barman says, "Sorry, we don't serve food in here."

A dyslexic man walks into a bra…

***

A man walks into a bar with a slab of asphalt under his arm and says:
   "A beer please, and one for the road."

***

Two cannibals are eating a clown.
   One says to the other: "Does this taste funny to you?"

***

"Doc, I can't stop singing 'The Green, Green Grass of Home'."
   "That sounds like Tom Jones syndrome."
   "Is it common, Doc?"
   "It's Not Unusual."

***

A guy walks into the psychiatrist wearing only Glad Wrap for shorts.
   The shrink says, "Well, I can clearly see you're nuts."

***

Deja Moo: The feeling that you've heard this bullshit before.

Did you hear about the Tasmanian who died and left his entire estate in trust for his beloved widow? She can't touch it 'til she's fourteen.

***

How many Aborigines does it take to eat a possum? Two. One to eat, and one to watch out for traffic.

***

Where was the toothbrush invented? Oklahoma. If it was invented anywhere else, it would have been called a teethbrush.

***

A new law recently passed in Tasmania – When a couple gets divorced, they're still brother and sister.

***

What do you have when you have 32 Queensland tradesmen in the same room? A full set of teeth.

***

Why is playing poker like sex? Because if you don't have a good partner, you'd better have a good hand.

How can you tell the difference between an oral and a rectal thermometer?

They taste different.

What's the first thing a battered woman does after she gets out of the women's shelter?

The dishes, if she knows what's good for her!

***

What's the best part about dating a homeless woman?

You can drop her off anywhere.

***

A man walks into doctor's office.

"What seems to be the problem?" asks the doc.

"It's…um…well… I have five penises." replies the man.

"How do your trousers fit?"

"Like a glove."

***

Our ice cream man was found lying on the floor of his van covered with nuts and hundreds 'n thousands. Police say that he topped himself.

***

What do you call a fish with no eyes?

A fsh.

Then there was the story of Trevor, the organ donor, who spent all night at the party looking for a willie recipient.

***

A vulture boards a plane carrying two dead rabbits. The flight attendant stops him and says, "I'm sorry, but you're only allowed one carrion per passenger."

***

Intelligent Questions to ask

Why can't women put on mascara with their mouth closed?

Why don't you ever see the headline 'Psychic Wins Lottery'?

Why is 'abbreviated' such a long word?

Why is lemon juice made with artificial flavor, and dish washing liquid made with real lemons?

Why is the man who invests all your money called a broker?

Why is the time of day with the slowest traffic called rush hour?

Why isn't there mouse-flavored cat food?

Why is it that most nudists are people you don't want to see naked?

When dog food is new and taste improved, who tests it?

Why do they sterilize the needle for lethal injections?

You know that indestructible black box that is

used on airplanes? Why don't they make the whole plane out of that stuff?

Why don't sheep shrink when it rains?

Why are they called apartments when they are all stuck together?

If flying is so safe, why do they call the airport the terminal?

How come Americans choose from just two people for president and fifty for Miss America?

***

How long is a minute? It depends which side of the bathroom door you're on.

***

You know you're ready to appear on The Jerry Springer Show when...

1. You let your twelve-year-old daughter smoke at the dinner table in front of her kids.
2. You've been married three times and still have the same in-laws.
3. You wonder how service stations keep their restrooms so clean.
4. Members of your family die right after saying: "Hey, watch this."
5. You think Dom Perignon is a Mafia leader.
6. Your junior high school has a daycare.
7. Your wife's hairdo was once ruined by a ceiling fan.
8. You think the National Anthem ends with: "Gentlemen, start your engines."

9. You lit a match in the bathroom and your house exploded right off its wheels.
10. The value of your truck goes up and down, depending on how much petrol is in it.
11. You have to go outside to get something from the fridge.
12. You only need one more credit on your card for a freebie at the House of Tattoos.
13. You can't get married to your lover because there's a law against it.
14. You think 'loaded dishwasher' means your wife is drunk.
15. Your toilet paper has page numbers on it

***

THE FOUR STAGES OF LIFE:
1. You believe in Santa Claus.
2. You don't believe in Santa Claus.
3. You are Santa Claus.
4. You look like Santa Claus.

WISE STATEMENTS

Marriage changes passion…suddenly, you're in bed with a relative.

"Old" is when the porn movie you bring home is "Debby Does Dialysis."

Home is where you can say anything you like, because nobody listens to you anyway.

Regular naps prevent old age, especially if you take them while driving.

Sex is hereditary. If your parents never had it, you won't either.

I have learned there is little difference in wives; you might as well keep the first.

If life deals you lemons, make lemonade; if it deals you tomatoes, make Bloody Marys.

There are two sides to every divorce: Yours and shithead's.

No one ever says 'It's only a game,' when their team is winning.

Middle age is when you choose your cereal for the fibre, not the toy.

***

What I've learned as I matured
I've learned that you cannot make someone love you. All you can do is stalk them and hope they panic and give in.

I've learned that no matter how much I care, some people are just assholes.

I've learned that it takes years to build up trust, and it only takes suspicion, not proof, to destroy it.

I've learned that you can get by on charm for about fifteen minutes.

After that, you'd better have a big willy or huge boobs.

I've learned that you shouldn't compare yourself to others – they are more screwed up than you think.

I've learned that you can keep puking long after you think you're finished.

I've learned that we are responsible for what we do, unless we are celebrities.

I've learned that regardless of how hot and steamy a relationship is at first, the passion fades and there had better be a lot of money to take its place.

I've learned that the people you care most about in life are taken from you too soon and all the less important ones just never seem to go away.

I've learned to say "Fuck 'em if they can't take a joke" in 6 languages.

*****

Good things to remember
1. Never raise your hands to your kids. It leaves your groin unprotected.
2. I'm not into working out. My philosophy is no pain, no pain.
3. I'm in shape. Round is a shape.
4. I'm still trying to figure out why Kamikaze pilots wore helmets.
5. Do you think illiterate people get the full affect of alphabet soup?
6. I've always wanted to be somebody, but I should have been more specific.
7. Ever notice when you blow in a dog's face he gets mad at you, but when you take him in a car he sticks his head out the window?

8. Ever notice that anyone going slower than you is an idiot, but anyone going faster than you is a maniac?

9. You have to stay in shape. My mother started walking five miles a day when she was 60. She's 97 now and we have no idea where she is.

10. I have six locks on my door, all in a row. When I go out, I lock every other one. I figure no matter how long somebody stands there picking the locks, they're always locking three of them.

11. One out of every three people is suffering from some form of mental illness. Think of two of your best friends. If they are OK, then it must be you.

12. On TV they show you how detergent takes out bloodstains. I think if you've got a tee shirt with bloodstains all over it, maybe your laundry isn't your biggest problem.

13. Ask people why they have deer heads on their walls and they tell you it's because they're such beautiful animals. I think my wife is beautiful, but I only have photographs of her on the walls.

14. A lady came up to me on the street, pointed at my suede jacket and said, "Don't you know a cow was murdered for that jacket?" I said, "I didn't know there were any witnesses. Now I'll have to kill you too."

15. Future historians will be able to study at the Jimmy Carter Library, the Gerald Ford Library, the Ronald Reagan Library, and the Bill Clinton Adult Bookstore.

DUMB QUESTIONS TO ASK...

If electricity comes from electrons, does morality come from morons?

Can you get cornered in a round room?

Why do we wash behind our ears? Who really looks there?

Why don't the hairs on your arms get split ends?

Why is it illegal to park in a handicapped parking space but it's ok to use a handicapped toilet?

How come we say 'It's colder than hell outside'? Isn't hell supposed to be fire and brimstone?

Why are women so scared of mice, yet they all love Mickey Mouse?

Why don't they make the sticky stuff on envelopes taste like chocolate?

Why is it that when things get wet they get darker, even though water is clear?

Why is it that when you get out of a swimming pool, your urine is hotter when you use the restroom?

Can mute people burp?

Why is 'Chopsticks' one of the easiest songs to play on the piano, but the hardest thing to eat with?

How come you play at a recital, but recite at a play?

If a fork was made of gold would it still be considered silverware?

If heat rises, then shouldn't hell be cold?

Why is there that little space inside strawberries meant for a pip, but the seeds are on the outside?

Why isn't chocolate considered a vegetable, if chocolate comes from cocoa beans, and all beans are a vegetable?

Do they have girl's bathrooms in gay bars?

Why is toilet bowl cleaning liquid only blue?

Why is it when we talk to God we are praying, but when God talks to us we are put into the loony bin?

Why do you go "back and forth" to town if you really must go forth before you go back?

Why do shaped macaroni taste better than the normal kind?

Why is vanilla ice cream white when vanilla extract is brown?

Why can't you get a tan on your palms?

Why do dogs sniff other dog's bums to say hello; why don't they just bark in their face or something?

Why do companies offer you 'free gifts?' Since when has a gift **not** been free?

If something 'goes without saying', why do people still say it?

You know the expression, "Don't quit your day job?" Well, what do you say to people who work nights?

How come car keys are the only keys with teeth on both sides?

Since bread is square, then why is sandwich meat round?

Why is it the Twelve Days of Christmas when there is only one day of Christmas?

If you die and you have a broken leg, do they take the cast off?

Is sign language the same in languages other than English?

Why is 'number' abbreviated as 'no.' when there is no "o" in number?

Why do they call the small candy bars the "fun sizes"? Wouldn't it be more fun to eat a big one?

Why do we teach kids that violence is not the answer and then have them read at school about wars that solved the World's problems?

Who gets to keep the pennies in a wishing well?

If you went back in time and killed your mother, would you disappear the moment you returned?

If money doesn't grow on trees then why do banks have branches?

How important does a person have to be before they are considered assassinated instead of just murdered?

Just what was the "Baby On Board" sign for? Did it help us decide which car not to hit in case of an accident?

If all of the Acme stuff doesn't work, why does Wily Coyote keep buying their products?

Why is it when we laugh in school the teachers say, "Do you find something funny?" when obviously we do?

Why do you have to 'put your two cents in' but it's only a 'penny for your thoughts'? Where's that extra penny going?

Since there is a rule that states 'i' before 'e' except after 'c', isn't 'science' spelled wrongly?

If the handicapped bathrooms are for people who can't walk, why do they put them at the end of the corridor?

Why do most people put more effort into their wedding than their actual marriage?

Do stuttering people stutter when they're thinking to themselves?

Why is it when we duck they call us chicken?

Are children who use sign language allowed to talk with their mouth full?

Why do people say, 'I've been working like a dog' when dogs just sit around all day?

When you see the weather report and it says 'partly cloudy' and then the next day it says 'partly sunny', what's the difference?

Why do people who don't want to go to hell bury themselves six foot closer?

MEN ONE-LINERS

What should you do if you see your ex-husband rolling around in pain on the ground?
Shoot him again.

***

How can you tell when a man is well-hung?
When you can just barely slip your finger in between his neck and the noose.

***

Why do little boys whine?
Because they're practicing to be men.

***

How many men does it take to screw in a light bulb?
Three – one to screw in the bulb, and two to listen to him brag about the screwing part.

***

What does it mean when a man is in your bed gasping for breath and calling your name?
You didn't hold the pillow down long enough.

***

Why do female black widow spiders kill their males after mating?
To stop the snoring before it starts.

Why do men whistle when they're sitting on the toilet?

Because it helps them remember which end they need to wipe.

***

What is the difference between men and women?

A woman wants one man to satisfy her every need.

A man wants every woman to satisfy his one need.

***

How do you stop a man from reading your e-mail?

Rename the mail folder to 'instruction manual'.

***

What is the difference between a Harley and a Hoover?

The position of the dirt bag.

***

Why is divorce so expensive?

Because it's worth it.

***

What's the difference between a girlfriend and a wife? 45 pounds.

What's the difference between a boyfriend and a husband?

45 minutes.

***

What's the fastest way to a man's heart?

Through his chest with a sharp knife.

***

Where does an Irish family go on vacation?

A different bar.

***

How do you get a sweet little 80-year-old lady to say the F word?

Get another sweet little 80-year-old lady to yell 'BINGO!'

***

What's the difference between a fairy tale told in the Northern states of the USA and a Southern fairy tale?

A Northern fairy tale begins "Once upon a time..."

A Southern fairy tale begins "Y'all ain't gonna believe this shit..."

What's the difference between an Australian zoo and a Chinese zoo? A Chinese zoo has a description of the animal on the front of the cage plus a recipe.

***

Why is there no Disneyland in China? No-one's tall enough to go on the good rides.

POLITICS

Osama Bin Laden has a heart attack and dies. He immediately goes to Hell, where the Devil is waiting for him.

"I don't know what to do with you" says the Devil. "You are on my list, but I have no room for you so I'll tell you what I'll do: I've got a few folks here who weren't quite as bad as you. I'll let one of them go, but you have to take their place. I'll even let you decide who leaves."

Bin Laden thought it sounded pretty good, so the Devil opened the first room. In it was Saddam Hussein and a large pool of water. He kept diving in and surfacing empty-handed. Over and over and over. Such was his fate in hell.

"No," said Bin Laden, "I don't think so. I'm not a good swimmer and I don't think I could do that all day long."

The Devil led him to the next room. In it was the Ayatollah Khomeini with a sledge-hammer and a room full of rocks. All he did was swing that hammer, time after time after time.

"No, I've got a problem with my shoulder. I would be in constant agony if I had to break rocks all day" said Bin Laden.

The devil opened a third door. In it, Bin Laden saw Bill Clinton, lying on the floor with his arms staked above his head, and his legs staked in a spread-eagle pose. Bent over him was Monica Lewinsky, giving him a blowjob. Bin Laden looked in disbelief and finally said, "Yeah... I can handle this!"

The Devil smiled. "OK, Monica...you're free to go."

***

Little Melissa comes home from first grade and tells her father that they learned about the history of Valentine's Day. "Since Valentine's Day is for a Christian saint and we're Jewish," she asks, "will God get angry at me for giving someone a valentine?"

Melissa's father thinks a bit, and then says, "No, I don't think God would get angry. Who do you want to give a valentine to?"

"Osama Bin Laden" she says.

"Why Osama Bin Laden?" her father asks in shock.

"Well," she says, "I thought that if a little Jewish girl could have enough love to give Osama a valentine, he might start to think that maybe we're not all bad, and maybe start loving people a little bit.

And if other kids saw what I did and sent

valentines to Osama, he'd love everyone a lot. And then he'd start going all over the world to tell everyone how much he loved them and how he didn't hate anyone anymore."

Her father's heart swells and he looks at his daughter with newfound pride. "Melissa, that's the most wonderful thing I've ever heard."

"I know," Melissa says, "and once that gets him out in the open, the Marines could blow the shit out of him."

***

A little boy goes to his dad and asks, "What are Politics?"

"Well son", says his father, "let me try to explain it this way:

#1. I'm the head of the family, so call me the President.

#2. Your mother is the administrator of the money, so we call her the Government.

#3. We're here to take care of your needs, so we'll call you the People.

#4. The nanny, we'll consider her the Working Class.

#5. And your baby brother, we'll call him the Future.

Now think about it all and see if it makes sense to you."

The little boy goes off to bed thinking about what his Dad said.

Later that night, he hears his baby brother crying and gets up to check on him. He finds that the baby has severely soiled his diaper. He goes to his parent's room and finds his mother sound asleep. Not wanting to wake her, he goes to the nanny's room. Finding the door locked, he peeks in the keyhole and see his father bonking the nanny. He gives up and goes back to bed.

The next morning, the little boy says to his father, "Dad, I think I understand the concept of politics now."

"Good, son, tell me in your own words what you think it's all about."

"Well... the President is screwing the Working Class while the Government is sound asleep. The People are being ignored and the Future is in deep shit.

***

A man spends many days crossing the desert without water. His camel dies of thirst. He crawls through the sand, certain that he has breathed his last, when suddenly he sees an object sticking out of the sand several yards ahead of him. He crawls to the object, pulls it out of the sand, and discovers an old brief case. He opens it and out pops a genie. But this is no ordinary genie. He is wearing a Tax Office badge and a dull gray suit. There's a calculator in his pocket. He has a pencil tucked behind one ear. "Well, my friend," says the genie, "You know how it works. You have three wishes."

"I'm not falling for this." says the man. "I'm not going to trust a Tax Officer auditor!"

"What do you have to lose? You've got no transportation, and it looks like you're a goner anyway!"

The man thinks about this for a minute, and decides that the genie is right. "OK, I wish I was in a lush oasis with plentiful food and drink."

The genie waves his wand and the man finds himself in the most beautiful oasis he has ever seen. And he is surrounded with jugs of wine and platters of delicacies. "OK, what's your second wish."?

"My second wish is that I was rich beyond my wildest dreams."

The genie waves his wand and the man finds himself surrounded by treasure chests filled with rare gold coins and precious gems.

"OK, you have just one more wish. Better make it is a good one!"

After thinking for a few minutes, the man says "I wish that no matter where I go beautiful women will want me, I will be able to get into their pants." The genie waves his wand. The man turns into a tampon.

The moral of the story

If the Government offers you anything, there's going to be a string attached!

***

Two Arabs are sitting in the Gaza Strip chatting over a pint of goat's milk. One pulls his wallet out and starts flipping through photos and they start reminiscing.

"This is my oldest son. He's a martyr. Here's my second son. He's a martyr too!"

After a pause and a deep sigh, the second Arab wistfully says, "They blow up so fast, don't they?"

The Australian media have just reported that an early morning raid today by Police has caught four Aboriginal terrorists.

Bin Smokin and Bin Drinkin were taken into custody along with Bin Bonkin and Bin Stealin. A fifth terrorist, Bin Workin, could not be found anywhere and is believed not to exist.

RELATIONSHIPS

Two lovers interested in spiritualism and reincarnation vowed that if either died, the one remaining would try to contact the partner in the other world exactly 30 days after dying. As fate would have it, a few weeks later the young man died in a car wreck. True to her word, his sweetheart tried to contact him in the spirit world exactly 30 days later. At the séance, she called out, "John, darling John; this is Martha. Do you hear me?"

A ghostly voice answered her, "Yes Martha, this is John; I can hear you."

"Oh John, what is it like where you are?" Martha tearfully asked.

"It's beautiful. There are blue skies, a soft breeze, sunshine most of the time."

"Well, what do you do all day there?" asked Martha.

"Well, we get up before sunrise, eat a good

breakfast, and there's nothing but sex until noon. After lunch, we nap until two and then have more sex until about five. After dinner, we go at it again until we fall asleep about 11pm."

Martha was taken aback. "Is that what heaven really is like?"

"I'm not in heaven Martha."

"Well then, where are you?"

"I'm a rabbit out in a field near Dubbo."

***

A husband and wife are traveling by car from Melbourne to Perth. After almost 24 hours on the road, they're too tired to continue and decide to stop for a rest at a nice hotel, planning only to sleep for four hours and then get back on the road. When they check out four hours later, the desk clerk hands them a bill for $350. The man explodes and demands to know why the charge is so high. He tells the clerk that although it's a nice hotel, the rooms certainly aren't worth $350. When the clerk tells him $350 is the standard rate, the man insists on speaking to the Manager. The Manager explains that the hotel has an Olympic-sized pool and a huge conference centre that were available for the husband and wife to use. 'But we didn't use them', the man complains. 'Well, they are here, and you could have,' explains the Manager. He explains they could have taken in one of the shows for which the hotel is famous. 'The best entertainers from New York, Hollywood and Las Vegas perform here,' the Manager says. 'But we didn't go to any of those shows,' complains the man again. 'Well, we have them, and you could have' the Manager replies. No matter what facility the Manager mentions, the man replies, 'But we didn't use it!' The Manager is unmoved, and eventually the man gives up and agrees to pay. He writes a cheque and gives it to the Manager. The Manager is surprised when he looks at the cheque. 'But sir,' he says, 'this cheque is only made out for $100.' 'That's right,' says the man. 'I charged you $250 for sleeping with my wife.' 'But I didn't!' exclaims the Manager. 'Well, she was here, and you could have.'

IF MEN WROTE THE RELATIONSHIP COLUMNS...

A guy in a mask bursts into a sperm bank with a shotgun.

"Open the safe" he yells at the woman behind the counter.

"But we're not a real bank" she replies. "We don't have any money; this is a sperm bank!"

"Don't argue! Open the safe or I'll blow your head off!"

She obliges and once she's opened the safe door the guy says, "Take out one of the bottles and drink it".

"But it's full of sperm!" she replies nervously.

"Don't argue just drink it or you die, here, now!" he says.

She takes the cap off and gulps it down.

"Take out another one and drink it too" he demands.

She takes out another and drinks it.

Suddenly the guy pulls off the mask and, to the woman's amazement, it's her husband.

"Now that wasn't so bloody difficult, was it?"

***

As the woman passed her daughter's closed bedroom door, she heard a strange buzzing noise. Opening the door, she saw her daughter giving herself a real workout with a vibrator.

"What in the world are you doing?" asked the shocked mother.

"Mom, I'm thirty-five years old, unmarried, and this thing is about as close as I'll ever get to a husband. Please, go away and leave me alone."

The next day, the girl's father heard the same buzz coming from the other side of the closed bedroom door. Entering the room, he saw his daughter making passionate love to her vibrator.

To his query as to what she was doing, the daughter said, "Dad, I'm thirty-five years old, unmarried, and this thing is about as close as I'll ever get to a husband. Please, go away and leave me alone."

A couple days later, the wife came home from shopping trip, placed the groceries on the kitchen counter, and heard the buzzing noise coming from the family room. She entered that area and saw her husband sitting on the couch, downing a cold beer, and staring at the TV. The vibrator was next to him on the couch, buzzing like crazy.

"What the hell are you doing?" she asked.

"I'm watching the Football with my son-in-law."

***

True bravery is arriving home at 2 am after a boy's night out, being assaulted by your wife with a broom, and still having the guts to ask,

"Are you cleaning, or are you getting ready to fly somewhere?"

***

An old man lived alone in Idaho. He wanted to spade his potato garden, but it was very hard work. His only son, Bubba, who used to help him, was in prison. The old man wrote a letter to his son and described his predicament.

"Dear Bubba, I am feeling pretty bad because it looks like I won't be able to plant my potato garden this year. I'm just getting too old to be digging up a garden plot. If you were here, all my troubles would be over. I know you would dig the plot for me. Love, Dad"

A few days later he received a reply from his son.

"Dear Dad, Don't dig up that garden, that's where I buried the bodies. Love, Bubba"

At 4am the next morning, FBI agents and local police showed up and dug up the entire garden without finding any bodies. They apologized to the old man and left. That same day the old man received another letter from his son.

"Dear Dad, Go ahead and plant the potatoes now. That's the best I could do under the circumstances. Love, Bubba."

RELIGION

A man is stumbling through the woods totally drunk when he comes upon a preacher baptizing people in the river. He walks into the water and bumps into the preacher. The preacher is almost overcome by the smell of alcohol and asks the drunk, "Are you ready to find Jesus?"

"Yes, I am!" the drunk answers. The preacher grabs him and dunks him in the water. He pulls him up and asks the drunk, "Brother, have you found Jesus?" "No, I haven't found Jesus" the drunk replies. The preacher, shocked at the answer, dunks him into the water again for a little longer this time. He again pulls him out of the water and asks again, "Have you found Jesus, my brother?"

"No, I haven't found Jesus." The preacher is at his wits end and dunks the drunk in the water again but this time holds him down for about 30 seconds. When he begins kicking his arms and legs, he pulls him up. "Have you found Jesus?" The drunk wipes his eyes, catches his breath and says, "Are you sure this is where the bastard fell in?"

***

A new Monk arrives at the Monastery. He is assigned to help the other monks in copying the old texts by hand. He notices, however, that they are copying copies, not the original books. The new monk goes to the head monk to ask him about this. He points out that if there was an error in the first copy, that error would be continued in all of the other copies. The head monk says, "We have been copying from the copies for centuries, but you make a good point, my son." He goes down into the cellar with one of the copies to check it against the original. Hours pass. Soon, one of the monks goes to look for him. He hears sobbing coming from the back of the cellar, and finds the old monk leaning over one of the original books crying. He asks the old monk what's wrong, and in a choked voice, comes the reply, "You were right...the word is "celebrate"...!"

***

First the Lord made man in the Garden of Eden.
Then he said, "There's something he's needing"
After casting about for a suitable pearl,
He kept messing around and created a girl.
Two beautiful legs, so long and slender,
Round, slim, and firm, and ever so tender.
Two lovely hips to increase his desire,
And rounded and firm to bring out the fire.
Two lovely breasts, so full and so proud,
Good Lord they're lovely, as he whispers aloud.
Two lovely arms, just aching to bless you,
And two loving hands, to soothe and caress you.
Soft, cascading hair hung down over her shoulder,
And two dreamy eyes, to make him grow bolder.
'Twas made for a man, just to make his heart sing,
Then he added a mouth: and ruined the whole damn thing.

A man is in front of a church, naked, with three packs of cigarettes.

He hears some nuns coming, and has nowhere to hide except in some nearby bushes. Unfortunately, his penis is sticking out. The four nuns walk by and one of the nuns notices his protruding penis. She goes over and pulls it. Thinking fast, the man hands over a pack of smokes.

"Oooh!" the nun exclaims, "free cigarettes!"

The other three nuns go over to collect their packs. The second nun pulls and gets her pack. The third one goes over and pulls and gets hers.

The man runs out of cigarettes to give. The last nun pulls and nothing happens. She pulls again. And again, and again. She wants her free cigarettes! Finally, after pulling a dozen or so times, she lets out an excited shout: "Oooh! Now it's giving hand lotion!"

***

Twelve priests were about to be ordained. As part of the ceremony, they each had to attach an electronic gadget to their penis and stand naked. If they got an erection, the gizmo would make a screeching sound. To prove that they were capable of self-control, the Bishop got a stripper to dance in front of each priest. All went well until the stripper got to the last priest. 'Screeeeeech' went the gizmo and it fell to the ground. The embarrassed priest bent over to pick up the gizmo...and eleven gizmos started screeching.

WHAT RACE WAS JESUS?

There are 3 good arguments that Jesus was Black:
1. He called everyone 'brother'.
2. He liked Gospel.
3. He couldn't get a fair trial.

But then there are 3 equally good arguments that Jesus was Jewish:
1. He went into his father's business.
2. He lived at home until he was 33.
3. He was sure his mother was a virgin and she was sure he was God.

But then there are 3 equally good arguments that Jesus was Italian:
1. He talked with his hands.
2. He had wine with every meal.
3. He used olive oil.

But then there are 3 equally good arguments that Jesus was a Californian:
1. He never cut his hair.
2. He walked around barefoot all the time.
3. He started a new religion.

But then there are 3 equally good arguments that Jesus was Irish:
1. He never got married.
2. He was always telling stories.
3. He loved green pastures.

But the most compelling evidence of all...3 proofs that Jesus was a woman:

1. He fed a crowd at a moment's notice when there was no food.
2. He kept trying to get a message across to a bunch of men who didn't get it.
3. Even when he was dead, He had to get up because there was more work to do.

***

A lady goes to her priest one day and says,

"Father, I have a problem. I have two female parrots, but they only know how to say one thing."

"What do they say?" the priest inquired.

"They say, "Hi, we're hookers! Do you want to have some fun?"

"That's obscene!" the priest exclaimed. Then he thought for a moment. "You know," he said, "I may have a solution to your problem. I have two male talking parrots, which I have taught to pray and read the Bible. Bring your two parrots over to my house, and we'll put them in the cage with Francis and Job. My parrots can teach your parrots to pray and worship, and your parrots are sure to stop saying…that phrase…in no time." The next day, she brought her female parrots to the priest's house. As he ushered her in, she saw that his two male parrots were inside their cage holding rosary beads and praying. Impressed, she walked over and placed her parrots in with them. After a few minutes, the female parrots cried out in unison: "Hi, we're hookers! Do you want to have some fun?"

There was stunned silence. Shocked, one male parrot looked over at the other male parrot and exclaimed, "Put the beads away, Frank. Our prayers have been answered!"

***

A new priest at his first Mass was so nervous he could hardly speak. After Mass he asked the Monsignor how he had done.

The Monsignor said, "When I'm worried about getting nervous on the pulpit, I put a glass of vodka next to the water glass. If I start to get nervous, I take a sip."

The next Sunday he took the Monsignor's advice. At the beginning of the sermon, he got nervous and took a big drink. He proceeded to talk up a storm! Upon his return to his office after Mass, he found the following note on his door:

1. Sip the vodka, don't gulp.
2. There are 10 Commandments, not 12.
3. There are 12 disciples, not 10.
4. Jesus was consecrated, not constipated.
5. Jacob wagered his donkey, he didn't bet his ass.
6. We do not refer to Jesus Christ as the late J.C.
7. The Father, Son, and Holy Ghost are not referred to as Big Daddy, Junior and the Spook.
8. David slew Goliath, he didn't kick the shit out of him.
9. David was hit by a rock and knocked off his donkey, He wasn't stoned off his ass.
10. We do not refer to the cross as the "Big T."

11. When Jesus broke the bread at the Last Supper he said, "Take this and eat it for it is my body." He did not say "Eat me"
12. The Virgin Mary is not called "Mary with the Cherry,"
13. The recommended Grace before a meal is not: Rub-A-Dub-Dub thanks for the grub, yeah God.
14. Next Sunday there will be a taffy pulling contest at St. Peter's, not a Peter pulling contest at St. Taffy's.

***

An old lady dies and goes to Heaven and is chatting to St. Peter at the Pearly Gates when all of a sudden she hears the most awful bloodcurdling screams.

"Don't worry about that," says St Peter, "it's only someone having the holes bored in their shoulder blades for the wings."

The old lady looks a little uncomfortable but carries on with the conversation. Ten minutes later, there are more bloodcurdling screams. "Oh my God," says the old lady, "now what is happening?"

"Not to worry," says St. Peter, "they are just having their heads drilled to fit the halo."

"I can't do this," says the old lady, "I'm off down to Hell."

"You can't go there," says St. Peter, "you'll be raped and sodomized."

"Yes, but I've already got the holes for that," says the old lady.

The priest of a small Irish village was very fond of a bantam cock rooster and ten chickens he kept in a hen house behind the parish manse. One Saturday night the rooster was missing, and as that was the time the priest suspected cock fights occurred in the village, he decided to say something about it at church the next morning. At Mass, he asked the congregation, "Has anyone got a cock?" All the men stood up. "No, no," he said. "That wasn't what I meant. Has anybody seen a cock?" All the women stood up. "No, no," he said. "That wasn't what I meant, either. Has anyone seen a cock that doesn't belong to them?" Half the women stood up. "No, no," he said. "Perhaps I should rephrase the question: Has anybody here seen **my** cock?" All the choir boys stood up.

***

Little April was not the best student in Sunday school and she usually slept through the class. One day the teacher called on her while she was napping, "Tell me, April, who created the universe?" When April didn't stir, little Johnny, a boy seated in the chair behind her, took a pin and jabbed her in the rear. "God Almighty!" shouted April. "Very good" said the teacher, and April fell back asleep. A while later the teacher asked, "April, who is our Lord and Saviour?," But April didn't even stir from her slumber. Once again, Johnny came to the rescue and stuck her again.

"Jesus Christ!" shouted April. "Very good," the teacher said and April fell back asleep. The teacher then asked April a third question; "What did Eve

say to Adam after she had her twenty-third child?"
And again, Johnny jabbed her with the pin. This
time April jumped up and shouted, "If you stick
that fucking thing into me one more time, I'll
break it in half and stick it up your arse!"

***

Three men died on Christmas Eve and were met
by Saint Peter at the Pearly Gates.

"In honor of this holy season," said Saint Peter,
"you must each possess something that symbol-
izes Christmas to get into Heaven."

The first man fumbled through his pockets
and pulled out a lighter.

He flicked it on. "It represents a candle" he said.

"You may pass through the Pearly Gates" Saint
Peter said.

The second man reached into his pocket and
pulled out a set of keys.

He shook them and said, "They're bells". Saint
Peter let him pass through the gates.

The third man started searching desperately
through his pockets and finally pulled out a pair
of women's panties. Saint Peter looked at the man
with a raised eyebrow and asked, "And what do
those symbolize?"

"They're Carols..."

***

On a tour of Scotland, the Pope took a visit to
the North coast on an impromptu sightseeing

trip. His 4X4 Popemobile was driving along the golden sands when there was an enormous commotion heard just off the headland. The Pope noticed a hapless man wearing an English football jersey just outside the surf, struggling frantically to free himself from the jaws of a twenty foot shark. At that moment a speedboat with three men wearing Scottish football tops roared into view from around the point. Spontaneously, one of the men took aim and fired a harpoon into the shark's ribs, immobilizing it instantly.

The other two reached out and pulled the Englishman from the water and then, using long clubs, beat the shark to death. They bundled the bleeding, semi conscious Englishman into the speed boat along with the dead shark and then prepared to leave, when they heard frantic shouting from the shore. It was the Pope, and he summoned them to the beach.

The Pope went into raptures about the rescue and said, "I give you my blessing for your brave actions. I had heard that there were some racist xenophobic people trying to divide Scotland and England, but now I have seen with my own eyes this is not true. I can see that your society is a truly enlightened example of racial harmony and could serve as a model for other nations to follow."

He blessed them all and drove off in a cloud of dust.

"Who was that?" the harpoonist asked his companions,

"That was His Holiness the Pope! He's in direct contact with God and has access to all God's wisdom" answered his friend.

"Well," the harpoonist replied, "he knows fuck

all about shark fishing! How's that bait holding up? Do we need to get another one?"

***

A little boy got on the bus, sat next to a man reading a book and noticed he had his collar on backwards. The little boy asked why he wore his collar that way.

"I am a Father." the priest said.

"My daddy doesn't wear his collar like that."

"I am the Father of many." said the priest, looking up from his book.

"My dad has four boys, four girls, and two grandchildren, and he doesn't wear his collar that way."

The priest, becoming impatient, said, "I am the father of thousands!" and went back to reading his book.

The little boy sat quietly. As he left the bus he leaned over and said, "Maybe you should wear your pants backwards..."

SEX

A sixteen-year-old girl told her mom that she had missed her period for two months. Very worried, her mother went to the chemist and bought a pregnancy kit. The test result showed that the girl was pregnant.

Shouting, cursing and crying, the mother said, "Who was the dirty pig that did this to you? I want to know!"

The girl then made a phone call to the prospective father. Half an hour later, a Ferrari stopped in front of their house and a mature, impeccably dressed and distinguished-looking grey haired man wearing an expensive suit stepped out and entered the house. He sat in the living room with the girl, her father and mother and said, "Your daughter has informed me of the problem. However, I can't marry her because of my personal family situation, but I'll be responsible. If a girl is born I will give her two retail stores, a townhouse, a beach villa and a $1,000,000 bank account. If a boy is born, my legacy will be two factories and a $2,000,000 bank account. If it's twins, I'll donate a factory and $1,000,000 to each. However, if there is a miscarriage..."

At this point, the girl's father, who had remained silent, placed a hand firmly on the man's shoulder and said, "If there's a miscarriage, you'll fuck her again mate!"

***

In ancient Greece, Socrates was reputed to hold knowledge in high esteem. One day an acquaintance met the great philosopher and said, "Socrates, do you know what I just heard about your friend?"

"Hold on a minute," Socrates replied. "Before telling me anything I'd like you to pass a little test. It's called the Triple Filter Test."

"Triple Filter?"

"That's right," Socrates continued. "Before you talk to me about my friend, it might be a good idea to take a moment and filter what you're going to say. The first filter is Truth. Have you made absolutely sure that what you are about to tell me is true?"

"No," the man said, "actually I just heard about it and..."

"All right," said Socrates, "so you don't really know if it's true or not. Now let's try the second filter, the filter of Goodness. Is what you are about to tell me about my friend something good?"

"No, the opposite..."

"So," Socrates continued, "you want to tell me something bad about him, but you're not certain it's true. You may still pass the test though, because there's one filter left: the filter of Usefulness. Is what you want to tell me about my friend going to be useful to me?"

"No...not really."

"Well," concluded Socrates, "if what you want to tell me is neither true nor good nor even useful, why tell it to me at all?"

This is why Socrates was a great philosopher and held in such high esteem. It also explains why he never found out that his best friend was screwing his wife.

***

A college teacher reminds her class of tomorrow's final exam.

"Now class, I won't tolerate any excuses for not being here tomorrow. I might consider a nuclear attack or a serious personal injury or illness, or a death in your immediate family, but that's it, no other excuses whatsoever!"

A smart-arse guy in the back of the room raised his hand and asked, "What would you say if tomorrow I said I was suffering from complete and utter sexual exhaustion?"

"Well, I guess you'd have to write the exam with your other hand."

***

A woman was having a daytime affair while her husband was at work.

One wet and lusty day she was in bed with her boyfriend when, to her horror, she heard her husband's car pull into the driveway.

"Oh my God – hurry! Grab your clothes," she yelled to her lover. "Jump out the window! My husband's home early!"

"I can't jump out the window!" he protested, "It's raining out there!"

"If my husband catches us, he'll kill us both!" she replied.

"He's got a quick temper and a very large gun! The rain is the least of your problems!"

He leapt out of bed, grabbed his clothes and jumped out the window! As he began running down the street in the pouring rain, he quickly discovered he had jumped right into the middle of the town's annual marathon and was running along beside 300 others. Being naked, with his clothes tucked under his arm, he tried to blend in as best he could. After a little while, several runners, who had been studying him with some curiosity, jogged closer.

"Do you always run in the nude?" one asked.

"Oh yes" he replied, gasping for air. "It feels so wonderfully free having the air blow over all your skin while you're running."

"Do you always run carrying your clothes with you under your arm?"

"Oh, yes" he answered breathlessly. "That way I can get dressed right at the end of the run and get in my car to go home!"

Another runner cast his eyes a little lower and queried,

"Do you always wear a condom when you run?"

"Only if it's raining..."

***

An Italian, a Jew and a Frenchman are bragging about their prowess as lovers. The Italian man says, "Last week, my wife and I had great sex. I rubbed her body all over with olive oil, we made passionate love, and she screamed for five minutes at the end."

The Frenchman boasts, "Last week when my wife and I had sex, I rubbed her body all over with butter. We then made passionate love and she screamed for fifteen minutes."

The old Jewish man says, "Well, last week my wife and I had sex too. I rubbed her body all over with kosher chicken fat, we made love, and she screamed for six hours."

The Italian and Frenchman were stunned. They

replied, "What could you have possibly done to make your wife scream for six hours?"

"I wiped my hands on the curtains."

***

Fred and Irene were getting a bit bored with things, so Fred went to an adult book shop and bought a book titled, 'New and Exciting Positions'. Fred fancied a position called the wheelbarrow. Irene was to lay on the floor, Fred was to pick up her legs and give it to her from behind while she would walk around on her hands.

"OK", agreed Irene, "but on two conditions. First, stop immediately if it hurts, and second, don't go past my mother's house!"

***

The spark had been lost in Darryl's marriage, and he was trying to think of a way to rekindle it. One night he came home and found his wife asleep in bed. He thought to himself, "I'll give her oral sex!" He crawled up under the covers and went down on his wife. Soon she began to gently squirm and moan in pleasure. After a few minutes, her body spasmed with ecstasy and a huge orgasm. Afterwards, Darryl went straight to the bathroom to brush his teeth. When he got there, the light was on and he saw his wife there, shaving her legs.

"What are you doing in here?" he said,

"Shhhh!" she answered pointing at the bed, "You'll wake mother."

Sallie lost her husband almost four years ago and still hadn't gotten out of her mourning stage. Her daughter was constantly calling her and urging her to get back into the world.

Finally, Sallie said she'd go out, but didn't know anyone. Her daughter said, "Mum... I have someone for you to meet."

The date was an immediate hit. They took to one another and after dating for six weeks, he asked her to join him for a weekend in the Bahamas. On their first night, they both undressed. She stood there nude except for a pair of black lacy panties, he was in his birthday suit. "Why the black panties?" he asked.

"My breasts you can fondle, my body is yours to explore, but down there I am still in mourning."

The following night, it was the same scenario, she standing with the black panties on, and he is in his birthday suit, except that on his erection he has a black condom.

"What's with this...a black condom?" she asks.

"I want to offer my deepest condolences."

***

After accumulating enough frequent flyer points, Mike and Maureen landed on Mars. They met a Martian couple and were talking about all sorts of things. Mike asked if Mars had a stock market, if they had laptop computers and how they made money. Finally Maureen brought up the subject of sex. "How do you guys do it?" asked Maureen.

The male Martian responded "Much the way you do."

A discussion ensued and finally the couples decided to swap partners for the night (for the sake of science, of course).

Maureen and the male Martian went off to a bedroom where the Martian stripped. She was disappointed to find that he had a teeny weeny dick.

"I don't think this is going to work," said Maureen.

" Why? What's the problem?"

"Well," she replied "it's just not long enough!"

"No problem," he said and proceeded to slap his forehead with his palm. With each slap his willie grew until it was the 'right' size.

"Well," she said "that's better, but it's still pretty narrow."

"No problem," he said and started pulling his ears. With each pull his dick grew wider and wider.

"Wow!" she exclaimed. They fell into bed and made mad passionate love. The next day the couples joined their normal partners and went their separate ways. As they walked along Mike asked, "Well, was it any good?"

"I hate to say it," said Maureen "but it was pretty wonderful. How was it for you?"

"It was horrible." he replied. "All I got was a headache. She kept slapping my forehead and pulling my ears!"

***

A mother took her daughter to the doctor and asked him to give her an examination to determine the cause of her daughter's swollen abdomen. It only took the doctor about two seconds to say, "Your daughter is pregnant."

The mother turned red with fury and argued with the doctor that her daughter was a good girl and would never compromise her reputation by having sex with someone. The doctor faced the window and silently stared at the horizon. The mother became enraged and screamed, "Quit looking out the window! Are you paying attention to me?"

"Yes... I am paying attention ma'am. It's just that the last time this sort of thing happened, a star appeared in the east, and three wise men came. I was hoping they would show up again and help."

STATISTICS

A 68-year-old accountant left a letter for his wife that read,

"Dear wife, I am 68, and by the time you receive this letter I will be at the Grand Hotel with my beautiful and sexy 18-year-old secretary."

When he arrived at the hotel, there was a letter waiting for him that read,

"Dear husband, I too am 68, and by the time you receive this letter I will be at the Breakwater Hotel with my handsome and virile 18-year-old gardener. Being an accountant, you will appreciate that 18 goes into 68 many more times than 68 goes into 18."

ROMANCE MATHEMATICS

Smart man + smart woman = romance
Smart man + dumb woman = affair
Dumb man + smart woman = marriage
Dumb man + dumb woman = pregnancy

***

OFFICE ARITHMETIC

Smart boss + smart employee = profit
Smart boss + dumb employee = production
Dumb boss + smart employee = promotion
Dumb boss + dumb employee = overtime

***

SHOPPING MATHS

A man will pay $2 for a $1 item he needs.

A woman will pay $1 for a $2 item that she doesn't need.

***

GENERAL EQUATIONS & STATISTICS

A woman worries about the future until she gets a husband.

A man never worries about the future until he gets a wife.

A successful man is one who makes more money than his wife can spend.

A successful woman is one who can find such a man.

***

Happiness

To be happy with a man, you must understand him a lot and love him a little.

To be happy with a woman, you must love her a lot and not try to understand her at all.

***

Longevity

Married men live longer than single men do, but married men are a lot more willing to die.

***

Propensity to Change

A woman marries a man expecting he will change, but he doesn't. A man marries a woman expecting that she won't change, and she does.

***

Discussion Technique

A woman has the last word in any argument.

Anything a man says after that is the beginning of a new argument.

The Geography of a Woman

Between the ages of 15–18 a woman is like China or Iran. Developing at a sizzling rate with a lot of potential but as yet still not free or open.

Between the ages of 18 – 21 a woman is like Africa or Australia. She is half discovered, half wild and naturally beautiful with bushland around the fertile deltas.

Between the ages of 21 – 30 a woman is like America or Japan. Completely discovered, very well developed and open to trade especially with countries with cash or cars.

Between the ages of 30 – 35, she is like India or Spain. Very hot, relaxed and convinced of her own beauty.

Between the ages of 35 – 40 a woman is like France or Argentina. She may have been half destroyed during the war but can still be warm and have desirable places to visit.

Between the ages of 40 – 50 she is like Yugoslavia or Iraq. She lost the war and is haunted by past mistakes. Massive reconstruction is now necessary.

Between the ages of 50 – 60 she is like Russia or Canada. Very wide, quiet and the borders are practically unpatrolled but the frigid climate keeps people away.

Between the ages of 60 – 70 a woman is like England or Mongolia. With a glorious and all conquering past but alas, no future.

After 70, women become like Iraq or Afghanistan. Everyone knows where it is, but no one wants to go there.

TOP TEN TIMES IN HISTORY THE 'F' WORD WAS APPROPRIATE

10th Scattered fucking showers, my ass"
  – Noah, 4314 BC
9th "How the fuck did you work that out?"
  – Pythagoras 126BC
8th "You want **what** on the fucking ceiling?"
  – Michelangelo1566
7th "Where did all those fucking Indians come from?"
  – Custer 1877
6th "It does so fucking look like her"
  – Picasso, 1926
5th "Where the fuck are we?"
  – Amelia Earhart, 1937
4th "Any fucking idiot could understand that"
  – Einstein, 1938
3rd "What the fuck was that?"
  – Mayor of Hiroshima, 1945
2nd "I need this parade like I need a fucking hole in the head!"
  – JFK, 1963

And the number 1 most appropriate time for using the "F" word...

"Aw c'mon...who the fuck is going to find out?"
  – Bill Clinton, 1997

***

Best Actual Headlines so far for the 21st Century:

1. Crack Found on Governor's Daughter
2. Something Went Wrong in Jet Crash, Expert Says

3. Police Begin Campaign to Run Down Jaywalkers
4. Iraqi Head Seeks Arms
5. Is There a Ring of Debris around Uranus?
6. Prostitutes Appeal to Pope
7. Panda Mating Fails; Veterinarian Takes Over
8. Teacher Strikes Idle Kids
9. Miners Refuse to Work After Death
10. Juvenile Court to Try Shooting Defendant
11. War Dims Hope for Peace
12. If Strike Isn't Settled Quickly, It May Last A While
13. Cold Wave Linked to Temperatures
14. London Couple Slain; Police Suspect Homicide
15. Red Tape Holds Up New Bridges
16. Typhoon Rips Through Cemetery; Hundreds Dead
17. Man Struck By Lightning Faces Battery Charge
18. New Study of Obesity Looks for Larger Test Group
19. Astronaut Takes Blame for Gas in Spacecraft
20. Kids Make Nutritious Snacks
21. Chef Throws His Heart into Helping Feed Needy
22. Local High School Dropouts Cut in Half
23. Hospitals Sued By 7 Foot Doctors

WHY I AM PROUD TO BE AUSTRALIAN

I'm proud to be Australian because…

Only in Australia…can a pizza get to your house faster than an ambulance or police car.

Only in Australia…do supermarkets make sick people walk all the way to the back of the shop to get their prescriptions while healthy people can buy cigarettes at the front.

Only in Australia…do people order double cheeseburgers, large fries, and a Diet Coke.

Only in Australia…do banks leave both doors open and chain the pens to the counters.

Only in Australia…do we leave cars worth thousands of dollars on the driveway and lock our junk and cheap lawn mowers in the garage.

Only in Australia…do we use answering machines to screen calls and then have call waiting so we won't miss a call from someone we didn't want to talk to in the first place.

Only in Australia…are there disabled parking places in front of a skating rink.

***

A little cheer for all from the Australian Bureau of Statistics

- 31 Australians have died since 1998 by watering their Christmas tree while the fairy lights were plugged in.
- 19 Australians have died in the last 3 years by eating Christmas decorations they believed were chocolate.
- Hospitals reported 4 broken arms last year after cracker pulling incidents.
- 101 Australians since 1999 have had broken parts of plastic toys pulled out of the soles of their feet.
- 18 Australians had serious burns in 2001 trying on a new jumper with a lit cigarette in their mouth.

- 543 Australians were admitted to Casualty in the last two years after opening bottles of beer with their teeth or eye socket.
- 5 Australians were injured last year in accidents involving out of control scalextric cars.
- 3 Australians die each year testing if a 9V battery works on their tongue.
- 142 Australians were injured in 2003 by not removing all the pins from new shirts.
- 58 Australians are injured each year by using sharp knives instead of screwdrivers.
- 8 Australians cracked their skull in 2004 after passing out while throwing up into the toilet.

STUPID PEOPLE

Driving to the office this morning on the motorway, I looked over to my right and there was a woman in a brand new BMW doing 120 kilometers per hour with her face up close to her rear view mirror, and putting on her eyeliner! I looked away for a couple of seconds and when I looked back she was halfway over in my lane, still working on that makeup! It scared me so much (I'm a man), that I dropped my electric shaver, which knocked the bacon roll out of my other hand.

In all the confusion of trying to straighten up the car using my knees against the steering wheel, it knocked my mobile phone from my ear, which fell into the coffee between my legs, causing it to splash and burn Big Jim and the Round Twins, making me scream and drop the cigarette out of my mouth, which ruined my shirt and disconnected an important call. Women drivers suck!

***

The Lone Ranger was ambushed and captured by an Indian war party.

The Indian Chief proclaims, "So, you are the great Lone Ranger. In honor of the Harvest Festival, you will be executed in three days. But, before I kill you, I will grant you three requests. What is your first request?"

"I'd like to speak to my horse."

The Chief nods and his horse Silver is brought before the Lone Ranger, who whispers in Silver's ear, and the horse gallops away. Later that evening, Silver returns with a beautiful blonde woman on his back. Her name is Polly. As the Indian Chief watches, Polly enters the Lone Ranger's tent and spends the night. The next morning the Indian Chief admits he's impressed. "You have a very fine and loyal horse, but I will still kill you in two days. What is your second request?"

The Lone Ranger again asks to speak to his horse. Silver is brought to him, and he again whispers in the horse's ear. As before, Silver takes off across the plains and disappears over the horizon. Later that evening, to the Chief's surprise, Silver again returns, this time with a voluptuous brunette, even more attractive than the blonde. Her name is Flossie. She enters the Lone Ranger's tent and spends the night.

The following morning the Indian Chief is again impressed. "You are indeed a man of many talents, but I will still kill you tomorrow. What is your last request?"

"I'd like to speak to my horse – alone!"

The Chief is curious, but agrees, and Silver is brought to the Lone Ranger's tent. Once they're alone, the Lone Ranger grabs Silver by both ears, looks him squarely in the eye and says, "Listen carefully, for the last time! I said...bring POSSE!"

***

A guy sticks his head into a barber shop and asks, "How long before I can get a haircut?"

The barber looks around the shop and says, "About 2 hours."

The guy leaves.

A few days later the same guy sticks his head in the door and asks, "How long before I can get a haircut?"

The barber looks around at the shop full of customers and says, "About 3 hours."

The guy leaves. A week later the same guy sticks his head in the shop and asks, "How long before I can get a haircut?"

The barber looks around the shop and says, "About an hour and a half."

The guy leaves. The barber looks over at a friend in the shop and says, "Hey, Bill, follow that guy and see where he goes. He keeps asking how long he has to wait for a haircut, but then doesn't come back."

A little while later, Bill comes back into the shop.

"Bill, where does he go when he leaves here?" the barber asks.

"He goes around to your house…"

***

I went to the store the other day, and I was in there for only about five minutes. When I came out there was a motorcycle cop writing a parking ticket. So I went up to him and said, "Come on, buddy, how about giving a guy a break?"

He ignored me and continued writing the ticket.

So I called him a pencil-necked Nazi. He glared at me and started writing another ticket for worn tires! So I called him a piece of horse shit. He finished the second ticket and put it on the windshield with the first. Then he started writing a third ticket! This went on for about twenty minutes. The more I abused him, the more tickets he wrote. But I didn't care. My car was parked around the corner.

***

Ken was on his deathbed and gasped pitifully. "Promise to fulfil my last request, Cindy," he said.

"Of course, Ken," his wife said softly.

"Six months after I die," he said, "I want you to marry Tim."

"But I thought you hated Tim," she said.

With his last breath, Ken said, "I do!"

Carlos calls his boss in the morning:

"Ey, boss I not come work today. I feel really sick. I got a headache, stomach ache and my legs hurt, I not come work."

The boss says, "You know Carlos, I really need you today. When I feel like you do, I go to my wife and tell her to give me a blowjob. That makes me feel better and I can go to work. You should try that."

Two hours later Carlos calls, "Boss, I did what you said and I feel great, I'll be at work soon. By the way, you got a nice house…"

***

A Mafia Godfather finds out that one of his underlings has screwed him out of ten million dollars. This underling happens to be deaf, so the Godfather brings along his attorney, who knows sign language.

The Godfather asks the underling, "Where is the ten million bucks you embezzled from me?"

The attorney, using sign language, asks the underling where the ten million dollars is hidden. The underling signs back, "I don't know what you are talking about."

The attorney tells the Godfather, "He says he doesn't know what you're talking about."

The Godfather pulls out a 9 mm pistol, puts it to the underling's temple, cocks it and says, "Ask him again!"

The attorney signs to the underling, "He'll kill you for sure if you don't tell him!"

The underling signs back: "OK! You win! The

money is in a brown briefcase, buried behind the shed in my cousin Enzo's backyard!"

"Well, what'd he say?" the Godfather asks the attorney.

"He says you don't have the balls to pull the trigger."

***

A small white guy gets into an elevator and notices a huge black guy standing next to him. The big black guy looks down on the small white guy and says, "7 foot tall, 350 pounds, 20 inch dick, 3 pound left ball, 3 pound right ball, Turner Brown." The small white guy faints! The black guy picks up the small white guy and brings him around by slapping his face and shaking him and asks, "What's wrong?" The small white guy says; "Excuse me, but what did you say?" The big black guy looks down and says "7 foot tall, 350 pounds, 20 inch dick, 3 pound left ball, 3 pound right ball, my name is Turner Brown." The small white guy says, "Thank god, I thought you said 'Turn around...'

***

A woman decides to have a facelift for her 47th birthday. She spends $15,000 and feels pretty good about the results. On her way home she stops at a newsstand to buy a paper. Before leaving she asks the salesclerk, "I hope you don't mind my asking, but how old do you think I am?"

"About 32," the clerk replies.

"I'm actually 47," the woman says happily.

A little while later she goes into McDonalds and asks the person behind the counter the same question. "I'd guess about 29." The woman replies, "No, I'm 47!"

Now she's feeling really good about herself. While waiting for the bus home, she asks an old man the same question. He replies, "I'm 78 and my eyesight is going. Although, when I was young, there was a sure way to tell how old a woman was, but it requires you to let me put my hands down your panties. Then, I can tell exactly how old you are."

They waited in silence on the empty street until curiosity got the best of the woman and she finally says, "What the hell – go ahead".

The old man slips both hands down her panties and begins to feel around. After several minutes she says, "Okay, how old am I?" He removes his hands slowly and says, "You are 47."

Stunned, the woman says, "That is amazing. How do you know?"

"I was behind you in McDonalds."

The salesman ran out of petrol on a country road. He started walking until he came to a farm house. He knocked on the door and a Chinese gentleman answered. "I've run out of petrol". Could you put me up for the night?" asked the salesman.

"Yes", said the Chinese man, "but I've heard about you salesmen, so you must promise not to touch my beautiful daughter."

"Agreed" said the salesman.

When he met the daughter, he was overcome by lust. She was gorgeous and was giving him a wink and a nod. As the salesman climbed the stairs to his bedroom, the Chinese gentleman reminded him. "Remember you promised not to touch my beautiful daughter. If you do, you will suffer the Third Degree of Chinese Punishment."

After the house was quiet, the salesman threw caution to the wind. This beautiful girl was worth the Third Degree of Chinese Punishment. He crept into her bedroom and they screwed wildly for several hours.

When the salesman woke next morning, a heavy rock was on his chest. A card said, "This is the First Degree of Chinese Punishment."

"Well, this isn't too bad", he thought as he picked up the rock and threw it out of the window.

On the bottom of the rock was another card which said, "Second Degree of Chinese Punishment – your right ball is tied to this rock."

Quick as a flash he leaped out of the window with the rock. "Phew, that was close", he thought. But as he went out of the window, he saw another card which said, "Third Degree of Chinese Punishment – your left ball is tied to the bedpost!"

***

A mute wants to buy a toothbrush. By imitating the action of brushing one's teeth, he successfully expresses himself to the shopkeeper and the purchase is done.

If a blind man wants to buy a pair of sunglasses, how could he express himself?

Simple – he just has to ask. He's blind, not mute.

A Londoner parks his brand new Porsche in front of the office to show it off to his colleagues. As he's getting out of the car, a truck comes speeding along too close to the curb and takes off the Porsche's door before speeding off. Distraught, the Londoner grabs his mobile and calls the police. Five minutes later, the police arrive. Before the policeman has a chance to ask any questions, the Londoner starts screaming hysterically, "My Porsche, my beautiful silver Porsche is ruined. No matter how long it would be at the panel beaters, it'll simply never be the same again!" After the Londoner finally finishes his rant, the policeman shakes his head in disgust: "I can't believe how materialistic you bloody Londoners are!" he says. "You lot are so focused on your possessions that you don't notice anything else in your life."

"How can you say such a thing at a time like this?" snaps the Londoner.

"Didn't you realize that your right arm was torn off when the truck hit you?"

The Londoner looked down in absolute horror.

"Hell! Where's my Rolex?"

***

Geoff really made a mess of himself at the office Christmas party. Next morning he woke with a terrible hangover.

"What happened last night?" he asked his flat-mate Ron.

"As usual, you made a fool of yourself in front of the boss" said Ron.

"Well...piss on him!" said Geoff.

"You did...and he fired you!" replied Ron.

"Well...fuck him!" said Geoff.

"You did...and he gave you your job back and promoted you!"

***

A woman and a man are involved in a bad car accident. Both of their cars are totally demolished but amazingly neither of them are hurt. After they crawl out of their cars, the woman says, "So you're a man. That's interesting. I'm a woman. Wow, just look at our cars! There's nothing left, but we're unhurt. This must be a sign from God that we should meet and be friends and live together in peace for the rest of our days".

Flattered, the man replies, "Yes, I agree with you completely, this must be a sign from God!"

The woman continues, "And look at this; here's another miracle. My car is completely demolished but this bottle of wine didn't break. Surely God wants us to drink this wine and celebrate our good fortune." She hands the bottle to the man.

The man opens it, drinks half the bottle and then hands it back to the woman. The woman takes the bottle and immediately puts the cap back on, and hands it back to the man.

The man asks, "Aren't you having any?"

"No. I think I'll just wait for the police..."

VIAGRA

Chris returns home from vacation with a severe case of sunburn, so he goes to see his doctor. After the examination the doctor prescribes chamomile lotion and Viagra.

Looking a little confused, Chris says, "I can understand you prescribing the chamomile lotion, but why the Viagra?"

"The Viagra is to keep the sheets off you at night."

***

A guy walks into a pharmacy and says, "I've got my new girlfriend staying overnight. Have you got something that will keep me horny all night?"

"Try this", replied the pharmacist, "it's Viagra Extra Strength".

Next morning the guy limped into the pharmacy, moaning and groaning.

"Did it work?" asked the pharmacist.

"Sure it did, but now my penis is black and blue and the pain is unbearable. Give me a tube of Deep Heat".

"You can't put Deep Heat there!" said the pharmacist.

"It's OK", said the guy, "it's for my arms. My girlfriend didn't turn up!"

***

In Pharmacology all drugs have two names, a trade name and a generic name. For example, the trade name of Tylenol also has the generic name of Acetaminophen. Aspro is called Asprin. Amoxil is also called Amoxicillin and Advis is also called Ibuprofen.

The FDA has been looking for a generic name for Viagra.

After careful consideration by a team of government experts it recently announced that it has settled on the generic name of mycoxafloppin.

Also considered were mycoxafailin, mydixadrupin, mydixadud, dixafix and ibepokin.

Do You Wish Your Partner Came With An Instruction Manual?

Why Men Lie & Women Cry

The sequel to the international bestseller *Why Men Don't Listen & Women Can't Read Maps.* Here the Pease's take lessons learned from the first book, and use them to explain common relationship problems.

Revealed in this book:
- Why men avoid commitment
- Why men everywhere feel women nag them
- Women's secret point scoring system
- Solving the seven biggest mysteries about the opposite sex

And the fabulous new MINI book ~

Why Men Can Only Do One Thing At A Time & Women Never Stop Talking

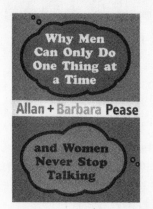

For anyone who has ever laid awake at night wondering why their partner just doesn't understand! The little book of sound advice from the world's foremost experts in relationships....

The perfect hardcover giftbook!

HOT DVD's and CD's

The Best of Body Language

A 60 minute DVD or VHS showing the highlights of over 15 years of hilarious television, based on the No. 1 best-selling book. This programme uses hidden cameras, live audience participation and newsreel of various human miscommunication, including real fight scenes, business interviews and people telling real lies!

How To Develop Powerful Communication Skills ~ Managing The Differences Between Men & Women

Containing a DVD and two CD's this programme shows -

- What men and women need to do to get on in business
- Why women read minds and men won't ask for directions
- The male boss; his female staff and the cold war
- How to avoid arguments, conflicts and disagreements
- Female Intuition; the walking radar detector
- How to persuade the opposite sex to say 'yes'

www.peaseinternational.com

How To Make Appointments By Telephone (CD Pack)

Your phone can create lots of cash!

This is an amazingly cost-effective, flexible and dynamic technique that will bring you spectacular results. This technique is used by many of the world's largest sales organisations and promises an average success rate of 7 out of 10 on cold calls. This is the most powerful appointments making tool you'll ever see!

Questions Are The Answers ~ CD or Cassette

Top level networkers are not 'natural' or 'born'. Top level networking is a skill - a learnable skill, and Questions are the Answers, gives you the techniques and shows you how to use them, how to measure and improve your progress and what to observe when dealing with people.

Now available to Direct Selling Groups around the world is some of the best training and development products ever including the best selling audio Questions are the Answers. This is THE sales programme to own and comes with a double sided laminated "Priorities Card".

GET YOURS TODAY!

www.peaseinternational.com